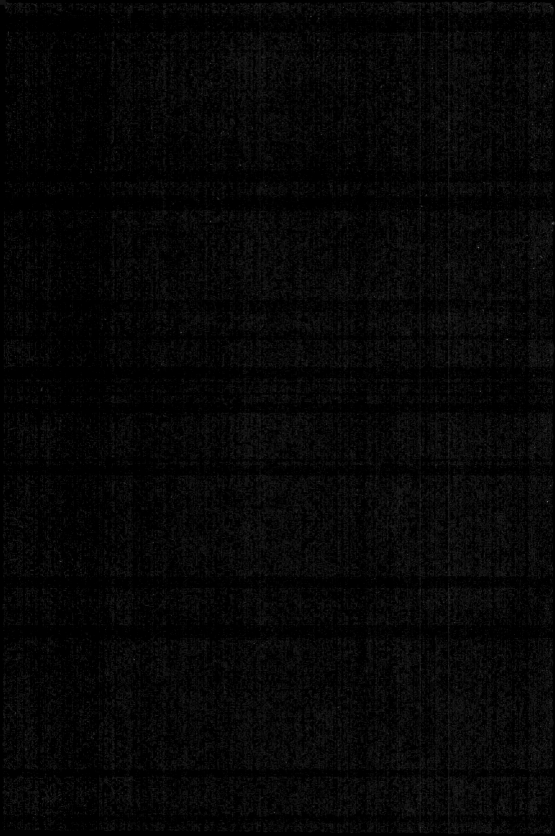

A Christmas Far from Home

A Christmas
Far from Home

**An Epic Tale of Courage and Survival
during the Korean War**

—⚏—

Stanley Weintraub

Da Capo Press
A Member of the Perseus Books Group

Designed by Jack Lenzo
Set in 12 point Caslon by The Perseus Books Group

Cataloging-in-Publication data for this book is available from the Library of
Congress.
ISBN: 978-0-306-82232-2 (hardcover)
ISBN: 978-0-306-82233-9 (e-book)

Published by Da Capo Press
A Member of the Perseus Books Group
www.dacapopress.com

Da Capo Press books are available at special discounts for bulk purchases
in the U.S. by corporations, institutions, and other organizations. For more
information, please contact the Special Markets Department at the Perseus
Books Group, 2300 Chestnut Street, Suite 200, Philadelphia, PA 19103, or call
(800) 810-4145, ext. 5000, or e-mail special.markets@perseusbooks.com.

10 9 8 7 6 5 4 3 2 1

For Phil Zimmer,
whose suggestions originated this book

The second law of thermodynamics dictates that every physical system tends toward maximum disorder.

Contents

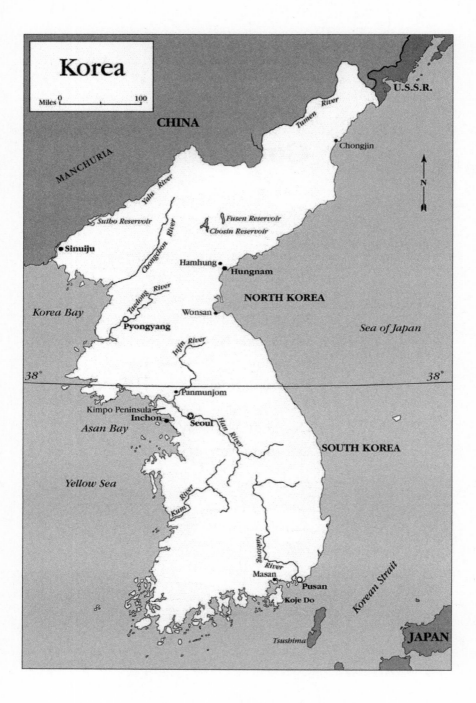

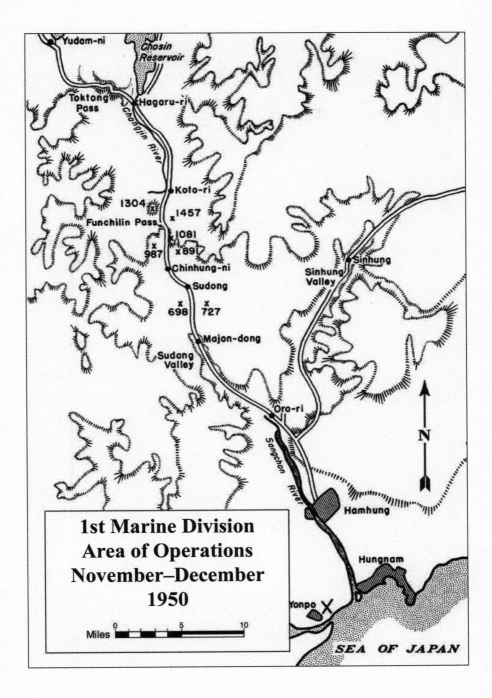

Yudam-ni

Chosin
Reservoir

Toktong
Pass

Hagaru-ri

Changjin River

Koto-ri

1304

x 1457

Funchilin Pass

x 1081

x
987

x 891

Chinhung-ni

Sudong

Sinhung

Sinhung
Valley

x
698

x
727

Majon-dong

Sudong
Valley

Oro-ri

N

Sangchon River

Hamhung

Hungnam

**1st Marine Division
Area of Operations
November–December
1950**

Miles

0   5   10

Yonpo X

SEA OF JAPAN

Preface:
Escape into Fantasy

"Gimee tomorrow."

A *Christmas Far from Home* is less a unit-by-unit history of an extraordinary and moving episode in the Korean War, from Thanksgiving Day to Christmas in 1950, than a narrative of two fantasies. General Douglas MacArthur, Supreme Commander in the Far East, gambled that he could end the war by Christmas and send the bulk of his armies home. In too public a fashion he promised as much. His troops in the frozen, windswept north of Korea, in the worst winter of their lives, believed despite all the evidence to the contrary that "Home for Christmas"—or at least their being shipped out of danger and voyaging home—was somehow possible. After all, MacArthur, his medal-embellished career long celebrated by the press, was the senior fighting general in the Army.

A more realistic wish was that of an embattled Marine in that frigid, barren waste who, when asked by *LIFE* combat photographer David Douglas Duncan, "If I were God, and could give you anything you wanted [for Christmas], what would you ask for?"

"Gimme tomorrow," he said.

Those two words may be the most memorable in what has been erroneously described as the "forgotten war." They will reappear when they actually happened.

"Over half a century later," David Halberstam wrote in 2004, "the war still remained largely outside American political and cultural consciousness. *The Forgotten War* was the apt title of one of the best books on it. Korea was a war that seems orphaned by history." While working on his own compelling book about the war that year, he added, "I chanced into the Key West, Florida library; on its shelves were some eighty-eight books on Vietnam and only four on Korea, which more or less sums up its fate in American memory."

Perhaps the library shelves lacked Korean War books because they were out being read. Rather than forgotten, the war has evoked shelves of notable histories and personal accounts, some of the latter by survivors still able to recall their roles, however small. Even this writer produced a war memoir, in distant 1964, when the events were still so sharply remembered that, respecting the privacy of the living, he disguised the identities of some who served with him. As the years pass, the memories of participants, in interviews and memoirs, become less acute, or are recalled with different passions, or are imaginatively recorded by yet another writer. Even quoting someone who was there often bumps up against another recollection that differs from an earlier account. Such anomalies are nothing new in historical narrative. There are many conflicting, dubious and fantastic accounts, despite the authority long given to Homer, of the Trojan wars.

Repelling naked aggression in the claimed national interest was the ostensible reason for Americans in Korea being seven or eight thousand miles from home. The proverbial line had to be drawn in the sand. Yet most soldiers in a combat zone, whatever the time and place, are not focused upon the complexities of geopolitics, patriot zeal, promotion in rank, medals and ribbons, nor even ultimate peace and demobilization. In the hierarchy of GI war aims, precedence always went to staying alive.

Priorities beyond tomorrow began with loyalty to your unit and to the guys at your side. Everything else, beyond enduring the war, was almost irrelevant. Finishing a war was why you fought it, and that meant, at the end or earlier, going home. No one swathed in winter gear and under relentless fire in Korea seemed interested in slogans. "Remember . . . anything" as a goad to action was meaningless. Rallying round the flag was absurdly antique. "Anti- . . . whatever," including despised Communism, was political talk motivating politicians who did none of the fighting and were only at hazard at the ballot box.

The term "Police Action" is often associated, still, with Korea—and Harry S. Truman. However, the blame for labeling innocuously what was a real and bloody war does not belong to President Truman at all. At a crowded press conference in Washington shortly after the North's invasion of the South and the beginnings of an American response, he was asked by a newsman, "Mr. President, would it be correct . . . to call this a police action under the United Nations?"

"Yes," said Truman, grateful for the euphemism. "That is exactly what it amounts to. We are not at war." Of course we were. Although associated since with Harry Truman, the unfortunate tag had come by way of ultraconservative California senator William Knowland, a Republican, who on the Senate floor had described the response to North Korean aggression "a police action against a violator of the law of nations and the charter of the United Nations." A reporter had picked the phrase up, and it made the newspapers. But what was not an official war declared by Congress under the Constitution was nevertheless a real war. It was General MacArthur who coined the only slogan, however since tinged with irony, worth remembering—"Home for Christmas."

Stanley Weintraub
Beech Hill, Newark, Delaware

1

A Turkey for Thanksgiving

"Turkey: a theatrical production that has failed"

"Organized resistance," General MacArthur predicted confidently, not for the first time, "will be terminated by Thanksgiving. . . . They are thoroughly whipped. The winter will destroy those we don't." The "they" were the North Koreans—and the general's boast was to President Truman, with whom he was conferring on Wake Island on Sunday, October 15, 1950. "It goes against my grain to destroy them," MacArthur deplored in mock sorrow, "but they are obstinate. The Oriental values 'face' over life."

After Thanksgiving, the general planned to return the Eighth Army, then moving up the western side of Korea toward the Yalu River frontier with Communist China, to Japan, "probably by Christmas." He would keep Major General Edward "Ned" Almond's X Corps, Army infantry units with a core component of the 1st Marine Division, then off the east coast waiting to disembark, as a security force until he returned order to a unified Korea. MacArthur neither saluted the President on arrival, despite long tradition, nor would he do so on Truman's departure.

After ninety minutes, the Supreme Commander reboarded his C-54, with *SCAP* emblazoned on its nose, to fly back to Japan and a late dinner at his posh, former Embassy home in Tokyo. With midterm Congressional elections approaching in early November, he did not want to be poster boy in the press for Harry Truman, who had only been a Missouri National Guard artillery captain in France in 1918 when MacArthur already was a division commander and brigadier general with a chestful of medals. "I have one more question," said Truman, according to the conference transcript by the general's aide, Colonel Laurence Bunker. "What will be the attitude of Commie China and the Russians to this? . . . Is there any danger of interference?"

MacArthur scoffed. "We are no longer fearful of their intervention." Red China, he claimed, had "no air umbrella" to shield its divisions should they cross the border from Manchuria. "There would be the greatest slaughter if China tried to put ground troops across. They would be destroyed." Ostentatiously consulting his watch after a few further exchanges with General Omar Bradley and Admiral Arthur Radford, MacArthur announced, "There are many pressing matters awaiting my return to Tokyo." He offered to accompany the President to the ramp of his plane. Pausing there for a brief ceremony, Truman's light fedora gleaming in the intense noonday sun eclipsed by the general's scrambled-eggs brass on his peaked hat, the President pinned a Distinguished Service Medal (the recipient's fifth) on MacArthur's tieless tunic.

The general boarded his plane and flew west, probably satisfied that every literate person in the United States scrutinizing a newspaper would notice that the President had to fly more than seven thousand miles to Washington from an isolated Pacific atoll while he had only a mere 1,900 miles back to his *Dai Ichi** headquarters in Japan, from which he oversaw the Occupation. He may have recognized, in Truman's political gaffe to go to Wake Island to meet him, Francis Bacon's centuries-old quip, "If the mountain will not come to Mahomet, Mahomet will go to the mountain."

By the time Omar Bradley returned with the President to Washington—a journey requiring two refueling stops en route—the chairman of the Joint Chiefs of Staff could radio plaudits to MacArthur about his "grand job"—as exemplified in "this morning's reports on the good news from Pyongyang." The enemy capital reportedly had just been occupied. North Korean remnants were fleeing toward the Yalu River frontier with China. MacArthur's forecasts appeared good indeed. Many GIs in Korea now anticipated Thanksgiving dinners back in Japan or on troopships heading further eastward toward Christmas at home. Yet the grandiose operations were already off schedule. As Pyongyang was being seized with little resistance, Almond's X Corps shiploads hovering off the eastern coast of northern Korea were belatedly reaching shore.

---

*The building was the prewar office of the *Dai Ichi* ("Number One") Insurance Company.

Despite open skepticism from the Pentagon, MacArthur's bold end-around strategy to land troops above Seoul at Inchon and cut off the North Koreans in the south had been, in September, thanks to Rear Admiral James H. Doyle, a conspicuous success. The general's follow-up was far less brilliant. Rather than exploit his momentum, he had chosen to divide his armies by sending the newly created X Corps up the eastern coast. Reboarding their ships, troops were to sail around South Korea to make amphibious landings well north of the 38th parallel. The operation, including reloading vehicles, weapons, fuel and rations, had cost six weeks, permitting the NKPA to regroup its remnants as well as the Chinese above the Yalu River in Manchuria to muster a dozen divisions and covertly slip them across into Korea.

Intelligence about Chinese troop movements was difficult to acquire, especially in Japan, where Major General Charles Willoughby at the *Dai Ichi* spun information his way. He listened to little of it from elsewhere. The Navy, not under MacArthur's thumb, had a small CIA operation ongoing at its base in Yokosuka. There, William Duggan monitored tips from Taiwan, where colleagues received clandestine radio messages from former Nationalist troops forced into the Communist ranks. Mao's Chinese were entraining toward Manchuria, toward the Yalu River border with North Korea. The refugee government in Taiwan had its obvious anti-Mao biases, but its contacts seemed genuine.

Tokyo paid little attention to the warnings; yet by early November, press dispatches from Korea were reporting that "North Korean forces, aided by Chinese troops and new weapons, were maintaining their pressure on the right flank of United Nations units on the west coast. Enemy troops were within twenty miles of key coastal roads." Since newsmen learned about it from General MacArthur's headquarters, it was less than accurate. Rather than North Korean, the enemy was predominantly Chinese and had no "new weapons." What they had was, to the complacent *Dai Ichi* bureaucracy, surprise. MacArthur soon charged, although the Chinese had given ample warnings about intervention, that "alien" Communist forces from Manchuria had crossed the Yalu River "without any notice of belligerency."

Long scheming to undermine the Truman presidency, ambitious Republicans like Harold Stassen, a perennial White House hopeful, charged with no supporting evidence that Truman had "a five-year record of coddling Chinese Communists, five years of undermining General MacArthur, [and] five years of snubbing freedom-loving Asiatics."* Feeding the sudden panic in the nation, a ham radio crank in the Bronx sent some New Yorkers into a frenzy by broadcasting, ostensibly from a "Citizen Defense truck," that "enemy planes" were approaching to drop atomic bombs on the city.

As early as ten days after MacArthur's Inchon success, General Nie Rongzhen, chief of the Chinese General Staff and its logistics expert, told K. M. Panikkar, Indian ambassador in Beijing, that the Chinese "did not intend to sit back with folded hands and let the Americans come to the border." On October 3, foreign minister Zhou Enlai gave Panikkar

---

*Presumably meaning Chiang Kai-Shek and his dwindling followers.

added confirmation of that warning, which was transmitted to London, then Washington, and finally to the *Dai Ichi*. MacArthur considered the threat a bluff. Even Truman observed that the ambassador "had in the past played the game of the Chinese Communists fairly regularly." Five days later, Chairman Mao Zedong, although realizing that intervention would postpone if not foreclose his gaining Taiwan, the island vestige of Chiang's China, cabled Kim Il Sung, about to flee Pyongyang, that the Chinese would enter the war.

Ignoring all warnings and blind to the increasing Chinese buildup across the Yalu River in Manchuria, MacArthur went ahead to pursue the unification of the two Koreas. "We were all deeply apprehensive," recalled Secretary of State Dean Acheson, but no one in Washington dared insist to the general that he halt, prudently, at a defensible line short of the Yalu. The intelligence failures from MacArthur's GHQ in Tokyo unsurprisingly coincided with his ambitions. "Neither the U.S. or the [South Korean] puppet forces have by far expected the entry of our Volunteers," Chairman Mao boasted to General Peng Dehuai. "That is the reason why they dare to advance in two separated lines." Nor did the *Dai Ichi* planners anticipate that the huge convoy to Wonsan on the northeast coast would be held up outside a harbor laced with enemy mines.

Admiral Doyle fulminated that X Corps could have moved faster on "shank's mare," and indeed, Bob Hope and his traveling USO show had arrived in Wonsan, below the primary landing site at Hungnam, only to find that the troops to be entertained were still bobbing at sea. "The fact that we beat the Marines to the beach," Hope recalled, "made the A.P. wire."

Rumors, however unfounded, arise easily and proliferate. Troops convoyed at tedious length around the peninsula to landfall above the 38th parallel soon shared an alleged explanation. The maneuver was to evade the fee that the corrupt Korean president Syngman Rhee charged for every American soldier transported anywhere on Korean rails. Maps, though inadequate, would have shown that however difficult were the mountain passes, no narrow-gauge tracks crossed the Korean waist from west to east. A ROK division did negotiate the rough terrain, on wheels and on foot, and was there, like Bob Hope, before the X Corps armada reached the coast.

By the time X Corps was ashore and deployed from Wonsan, Hungnam, and Iwon, even farther northeast, early winter was setting in. North Korea acquired its severe chill from Manchuria and neighboring Siberia. Shuddering troops would soon be calling the below-zero gales "the Siberian express." Hal Boyle in an AP dispatch quoted "a philosophic private" as saying, "Hell, it's better to freeze going forward than to freeze on your rump"—he probably used a stronger noun, but AP served family newspapers—"waiting for the Chinese to make up their minds." The troops, Boyle closed, "have great faith in General Douglas MacArthur. They feel that he is the Santa Claus in uniform who will lead them to final victory by Christmas."

MacArthur's diminishing reserves of shrewdness were at odds with his disproportionate ego. He could not be wrong. To the general, wars didn't ebb and flow and eventually reach accommodation. There was only victory or defeat. He had expected to intimidate Mao's arrogant new China by creating irretrievable facts on the ground below the Yalu. Home by

Christmas would be a personal public relations triumph as well as a sweeping victory over Communism. A presidential campaign was now little more than a year away. MacArthur hoped to be a candidate. Christmas meant little to the general yet much to the American electorate—and to his troops. Religious observance was never important to MacArthur except for exploitation as metaphors and slogans and for biblical cadences employed in his speechmaking—but for the catastrophe of Christmas 1941.

Except in his communiques, which he largely wrote himself, his bungling the defense of the Philippines had reached its nadir just prior to the Christmas after Pearl Harbor, when he was forced to evacuate his headquarters and hotel penthouse and flee to the fortress island of Corregidor in Manila Bay. Except to intimates, he had kept secret his decision to declare helpless Manila an Open City, abandoning it to the Japanese without a fight. His young son, Arthur, not quite four, expected gifts from Santa Claus under his tree, like other American kids.

As Christmas approached, Jean MacArthur unwrapped her own presents, hurriedly acquired and delivered the day before by Lieutenant Colonel Sid Huff on orders from her husband. "Sid," MacArthur had told his aide, "I've forgotten to buy Jean a Christmas present." Loyally, Huff had gone to shops still open for business where Mrs. MacArthur's size in dresses and lingerie was known, and returned with red-ribboned purchases less than useless on the beleaguered, tadpole-shaped island. The general advised her to open the boxes right away. Christmas Eve would be too late.

War tension was lost on Arthur IV, who would celebrate his next birthday in February in a dank tunnel on the fortress island of Corregidor in Manila Bay. Although it was past the child's bedtime, his father announced a day early that it was already Christmas Eve. Eagerly, Arthur pulled the wrappings off his presents. One was a tricycle, which he pedaled happily around the penthouse and its balconies. On Christmas Eve, Sid Huff carried the tricycle from the trunk of MacArthur's abandoned Packard, from which its four-star flag had been removed, to the interisland steamer *Don Esteban*, which weighed anchor from the Cavite docks at 7:00 p.m. The glow of harbor fires from enemy daylight bombing was receding. A few of the general's staff aboard, unwilling to relinquish the holiday, sang "Silent Night" from the forward deck as the ship plowed into the bay in the darkness toward Corregidor.

—⁂—

Christmas 1950 augured to be more rewarding in occupied Tokyo, seven hundred air and sea miles from unanticipated disaster in North Korea. The commanding general of X Corps, deliberately created independent of Eighth Army to the west, was Major General Edward "Ned" Almond, MacArthur's Far East Command deputy now distant from the *Dai Ichi*. Both generals were envisioning a third star for him. Neither expected to encounter massive, if any, intervention from Red China, and when a few Chinese were taken prisoner and minimized the dimensions of their infiltration, Almond advised troops that the intruders claimed only to be from battalions of

volunteers. An Associated Press wirephoto in newspapers on
November 7 depicted the general interviewing a Chinese pris-
oner through an interpreter on the same day that a headline in
The New York Times reported, "MAC ARTHUR IDENTI-
FIES RED UNITS; FOE WITHDRAWS IN SURPRISE
MANEUVER."

As the Chinese vanished as suddenly as they had entered, the Eighth Army regained ground in the west. The
South Korean Capital Division, to little opposition, disembarked at Iwon in the far northeast and "moved up a coastal
road toward the Soviet frontier [in Siberia]." The Red Chinese
comings and goings seemed baffling in Tokyo. The press head-
lined, "U. N. UNITS RESUME ADVANCE IN KOREA
AFTER SLIGHT LOSS." Although the "units" were largely
American, the emphasis from both Washington and Tokyo
was on the international coalition, some of it token, to reverse
aggression.

The first military abbreviation for the "alien" enemy would
be CCV. Chairman Mao referred to them as CPV—Chinese
People's Volunteers. No volunteers, they were conscripts, including former soldiers of Chiang Kai-Shek taken prisoner
and forcibly turned. On October 8, Mao had instructed the
military command, "The Northeast Border Defense Force is
renamed the Chinese People's Volunteers and it should get
ready to move into the [North] Korean territory immediately."
There would be hundreds of thousands of "volunteers."

General Peng Dehuai had slipped over the Yalu with one
of his units after dark on October 18. By sunrise, thousands of
foot soldiers were quietly across and concealed, and they kept

coming nightly—four infantry armies, three artillery divisions and an anti-aircraft regiment. A concrete road atop the massive dam at the Suiho power plant remained intact and was used after dark. MacArthur had been ordered, to avert a provocation with Mao, to leave the Chinese side of the river unbombed. Even his orders to attack "the Korean end" were contravened briefly by Washington, which reminded MacArthur of the need to consult the British before taking any action affecting Manchuria. (Apparently the British were protecting their interests in indefensible Hong Kong.) The Pentagon's maintaining the letter of that agreement was sheer blindness, inviting intervention without penalty. Precise high-altitude bombing of the Korean ramps without collateral damage was an absurdity, and MacArthur must have realized that if he chanced it, a claimed targeting error could be apologized for yet the necessary damage done. It would not be the first time in warfare, and the Chinese were in no need of excuses to involve themselves. In reality they had already intervened.

When B-29s dropped flares in the darkness on the Korean side, no Chinese troops could be identified in reconnaissance photos. The Chinese knew how and where to hide when over the Yalu—and how to cross unseen. According to Xue Li of the 4th Engineering Corps, his commanding officer, Du Ping, was ordered to construct additional crossings which could not be bombed because they could not be detected. His prefabricated wooden bridges, painted "the color of the water," were submerged just below the surface. Trucks could cross at night at wheeltop depth with their cargoes, and hardy troops could wade on the platforms through the icy water.

Peng Debuai, left, commander of the Chinese Communist Forces, meets with Kim Il Sung, premier of the Democratic People's Republic of Korea. *Marine Corps Historical Center*

Although the temperatures hovered at subzero levels, Chinese soldiers and officers, fortified by "strong wine," worked in the darkness nearly naked, allegedly shouting to each other, "It isn't cold! It isn't cold!" When they emerged for rests, Xue and others rushed to them with dry padded overcoats, and "when we poured wine into their mouths, the teeth of these heroes clattered and they could not hold on to their flasks." A Chinese account gushed that "in temperatures lower than-10C in a winter light, . . . volunteer soldiers with ice hanging on their bodies emerged from the river like gods in silver armor." Troops had crossed "without hesitation, taking off their padded trousers, shoes and socks, and tieing them to their backs, . . . even the female soldiers responsible for first aid." By order of General Peng, the locations of the submerged bridges were kept secret. After river water had frozen hard, the hidden spans were no longer needed, but when in use they forded tens of thousands silently southward.*

Mao had prescribed that "every day the troops should start crossing the river at dusk, cease action at 4:00 A.M., and finish covering up before 5:00 A.M., and every unit must strictly and carefully follow up that plan." Like the engineering cadres, they hid by day and moved by night. They concealed themselves in hillside caves, railway tunnels, mine shafts and village huts and then proceeded in darkness on foot. Eighteen divisions of about 180,000 men crossed in the west; in the east twelve divisions of about 120,000 men somehow took cover during October and November and waited. The X Corps landings were long expected by the enemy, as the convoys, impossible to hide, were not contested—but for the unanticipated mines. It would have taken little strategic imagination—yet there was none—to predict that MacArthur's divisions were being sucked into a trap. "When it paid to be aggressive, Ned [Almond] was aggressive," an operations officer recalled. "When it paid to be cautious, Ned was aggressive."

In their first encounters with the Americans and South Koreans moving inland, on October 25, the Chinese employed their "pocket artillery" of grenades and satchel charges, attacking by

---

*In their brief Mongolian-Manchurian war of 1939 with the Japanese, the Russians built bridges across the Halha and Holsten Rivers with their surfaces ten to twelve inches below the water level so enemy aircraft could not spot them. Although the Red Chinese military, some of them Soviet educated, may have learned from that example, the stealthy strategy dates back to antiquity.

night after eerily summoning their forces with bugles, cymbals and whistles and firing flares into the night. The Red offensive was low in technology but effective in timing and surprise. The "volunteers" took prisoners as astonished forward units pulled back, sometimes abandoning vehicles, guns and supplies. Assembling captives, a Chinese captain identifying himself as Lao tried out his long-unused mission-school English, and a Marine, discovering he was a prisoner of the Chinese rather than the North Koreans, exclaimed, "For God's sake! This isn't *your* war!"

"It is now," said Lao.

The initial attacks on both Korean fronts, west and east, had ended abruptly. The Chinese withdrew, partly to regroup, now that they understood American tactics and weaknesses, but more significantly to create a vacuum into which they could entice and ambush the better-equipped enemy. Peng wanted to give the enemy the false impression that "we are being intimidated into retreat." In a few cases the enemy retreat was real. Moving up to the Chosin Reservoir region in the east, Colonel Homer Litzenberg's 7th Marines had encountered a regiment of the Chinese 124th Division. Five days and nights of artillery barrages and air strikes had driven the Chinese from the hills south of the Funchilin Pass, on the zigzag uphill road to Koto-ri and the ominously dragon-shaped and Japanese-built Chosin Reservoir. (The Japanese had occupied Korea from 1910 until the end of the Pacific war in 1945. The Korean name for the reservoir was Changjin, but the U.S. Army had reproduced the maps it had.*) Chosin was reputed to be the coldest place in

---

*The Navy settled the name matter on its own in 1992 when it christened the fourteenth *Ticonderoga* class guided missile cruiser USS *Chosin*.

Korea, a rare region where rice, the staple of the national diet, could not grow.

In the first encounters, about 1,500 Chinese in their quilted winter uniforms and earflap caps and canvas shoes with rubber soles lay dead, frozen awkwardly where they fell. Each had what remained of a five-day supply of rations, mostly precooked rice and beans, to eliminate the need for identifying fires. About fifty Marines lay dead, and two hundred were wounded.

In a light L-5 reconnaissance plane General Almond touched down with an aide to inspect the scene and noticed the barrels of eighteen regimental howitzers poking up at high angles to fire over the nearby hills. "I didn't know," he remarked blindly to the puzzled Litzenberg, "that you had anti-aircraft guns up here."

Commanding the 1st Marine Division was Major General Oliver Prince Smith, a lean, prematurely white-haired veteran of bloody Peleliu in September 1944. Intending to be ready for the worst, Smith, with the cooperation of Major General Field Harris, who ran Marine air operations, resorted to what he felt certain was only a respite in the war to prepare a runway on the outskirts of Hagaru, sixty-four miles of rugged, winding road upland from the harbor at Hungnam. When completed, the crushed stone airstrip, Harris assured Almond, would accommodate transport of equipment and supplies as well as evacuation of casualties.

"What casualties?" Almond asked. The Chinese incursion, seemingly a feint or a failure, seemed over. The few of O. P. Smith's dead and wounded were hardly worth notice. Almond's lack of alarm coincided with the smug skepticism in the *Dai Ichi*.

Major General Oliver P. Smith, commander of the 1st Marine Division during the Chosin Reservoir campaign. *Department of Defense*

Despite Almond's confidence, Smith and Harris had arranged for Army engineer captain Philip A. Kulbes to bring seventy-seven GIs and ninety ROKs to convert the frozen, boulder-strewn bean field into a runway that would take sturdy twin-engine C-47s, the commercial DC-3. Exploiting the lull, floodlights were employed to continue work after dark. Smith foresaw a tough campaign ahead and, fearing entrapment, quietly ordered his regimental commanders to move cautiously toward the jump-off locations for the assaults north from the crooked, mountain-shrouded Reservoir. He also wanted to concentrate his forces west of Chosin, insisting upon the deployment of some 7th Division troops on the east. Almond considered Smith's precautions as obstructionism.

In his command diary for November 6, with more than two weeks to go before MacArthur's grand design was to be initiated in the increasing pre-winter cold, Almond continued to ignore the Chinese, although now more than a threat, instead writing in his field diary happily about his posh headquarters amenities: "Inspected the Pullman and [the] coach car which are to be prepared for the use of the X Corps staff." Also flown in to the Yonpo airbase south of Hungnam, from Inchon, where it had been shipped from Japan, was his personal van—a large trailer equipped with bathtub and shower, flush toilet, refrigerator, fine linen complete to napkin rings, and silverware and fine china. Flights from Tokyo airlifted fine wines, fruit, fresh vegetables and steaks. Troops who slept in flimsy tents and dined on C-rations and hasty cookstove fare resented his openly cushy *Dai Ichi* style.

To ingratiate himself with the Marine command once his amenities had been installed at Hungnam, Almond had invited Smith and his three regimental commanders to a dinner at which the four Marines sat in shock. Enlisted men in white jackets provided the service and Japan the rest. Almond had imported the Tokyo tone to the wrong place and time. Colonel Lewis "Chesty" Puller of the 1st Marines suppressed his usual obscenities in deploring the compound as "an unconscionable waste in a war zone." Profligacy on a larger scale was Almond's overstaffed Corps headquarters, which Puller estimated, a bit broadly, could populate a regiment. It was the *Dai Ichi* way of war.

MacArthur, whose lifestyle lacked no comforts and who never spent a night on Korean soil, remained outraged by the JCS mandate to avoid provoking China. Reluctantly acknowledging the Chinese presence, he had warned on November 7—still the 6th in Washington—of a possible "calamity of major proportions" if China had a free hand and went unpunished—a term he used provocatively to suggest whatever might harm Mao's regime.

Although Washington permitted MacArthur to cross the 38th parallel, which the Chinese regime considered provocative, the Joint Chiefs of Staff directive of September 27 had cautioned the general not to send American troops close to the Manchurian border—to use only Koreans. Even that was too much for Zhou Enlai. On September 30, he charged, "The Chinese People will not look on idly while their neighboring country is being barbarously invaded by Imperialists." Zhou was reversing the reality, for the neighboring country to the north had initiated the aggression. Modifying his position on intervention, Mao had warned on October 23, "If U.S. forces do not advance toward our frontier, the Chinese People will not fight or resist them." Yet his troops had already crossed the Yalu into Korea in secret without at first engaging the Americans.

Mao expected MacArthur to ignore both Washington and Beijing. The general's alarmist message once the Chinese had come in, intended to promote attacks on Manchurian targets, prompted agonized reconsideration by Truman and the JCS. MacArthur's air chief, Lieutenant General George Stratemeyer, was reluctantly authorized to bomb the Yalu spans but only on the Korean approaches. However, the Yalu was freezing over, minimizing the importance of the bridges. If MacArthur could inhibit massive Chinese involvement, he thought, the war might end quickly. He had no idea how many Chinese were already in Korea.

Early in November, General Peng radioed Mao that the preliminary "counteroffensive" was now on hold. His troops had pulled back out of artillery range. For the next phase, Peng had to move men, munitions and supplies into position. Roads were few and narrow, and early winter had set in. It was "increasingly difficult to preserve the strength of our troops who have to sleep outside and in the snow." The Third Field Army's Russian-made heavy machine guns froze in the bitter cold, and many of the troops, veterans of the civil war in eastern China, had never experienced below-zero weather. (On November 20, as the ostensible lull in the northwest continued, Colonel Mariano Azurin of the Philippine-reinforced battalion, complained to the EUSAK* command, "The morale of our troops is very low. They have never been in even a mild climate before. I will not remark on the shortage of winter clothing." Yet he did.)

When the 7th Marines began the new day's operations below the Chosin Reservoir on November 7, troops had found that the Chinese opposite them the day before were out of close contact just as they had disappeared above the Chungchon River opposite the Eighth Army in the west. No one in the distant *Dai Ichi*, from which the two commands were

---

* Eighth United States Army, Korea.

ineffectively coordinated, perceived anything significant in what had to have been planned, simultaneous Chinese pull-backs. For several days, brief exchanges of fire on both fronts continued, then silence. The Chinese had come and gone.

After having been called off by Washington then permitted after an appeal from MacArthur, on November 8, a flight of B-29s from Japan plus three hundred fighter-bombers in several sorties attacked the Yalu bridges in the northwest. Ramps on the Korean side were damaged and the river town of Sinuiju largely destroyed. The raids seemed less in support of holding EUSAK gains in the north than in provoking a collision with Mao's forces that might release MacArthur from UN restraints. Despite years of Air Force brag, bombsights guarded like gold ingots were inaccurate, and bombs went awry in any case from wind turbulence. Although the Chinese complained about explosives detonating on their side of the Yalu, they viewed the targeting errors in the same vein as MacArthur, who sought provocation although the Pentagon did not.

The next day, MacArthur sent a top-secret cable to Washington requesting the rubber-stamping of his end-of-war objectives. He planned to drive the Chinese back across the Yalu and reunify Korea and to begin his parallel offensives before Thanksgiving Day. "I plan to launch my attack for this purpose," he announced, as if a hard winter was not already setting in, "on or about November fifteenth. . . . Any program short of this," he went on in his penchant for extreme rhetoric, "would completely destroy the morale of my forces and its psychological consequences would be inestimable. It would condemn us to an indefinite defense line in North Korea and would unquestionably arouse such resentment among the South Koreans that their forces would collapse or might even turn against us."

MacArthur predicted even further horrors if the Pentagon "deserted" him, invoking Munich and the sellout of Czechoslovakia in 1938, lecturing Washington on the "lessons of history." Yet the Chinese would soon rout the ineffective ROK troops, and MacArthur's own forces, rather than struggling in mountainous subzero conditions below the Yalu and uninterested in history, would rather have gone home for Christmas, leaving a shaky defensive line somewhere for the flight-prone South Koreans.

An ocean and a continent away, unaware of the realities and without adequate intelligence from the war zone, was MacArthur's only peer in the command structure, Defense Secretary George C. Marshall, Army chief of staff from 1939 to 1945. Duped by MacArthur's shrill anxieties, Marshall replied in a "very personal and informal" message sympathizing about the problems "in trying to direct a multinational army in a war fought in difficult terrain" with "limiting" diplomatic factors. The conflict, nevertheless, had to be restricted to Korea. "Everyone here, Defense, State, the President, is intensely desirous of supporting you." Yet the delicate international balance could not be disrupted, even if Korea was Josef Stalin's proxy war. That equilibrium had already been strained by MacArthur's reckless push toward the Yalu and repeated threats from Red China.

In Tokyo, MacArthur wavered between hysteria over the Chinese intervention and the puzzling pullback as well as his intelligence chief's soothing misreading of the apparent and unfathomable Chinese withdrawal. His ambitions wavered between unifying Korea at the Yalu and provoking a wider war, drawing in reluctant allies, to further his dream of reversing Communism in Asia. General Willoughby's advice was always what MacArthur wanted to hear. On the evidence of General Peng's relative quiescence, MacArthur's operations chief, Brigadier General Edwin K. Wright, sent a message for MacArthur to Ned Almond, with copies to Major General Walton Walker at the Eighth Army and to the Pentagon, urging that X Corps, limited in numbers, exploit the pause to do everything possible to assist Walker's forces across the forbidding Korean spine to the west.

Upbeat despite the worsening winter conditions his troops faced, Almond replied that he could best help EUSAK by continuing north beyond the reservoir highlands to the Manchurian border, after which his divisions could turn west to support "Johnnie" Walker. Although Almond emphasized the drawbacks of the stark wintry terrain, MacArthur, encouraged that the Chinese could not be located by reconnaissance flights, urged a quick close to the war, before arctic weather would handicap both sides. Lieutenant Colonel John H. Chiles, Almond's operations deputy, flew Almond's X Corps plan, which Marine commander Smith was at first not shown, to Tokyo. From there, to assist Walker on paper, MacArthur redrew the proposed boundary between Korean commands to stretch the Marines further west. (Smith had resisted separating his troops.) Despite the seemingly brief Chinese scare, MacArthur was eager to initiate his end-the-war offensives to push to the Yalu and preempt the looming Chinese. An exit by Christmas was still on.

Some brass in Korea believed him. Reporting from the Chongchon River front in the EUSAK west, Colonel Ernest V. Holmes, an Ohioan, told Hal Boyle, who put it in an AP dispatch dated November 15, that he believed the war would end the first week of December. "I doubt that we will ever go near the Manchurian border. Some damn fool might cross it and cause trouble. I will see you in Hawaii on Christmas Day."

Mao and Peng had cultivated MacArthur's illusions. *Dai Ichi* intelligence had no idea what numbers the Chinese had put across and assumed that they had little armor or artillery, limited motor transport and hardly any aircraft. Although no Soviet planes had been downed (Stalin had ordered nine MIG-9 and MIG-15 divisions to Manchuria), it was assumed from overheard air-to-ground conversations that Russians (instructing the Chinese) were flying along the Yalu frontier, whatever the MIG markings. The MIG-15, based on a wartime German design, had appeared in November and was so much faster than the F-80C that it could climb away from the now-inadequate *Shooting Star*, according to an Air Force historian, "as if it were anchored in the sky." Seldom making more than two passes, a MIG would then streak back across the border. Anti-aircraft fire based upon a Soviet radar warning net came from across the border in Manchuria. Counting upon MacArthur's public boasts about an end-by-Christmas offensive, Mao confidently radioed Peng on November 9 that he expected "one or two battles on the eastern and western fronts between late this month and early December to destroy another seven or eight regiments."

Returning to Beijing on the 13th, Peng told a conference of generals which Chairman Mao had convened, "We will employ a strategy of luring the enemy forces into our internal lines and wiping them out one by one." He would "fundamentally" turn the war around. For the entrapment he envisioned, the other side had to push forward. He would encourage that movement.

Reluctant to shift from an amphibious force to slogging inland infantry, O. P. Smith had to accept, nevertheless, orders from MacArthur via Almond which seemed, in the frozen terrain, utterly stupid. Moving forward with caution, to Almond's exasperation only about a mile a day, the Marines established operational and supply camps at Chinghung-ni, at the base of the climb into the Taebek range, and at Hagaru-ri, into the hills just below the Chosin Reservoir. On a flying visit to Smith at Hagaru on the 15th, Almond pointed to the north and urged, "We've got to go barreling up that road." Then he flew back to his posh compound.

"That road"—the iced-over dirt-and-gravel route from Hungnam, Hamhung and the sea—reached Hagaru over the Funchilin Pass, a narrow hairpin stretch over a chasm through which four huge conduits carried water from the reservoir to a power plant a half-mile under a narrow concrete bridge. Had the enemy blown the bridge, American tanks, trucks and motorized artillery could not have continued to Chosin and beyond. That the span remained intact—for the moment—suggested either a bizarre tactical blunder by the enemy—or a shrewd inducement to proceed riskily beyond. Smith worried that it was not a lapse but a lure.

"As I indicated when you were here," he wrote with unconcealed concern to the Marine commandant, General Clifton Cates, now back in Washington, "I have little confidence in the tactical judgment of the [X] Corps or in the realism of their planning. . . . Manifestly, we should not push on without regard to the Eighth Army. We would simply get farther out on a limb. . . . I believe a winter campaign in the mountains of North Korea is too much to ask of the American soldier or Marine." Smith had bypassed his immediate chief in Tokyo, assuming correctly that Lieutenant General Lemuel Shepherd was in MacArthur's pocket. Cates would claim later to have mislaid the letter before he could respond to it, recovering it, conveniently, only the next February. It was more politic than to contest the *Dai Ichi*.

The "limb" was real. To the north, under cover of the long pre-winter night, the Chinese 20th, 26th and 27th Armies, with 150,000 men, continued crossing the iced-over Yalu. Unseen, they deployed in the Chosin Reservoir highlands while thousands of Chinese service personnel moved supplies on foot southward and also, in near darkness, repaired roads, highways and bridges. They exploited intelligence from village informants and from their own advance men, supplemented by press and radio reports picked up from American correspondents, often complete to identification of units and soldiers. (The folks at home wanted to know how their boys were doing, and naming names was morale boosting.) When Lieutenant Colonel Robert Taplett, commanding the 3rd Battalion of the 5th Marine Regiment, helicoptered forward on the east bank of the reservoir, unhindered by ground fire, he could see crisscrossing tracks in the mountain snow and the deep shadows of foxholes. Flying low, his pilot confirmed the evidence. "Those damn holes," he agreed, "are just crawling with people."

Returned below the Yalu from Beijing on November 16, General Peng ordered each of his armies to continue the deception "that we are being intimidated into retreat." Meanwhile, according to the memoirs of Nikita Krushschev, Peng "composed lengthy telegrams [to Mao] expounding elaborate battle plans. . . . The enemy would be surrounded and finished off by decisive flanking strikes." Mao wired copies to Stalin. To spread further disinformation, Peng ordered the circulation of "safe-conduct passes"—a device employed in every war by every combatant. They included an image of a dead soldier on one side and a bloated, cigar-smoking, wine-swilling capitalist on the other, with the caption, in English,

> Korea's where the GIs die,
> Home's where the politicians lie . . .

Left by infiltrators or co-opted villagers, they offered assurance that troops surrendering would find "peace and safety," be permitted to write to their families, and receive food and medical care. "We have already set free many American and British prisoners, the "pass" promised. "You will certainly be freed and get home in the end."

The "trick"—in Peng's terms—followed up a suggestion he and his staff had made to Chairman Mao on November 17, 1950:

> We are proposing to release 100 American and puppet
> Rhee's prisoners . . . including 30 Americans and 70 puppet prisoners. . . . Our main objective is to publicize our

lenient treatment policy toward POWs in order to overcome the enemy troops; for fear of being murdered once
captured. We plan to send these prisoners back through
the front line positions during the night of the 19th. Please
instruct us immediately whether it is all right.

Mao approved. As Peng explained to General Du Ping,
"We can tell the prisoners that we are short of food supplies,
that we are starving, and probably are going to withdraw back
to China. . . . To hook a big fish, you must let the fish taste
your bait."

2

Upbeat Thanksgiving

GIs joked about being
"fattened up for the slaughter"

L ittle resistance from the apparent remnants of the North
Korean People's Army was encountered as, on the 19th,
troops from the Seventh Division's 17th Regiment reached the
village of Kapsan, northeast of the Chosin Reservoir. Trudging beyond, they were only twenty-three miles from the Yalu
and the Manchurian frontier. Intending to push further in the
intense cold, the regimental command radioed for airdrops of
250 squad tents and 500 oil-burning pot-belly stoves to heat
them. (They arrived on schedule, but because of parachutes
inadequate to slow the drop sufficiently, many of the stoves
shattered on impact.) Moving ahead, Korean troops from the
ROK Capital Division reached the river farther to the east,
hacked through the ice and filled a bottle with Yalu water to
send symbolically to Syngman Rhee.

Without opposition, soldiers from Colonel Herbert
Powell's 17th advanced further on foot the next day over the

snow-covered hills, and by ten in the morning of the 21st were in the village of Hyesanjin, nearly destroyed the week before by carrier planes. Ned Almond and division commander Major General David Barr flew in for the occasion, following the lead company two miles down the dirt road from the crest overlooking the Yalu. The river, little more than fifty yards wide near its eastern source on the slopes of 8,000-foot Nam P'otae-san, was frozen but for a narrow channel midstream. That, too, would soon ice over.

Although it was well below zero (Fahrenheit), some jubilant Americans expressed themselves in the traditional soldiers' gesture that press cameramen spared photographing for the folks back home. Standing at the snow-covered riverbank within sight of the Chinese side, troops urinated in unsteady unison into the frozen Yalu. (No penile frostbite is recorded.) For the front pages, an Associated Press wirephoto would depict, distantly and modestly, from the rear, a cluster of 17th Regiment troops ostensibly looking out across the Yalu at the snow-covered hills of Manchuria.

Almost certainly without reference to the hallowed ritual, MacArthur radioed to Almond, "Heartiest congratulations, Ned, and tell Dave Barr that the 7th Division hit the jackpot." Press reports from Tokyo on November 22 indicated that the troops at the Yalu had "dug in"—but that was *Dai Ichi* exaggeration. The advance was more symbolic than real. Also erroneous—obviously a Chinese plant—were "intelligence reports that the Communists are hastily recruiting all males 18 to 45 years old in the northeastern provinces in an attempt to recreate their wrecked divisions." Luring the enemy into false complacency worked well in gullible Tokyo. "Official accounts" from GHQ were that troops were "pushing ahead to clear northeast Korea." From Taiwan, Chiang Kai-Shek's island domain, came charges that Moscow had "taken over" mainland China as a "colony"—disinformation from a different source. In reality, but for the military hardware it could solicit, Mao's regime was distancing itself from Stalin.

Thanksgiving was only two days away. Impelled by renewed optimism about the war, the rush in the United States for airline tickets for holiday travel exceeded all previous records. Another cause for optimism came from Princeton, where *New York Times* science writer William L. Laurence reported on "a new type of electronic brain that will save years of time and millions of dollars" and was described as "the largest and most accurate analogue computer ever built." Constructed under contract for the Navy's Bureau of Aeronautics for advanced weapons design, it used "4,000 electronic tubes and several miles of intricate wiring." Such futuristic weaponry seemed unnecessary for Korea, where the most advanced technology employed was to deliver by air, land and sea tens of thousands of Thanksgiving dinners. According to the *Dai Ichi* victory estimates, most troops would be heading Stateside somehow by Christmas, making another vast holiday dinner operation unnecessary.

Even without field glasses, Barr and Almond when briefly at the Yalu, could see Chinese sentries in the village on the other side impassively walking their rounds. No other evidences of activity were apparent. The frozen Yalu, Almond would recall, seemed "very little of an obstacle" to a Chinese

US Army X Corps commander, Major General Almond, center, in front of the Yalu River with 7th Infantry Division officers, from left to right, Brigadier General Homer Kiefer, division artillery commander; Brigadier General Henry I. Hodes, assistant division commander; Major General David G. Barr, division commander; and Colonel Herbert B. Powell, RCT-17 commander. *National Archives*

crossing, "but otherwise there was no serious concern." That should have been concern enough.

Returning in his L-5 to Corps headquarters at Hungnam, well south of the Barr's beachhead on the north coast, Almond formally congratulated the 7th Division's commander early the next day in a radio message very likely meant more as a brag to MacArthur, who also received it. "The fact that only twenty days ago," Almond began in heroic mode, "this division landed amphibiously on the beaches at Iwon, and advanced 200 miles over torturous mountain terrain and fought successfully against a determined foe in subzero weather will be recorded in history as an outstanding military achievement."

Private Bob Hammond of the 57th Field Artillery turned eighteen as his battalion reached the Yalu. "This is it!" he was told, as if their mission was accomplished. "The top of Korea! You can't go any further than that, or you wind up in China."

The 7th's other regiments, the 31st and 32nd, were moving up well to the rear of the 17th, which, after its exploratory probe, had backtracked cautiously south from the Yalu. Scattered North Korean units stubbornly impeded the 17th, blowing up bridges and cratering the already poor, narrow roads before slipping in darkness toward hideouts in the Chosin highlands. Yet the real foes seemed the arctic temperature and the strategic vacuity in Tokyo. Frostbite was causing more casualties than gunfire and grenades. It was easy to order troop advances in frigid Korea from the upper floor of the *Dai Ichi*, with its placid view across renamed First Avenue to the Hibiya Park palace gardens of the figurehead Emperor.

Almost nothing kept the efficient military logistical services from furnishing elaborate Thanksgiving dinners sometime from Thursday through the weekend for all troops in Korea, even if the dinners, complete to the holiday trimmings, had to be air-dropped. From Pusan in the south almost to the Yalu, celebrating the occasion was a triumph of American ingenuity. Spare parts for vehicles and spare socks for men as well as stockpiled fuel and anti-freeze were lacking, but trestle tables up and down the peninsula were heaped with aluminum containers of roast turkey with gravy, cranberry sauce, shrimp cocktail, asparagus, stewed tomatoes, "snowflake" and candied sweet potatoes, green peas and whole kernel corn, stuffed

olives, sliced pineapple, fruitcake and pumpkin pie, most of it
prepared in Japan from ingredients shipped from the States.

In the EUSAK west, Thanksgiving was complicated by
MacArthur's orders that the jump-off hour would be at 1000
the next day. Front-line units had to prepare for "go" almost
as they attacked their lavish holiday trays in what seemed un-
earthly quiet.

A world away, in Manhattan, General Alfred Gruenther, Dwight Eisenhower's SHAEF deputy in 1944–45, was
visiting his former boss at Ike's presidential residence at Columbia University. Gruenther's eldest son, Dick, class of 1946
at West Point, was a platoon leader in the 7th Division's 17th
Infantry. Although his father did not yet know it, he had
been severely wounded four days before units of his regiment
reached the Yalu. As a power within the Joint Chiefs of Staff,
Gruenther realized that trouble was brewing in Korea and that
MacArthur was ignoring the evidence. He had already over-
reached. His troops in the north were about to be confronted
by Mao's innumerable Chinese.

Gruenther had invited himself to Thanksgiving dinner
to consult with Eisenhower. The activation of NATO was
imminent, and Gruenther would be deputy, again, to Ike, in
the counter-force to Soviet ambitions in Europe. John Eisenhower, then a young instructor at West Point, was also at the
table. Once Gruenther left, Ike confided to his son that he
had never been so depressed about the war in Korea. Leaving the next morning to return to the Academy, Lieutenant
Eisenhower switched on his car radio and heard a newscaster
reporting MacArthur's "home for Christmas" promise. After

two further Christmases had passed, young Eisenhower would be in Korea himself, with the 15th Regiment of the 3rd Division.

After landing at Iwon, the division was far above the 38th Parallel in Almond's X Corps. Red Chinese historian Hu Hai Bo fictionalized imaginatively, "On the northeast front of the U.S. Army, each command printed nice menus. There were tablecloths on the tables, and festive candles were set up at the ruins of burnt down villages. Some units even gave out whiskey, and the officers and soldiers had hot baths and changed to new uniforms." But for the battered villages, nothing in his account was remotely accurate. In that "northeast" sector, where the start of the X Corps offensive would be delayed several days beyond EUSAK's launch, the 5th Marines regimental diary described brief Thanksgiving services at several companies and noted apples and mince pie on the menu shared by the 1st and 2nd Battalions. Chesty Puller's 1st Regiment at Koto-ri, eleven miles south of Hagaru, attacked their Thanksgiving dinners near a rapidly running stream that was still unfrozen.

"Each day it had gotten colder," Staff Sergeant Lee Bergee recalled. "To the north and west I could see high, snowcapped mountains. We ate turkey and all the trimmings. The night before, I had watched the cooks working, their area illuminated by truck headlights. Before dinner I refereed a tackle-football game on a field two bulldozers had leveled for us. In the afternoon Colonel Puller pinned decorations on the chests of men who'd won* them at Inchon or Seoul. . . . One [medical] corpsman with our battalion shook his head from side to

---

*One is *awarded* a decoration. In "won," Bergee uses a familiar service term.

side while they read his citation for bravery. I washed some clothes in the stream; the water was very cold. Each night was below freezing. I hoped we'd be out of Korea before the worst of winter fell on us."

In some subzero sectors, the festive fowl had to be thawed for consumption the next day. At Hagaru-ri, at the base of the Chosin Reservoir, Lieutenant Colonel Raymond Davis's 1st Battalion of the 7th Marines found their turkeys as "frozen hard" as the weather, but the night before Thanksgiving an officer at headquarters "came up with an idea. He made a mountain of the frozen birds around two field kitchen stoves that had been fired up. Next he covered the whole thing with two pyramidal tents that he sealed tight with snow and brush. By morning the birds were thawed enough for them to be cut up and cooked." In the 3rd Battalion, Sergeant Emilio "Ray" Aguirre discovered that a patrol from George Company, his own unit, would be ordered out on reconnaissance, delaying their share of turkey and trimmings. "I guess no one wanted to volunteer, so Ernie [the platoon leader] looked at us and said, 'I guess you have to go, Ray. And Gordy is going with you and the third squad. . . . I'm sorry all this had to happen, but those are my orders. . . . They have reported some enemy activity on that hill. I know how you men feel going out on patrol, especially on Thanksgiving, but you know that this business doesn't take time off for the holidays. Maybe you can get to eat your Thanksgiving dinner when you come back."

They griped all the way forward, found an abandoned jeep that was "pretty well shot up," heard "artillery coming down at us on every side"—probably mortar fire—and raced back to the

A 5th Marine cook prepares Thanksgiving pie at Hagaru-ri combat base. *National Archive*

Thanksgiving dinner is served near Hamhung, where the weather
was not as severe. *Department of Defense*

edge of their hill, "hoping to get a bit of that turkey." The last at the chow wagon, "they couldn't even find the meat under all the green peas and potatoes." Aguirre opened a rations can of tamales.

Corporal Harley Trueblood's Baker Company, 1st Tank Battalion, with Chesty Puller's 1st Marines, looked forward to its first hot meal since coming ashore, but the Siberian winds froze the steaming slices of turkey between mess kit and mouth. "What you had," he recalled, "was a kind of a turkey popsicle." Charlie Company's watch below Toktong Pass would be on a knoll designated as Hill 1419—its elevation in meters—but called Turkey Hill because Baker Company, which had occupied it on Thanksgiving Day, had dumped its scraps there, inadequately covered with soil too frozen to break up. When the Chinese attacked, Charlie Company's survivors abandoned the hill, and the turkey bones.

The 192 officers and men of Captain William Barber's Fox Company in the 7th Regiment's 2nd battalion had welcomed Thanksgiving dinner as a rare respite from the greasy stuff usually served by mess cooks, itself a relief from canned rations, but by the time they took their trays to their foxholes, the candied sweet potatoes, sausage stuffing and turkey smothered in gravy were frozen. Mentioning only the positive aspects, Lieutenant Lawrence Schmitt, the company communications officer, wrote fervently that night to his wife, "We sang the 'Star-Spangled Banner,' 'America [the Beautiful],' and 'My Country 'Tis of Thee.' The Chaplain said a prayer, and the [regimental] colonel gave a talk. I have a lot to be thankful for: my wonderful wife and boy, our house, our health, and our faith. May the Good

Lord continue to be generous to us." (A few days later his shin-bone would be shattered by sniper fire, but he would survive.)

The next morning, their trench latrine and the paths to it were littered with frozen diarrhea. Because the battalion had moved on Thanksgiving morning toward Yudam-ni, four-teen steep miles above Hagaru, some Marines could not get at their turkey trays until the evening after the holiday, but, medic William Davis recalled, "no one minded." As they approached Yudam-ni, west of the reservoir, through Toktong Pass, they were confronted by about two hundred Chinese, who were scattered by artillery and a called-in air strike. Once the Marines secured the forlorn village, their dinners followed from Hagaru. Cooks worked by truck and jeep headlights, and troops ate in the glare from tin trays "just like aboard ship. Darker than pitch. We stood or sat on the [warm] hoods of the vehicles and ate our meal. . . . You had to eat fast because everything was turning cold. The gravy and then the mashed potatoes froze first. The inside of the turkey was still warm. Boy, you ate fast. And all the time the snipers [fixed on the distant headlights] were shooting at us."

Harsh and hazardous circumstances almost everywhere complicated the rough but festive interlude. No one had to worry about interruptions from the air. Soviet planes in Man-churia did not risk flying below the Yalu, as downing a Rus-sian pilot would expose the open secret of their presence. In the hiatus after the unexplained Chinese withdrawal—but for brief interruptions as at Yudam-ni—lights attracted little en-emy fire. It was as if the enemy was abetting Thanksgiving. GIs joked about being "fattened up for the slaughter."

The Navy dined well when aboard ship. Rear Admiral James H. Doyle, out in Hungnam Harbor, sent General Smith a roasted turkey for his staff mess. Smith looked forward to "a family Thanksgiving dinner" with a bird that would not have to be thawed. The staff would enjoy Doyle's gesture, but not their chief. He had to be elsewhere.

Few troops were aware of the dining excess prepared for X Corps high brass. Twenty-eight guests sat at General Almond's tables in his heated trailer compound at Hamhung, eight miles up the main supply route from Hungnam. Included were Almond's top Army subordinates, Marine generals O. P. Smith and Field Harris, and colonels Chesty Puller and Alpha Bowser. Smith's party had jeeped down the MSR from Hagaru-ri, his command post near the airstrip under construction, where more than a thousand Marines guarded the working site, a barren bean field of rock-strewn black loam already deeply frozen. (The command post nearby was a Japanese-built house with a portrait of Stalin prominent on one wall. Smith let it remain.) Colonel Puller jeeped fifty-three icy miles south from Koto-ri, below Hagaru, where he oversaw 2,500 Marines, 1,500 soldiers and 250 British Royal Marines.

Almond's festive board "was a plush state of affairs," Bowser recalled unappreciatively. (The dinner may have prompted Hu Hai Bo to apply its lavish ambience to all of X Corps.) According to Smith, "The meal itself included all the appointments one would expect in, say, a formal luncheon in Washington: a cocktail bar, white tablecloths and napkins, china, silverware, place cards." He felt awkward amidst the grotesque luxury, realizing where the Marine regiments were or were going.

Portrait of Soviet dictator Joseph Stalin found inside a Chinese command bunker. *National Archives*

The 3rd Battalion of the 7th Marines, with Homer Litzenberg's regimental staff, took up positions to the north in the forlorn, frozen village of Yudam-ni the next day. General Smith intended to have Lieutenant Colonel Raymond L. Murray's 5th Marines pass through Litzenberg's 7th at Yudam-ni, with Puller's 1st in reserve behind both. But for probing patrols, they would go no farther.

Relenting under Smith's pressure to consolidate his forces, Almond ordered a regimental combat team from General Barr's 7th Division, RCT-31, to replace the 5th Marines on the east side of the reservoir by Monday the 27th. It would be the very day, Stateside, that newspapers published the triumphal photo of Barr's troops at the Yalu. Once they had withdrawn, trouble loomed from the Chinese lurking near both banks of the iced-over reservoir. However worried by reports of enemy sightings from villagers above Chosin, General Barr, with his forward units drawn back, issued Almond's unnerving deployment instructions to Colonel Allan D. MacLean, who began supplementing his 31st Regiment with a tank company, a field artillery battalion, and the 1st battalion of the 32nd Infantry, commanded by Lieutenant Colonel Don C. Faith, Jr. It was no longer a secret that many Chinese had already crossed the frozen Yalu from Linchiang in Manchuria, where the river angled north about a hundred miles above Yudam-ni, then dropped to the southeast. Although the terrain was rough and the ground frozen, the Chinese were used to moving without wheels and hiding by day.

On the 25th, just after Thanksgiving, a Marine chaplain, Navy lieutenant Cornelius J. Griffin (who would be wounded two weeks later), asked a mess sergeant "to save the red cellophane the frozen turkeys came wrapped in . . . , and, once dinner was over, to wrap all the bones he could find in it." When the sergeant wondered why, Griffin explained in service unchaplainese, "When we get up farther north, if we have to, we can boil the hell out of these bones in melted snow and make some damned good turkey broth." (Within the week, the bones were recycled, and also the wrappings. "We took the red cellophane and reused it a second time to cover up all the holes and loose corners in the sick bay [tent]s during blackouts.")

Morale remained high despite frigid winds and pelting snow. Huddled in their tents, troops talked between

Lieutenant Colonel Don C. Faith, right, commanding officer of the 1st Battalion, 32nd Infantry, 7th Division, pictured with the regiment's commanding officer, Colonel Alan D. MacLean, in Japan in the spring of 1950. *Marine Corps Historical Division*

mouthfuls, in less than holiday circumstances, of the slim chances of enjoying Christmas dinner back home—or even en route home. That fading fantasy had been sustained by the *Dai Ichi*, a military equivalent of the land of Oz. "Regardless of Chinese intervention," MacArthur had assured a *Chicago Tribune* reporter the day before Thanksgiving, "the war will be finished by the end of the year."

Arriving on the coast at Iwon, the northernmost debarkation site, with self-propelled 155mm howitzers mounted on tank tracks, Lieutenant James H. Dill of B Battery, 31st Field

Artillery, 7th Division, climbed icy, switch-backed mountain roads with his battery as far as the village of Kapsan before withdrawing south without incident. Thanksgiving, he wrote, was "an unbelievably joyous break" from canned corned beef hash. At their turkey dinner, a memo distributed from higher-level brass, apparently with origins in Tokyo, informed the battery "that the war was almost over, and that we should prepare for a return to Japan. The advisory also included an example of how forms should be made up for returning our ROKs to their own army. We were to tell them that most would soon be discharged and sent home." (Republic of Korea soldiers added numbers but little else to the division.) Another bulletin recommended brushing up on close order drill "since the 7th Division would be expected to take part in a Grand Victory Parade as soon as we reached Japan."

Victory meant pursuing alleged North Korean remnants to the Yalu, west to east. Ten days before Thanksgiving, Mac-Arthur had explained to William Sebald, the State Department's representative in Japan, that it was crucial to reach the frontier before the river froze over, as the Chinese might then be tempted to cross, massively, on the ice. Visiting Tokyo from Seoul, John Muccio, the dapper American ambassador to South Korea, shared his worries with the general that the Chinese may not have been merely blustering about intervention. Nevertheless, MacArthur was "satisfied," according to Muccio's notes, that "our Air Forces and our Intelligence" would have detected the movement of large forces across the Yalu. Covertly, MacArthur conceded, the Chinese might have managed to move "25,000, and no more than 30,000, soldiers across the border." He knew there had been exchanges of fire. He had even estimated enemy numbers earlier at 60,000, but the Chinese seemed to MacArthur to have had second thoughts and slipped away. If they tried to put more troops across, he assured Muccio, General George Stratemeyer's planes would bomb the hell out of them and the area "will be left a desert."

MacArthur and his staff seemed ignorant of Mao's shrewd *On Protracted War*, in which he advised, "To achieve quick decisions we should generally attack not an enemy force holding a position, but one on the move." That meant concentrating, "under cover, a big force along the route through which the enemy is sure to pass, [then] suddenly descend on him while he is moving, encircle and attack him before he knows what is happening, and conclude the fighting with all speed."

Unknowingly fulfilling all of Mao's prior conditions, MacArthur made a dramatic flying visit to Korea on the morning after Thanksgiving to announce his imminent offensive. As it was a smug, self-promotional strategy for the media, he would take newsmen and photographers with him as well as a few of his courtiers at the *Dai Ichi*. Early on Friday morning, November 24, his four-motored, personal *SCAP* flew to the airfield at Sinanju, about fifty miles north of the occupied North Korean capital, Pyongyang. Sinanju was one of the few prewar NK airstrips with a runway lengthy enough for his sleek newly delivered Lockheed *Constellation*. Although the strip abutted Major General Frank Milburn's I Corps headquarters, MacArthur could not wait for touchdown and his usual photo-op performance of GHQ announcements. From Tokyo, as he took off, the *Dai Ichi* issued what seemed intended as his next-to-last declaration about the future of the conflict. The final bulletin would confirm the end of the war.

Curiously, while MacArthur had denied any substantial involvement by Mao or Stalin in Korea, he sweepingly suggested otherwise in his self-congratulatory new communique, which took a broad swipe at world Communism:

> The United Nations massive compression envelopment in North Korea against the new Red Armies cooperating there is now approaching its decisive effort. The isolating component of the pincer, our Air Forces of all types, have for the last three weeks, in a sustained attack of model coordination and effectiveness, successfully interdicted enemy lines of support from the North so that further reinforcement therefrom has been sharply curtailed and essential supplies markedly limited. The [X Corps] eastern sector of the pincer, with noteworthy and effective Naval support, has steadily advanced in a brilliant tactical movement and has now reached a commanding enveloping position, cutting in two the northern reaches of the enemy's geographic potential. This morning the western sector of the pincer moves forward in general assault in an effort to complete the compression and close the vise. If successful that should for all practical purposes end the war, restore peace and unity to Korea, [and] enable the prompt withdrawal of United Nations military forces.

"In the history of war," the Maoist historian Hu Hai Bo writes, "no military commander [until MacArthur] would review his plan of attack publicly before the attack. The route, scale, force, destination, were disclosed like a travel itinerary. A British newspaper observed that promoting his strategy so widely 'is certainly a strange way to fight.'" Those aware of the potential for catastrophe in MacArthur's confident misjudgments were alarmed as they read the handout duplicated for everyone flying with him. Yet few could confide any anxieties even to each other. MacArthur could suspend a correspondent's accreditation or abort an officer's career. A reporter assigned to the British 27th Brigade in the west wrote later that "this document filled us with alarm and despondency."

In his command diary, O. P. Smith, east of the frigid Taebek peaks of Korea, referred privately to MacArthur's "usual flowery communique." Smith's operations chief, Colonel Alpha Bowser, called it "goofy." Despite later misgivings, Major General Clark Ruffner, MacArthur's hand-picked chief of staff for Almond, loyally backed the operation. Korea had been Ruffner's first combat zone experience. He had spent World War II as deputy to his father-in-law, Lieutenant General Robert "Nelly" Richardson, an old friend of MacArthur, in rugged Hawaii.

Leading a fleet of jeeps to tour rear areas, Eighth Army commander Walton Walker, with Frank Milburn, ceremonially met MacArthur's party at the airstrip just south of the Chongchon River. In the fifteen-degree frost and gloom, MacArthur pulled on a parka and fastened a checked scarf around his neck, never removing his trademark sunglasses. Because of his attack orders, few senior officers were present, as troops were already positioning for the push further north.

While Major General Frank Church and Major General John Coulter and others gathered around MacArthur's jeep, reporters clustered nearby for MacArthur's briefing and for follow-up comments from his top brass. Milburn prudently predicted tough going on both sides of the peninsula, reporting that patrols had found Coulter's IX Corps sector "heavily defended," while Church loyally noted that his 24th Division had faced little resistance and might make it all the way to the Yalu. "Well, if they go fast enough," MacArthur quipped, "maybe some of them could be home by Christmas."

Colonel John Austin of the I Corps staff recalled the general on his rounds as "erect and supremely confident, absolutely at his peak." He was "walking history." To the assembled officers at Corps headquarters, he began, "Gentlemen, the war is over. The Chinese are not coming into this war. In less than two weeks, the Eighth Army will close on the Yalu across the entire front. The 3rd Division will be back in Fort Benning for Christmas dinner." No one questioned the logistical impossibilities, Austin told the historian Robert Smith decades later when Smith was writing a book about MacArthur in Korea. "It would have been like questioning an announcement from God." But the 3rd Division was on the other Korean front, in the northeast, not with the Eighth Army, and two weeks hence, even victory would have left no time for disassembling a division and returning it for Christmas dinner nine thousand miles away in Georgia.

General Stratemeyer recalled that MacArthur "was thrilled with the entire operation as was everyone in his [GHQ] party. Complete victory by Christmas seemed assured." Recalling that he had already made such promises,

General Douglas MacArthur in jeep with Lieutenant Walton H. Walker, in rear seat, commander of the Eighth Army, in Korea on November 24 to announce the offensive that was to end the war. *National Archives*

even to President Truman when he met him at Wake Island in mid-October, MacArthur added to General Church, "Don't make me a liar." The United Press quoted MacArthur remarking buoyantly to John Coulter, as overheard by Earnest Holbrecht of the United Press, "You can tell them"—the troops—"that when we get up to the Yalu, Jack, they can all come home. I want to make good my statement that they will get a Christmas dinner at home." The Associated Press reported his saying, "I hope to keep my promise to the GIs to have them home for Christmas."

Brigadier General Courtney Whitney, MacArthur's all-purpose aide since Manila days, years afterward recalled the boasts cautiously as "half in jest but with a certain firmness of meaning and purpose." MacArthur would later describe all his references to Christmas as press misquotes. His promising troops Christmas dinner at home, a skeptical Pentagon official cracked privately, was a confusion of domiciles. The general hadn't been back in the States since 1937. "General MacArthur has been in the Far East so long he's come to think of Japan as home."

Veteran newscaster Lowell Thomas, who had known MacArthur since 1918, reported on radio that when he saw the story that had come over the wire, "I shook my head and told my associates I was positive that MacArthur had never made any such statement. Today the correction came. The General says he was misquoted." Since he always invented his own reality, he would allege afterward that he displayed far less optimism than reported. Once foreboding seemed more appropriate than self-congratulation, he claimed, "What I had seen at the front worried me greatly. The ROK troops were not yet in good shape, and the entire line was deplorably weak in numbers." Having it both ways, MacArthur also alleged inventively, years later, that the home-by-Christmas boast, "twisted by the press into a prediction . . . with which to bludgeon me," was really intended to assure the Chinese that we would get out of Korea the moment the Manchurian border was reached."

Five hours by jeep convoy through what seemed safe areas concluded MacArthur's pre-offensive EUSAK tour at the Sinanju airstrip where it had begun. Walker and his staff saluted good-byes at the ramp of the *SCAP*. As the cabin door closed, Walker murmured about the home-by-Christmas brag,

"Bullshit!" Then he rumbled back to his command post. Mike Lynch, his L-5 pilot accompanying him in a jeep, had never before heard a derogatory word from his boss about anyone. Privately despondent, Walker knew better than to share Mac-Arthur's grandstanding optimism in the face of oncoming winter and unseen and numberless Chinese, but he was cowed in the general's presence. Within ten days, Walker's Eighth Army would retreat, disastrously, 120 miles.

To enhance security during MacArthur's tour, the Far East Air Force had intensified its activity below the frontier, following up aircraft strikes mounted from the carrier *Leyte*, attempting to bomb the southern spans of the Yalu bridges. (The attacks were intended as a protective distraction from MacArthur's presence as well as part of the pre-offensive buildup.)

Air strikes could—and do—have unanticipated consequences. The Chinese People's Volunteers headquarters area was unlocated by *Dai Ichi* surveillance. Pilots had only suppositions that it existed. Chairman Mao's eldest son, Mao An Ying, twenty-eight, had enlisted, with his father's permission, in the CPV. Ambitious to rise in politics, he wanted to command an infantry regiment, but General Peng, realizing that Soviet-educated young Mao's experience was only as party secretary of the Beijing Machinery Factory, named him instead his military assistant and Russian language translator. A headquarters post seemed safe.

At dawn on the morning following Thanksgiving, a holiday the Chinese ignored, sirens sounded at Taeyudong, below the Yalu in the west. Peng's deputy, Hong Xue Zhi, urged him to rush to a shelter in a nearby mine shaft. "Big Hong," said Peng, "Why? If you are afraid, you should go!"

"We do not count," said Hong. "But you are the chief commander. Of course you have to go. It would be unfortunate if anything happened. Go, go, go!"

After Peng was half-dragged to shelter, bombs fell, one destroying the wood-plank structure he had just left. Mao An Ying and another junior officer, Gao Rui Xin, had remained in the farm cabin—Peng's office. It was hit before they could flee. Both were killed. An Ying's body could be identified only by the German revolver he owned, lying at his side.

Despite the certain embarrassment to his command, Peng realized that he could not withhold the news from the Chairman. Peng radioed Mao's deputy, Zhou Enlai, that An Ying's body could not be treated differently from other casualties. He would be buried in North Korea. "I, on behalf of the CPV command, will inscribe a tombstone tablet indicating that he joined the CPV on his own free will and died on the battlefield, and [that] he has proven himself as a fine son of Mao Zedong."

After consulting with such officials as Deng Xiaoping (who would be Mao's successor), Zhou agreed, but the Chairman was not immediately informed. Months later, when Peng apologized in person for not better safeguarding young Mao, his father appeared grieved but conceded, "An Ying has just done his duty." It was "characteristic of our revolutionary spirit to share weal and woe." An Ying remained in North Korea under his wooden red star.

Like O. P. Smith on the X Corps front, Walker had delayed the opening of his offensive as long as he dared disobey

MacArthur. General Smith operated under his own Mac-
Arthur surrogate, Ned Almond, who conceded that there were
a few Chinese self-confessed volunteers. All Walker could do
was offer an anxious message to General Church for Colonel
Richard W. Stephens, whose 21ˢᵗ Infantry would lead the 24ᵗʰ
Division's advance: "You tell Stephens that the first time he
smells Chinese chow,* [he should] pull back immediately." Yet
when Walker's deputy, Major General Leven Allen, returned
from Sinanju to Eighth Army headquarters, he remarked to
staff officers, "I think the attack will go. General MacArthur
would not have come over if he did not think so."

Once the *Constellation* was airborne, MacArthur instructed his pilot, Lieutenant Colonel Anthony F. Story, as
he began the three-hour flight back to Tokyo, "Head for the
west coast and fly up the Yalu." MacArthur wanted to reach
the mouth of the river and then swing along it, just below the
Manchurian border, eastward.

"I don't think we should do it, General," said Story.†

"I don't care," said MacArthur. "I don't want to go right
back to Japan. I want to follow the Yalu River all the way to
the other side [of Korea]." From about five thousand feet—it
was cold and clear—he wanted personal confirmation before
winter darkness settled in that there was no buildup of enemy forces in the Korean north. He lit his pipe and calmly

---

* A Chinese account quotes Walker as referring to "fried noodles."

† Loyally, Story afterward changed his tune. MacArthur "told me a couple of
days ago he had it in mind. He is the boss. And I would take him any place he
wants to go." Had that been the case, the jets from Kimpo would have been
circling above.

settled back. An officer brought him a sheaf of topographical maps. In the glare of the snow and ice below no one aboard saw anything move. Not a shot was fired from north of the Yalu, nor did enemy aircraft appear, although on earlier flights by border-hugging jets, the voices of Russian-speaking pilots were often overheard.

Those apart from MacArthur's *Dai Ichi* entourage openly lacked his confidence. "Sid," an anxious correspondent appealed to one of MacArthur's Manila-vintage aides, Lieutenant Colonel Huff, "is this trip really necessary?" MacArthur would not harness a parachute, although others did. "You gentlemen wear them if you care to do so," he said. "I'll stick with the plane."

Once Tony Story urgently radioed for a fighter escort, jets from Kimpo airbase near Seoul quickly caught up to the *Constellation*, flying at nine thousand feet. Story had lingered back awaiting them. "At this height," MacArthur later claimed extravagantly, "we could observe in detail the entire area of international No-Man's Land"—a curious term for sovereign territory—"all the way to the Siberian border. All that spread before our eyes was an endless expanse of utterly barren countryside, jagged hills, yawning crevices, and the black waters of the Yalu locked in snow and ice. It was a merciless wasteland. If a large force or massive supply train had passed over the border, the imprint had already been well covered by the intermittent snowstorms of the Yalu valley." Yet this was the forbidding wintry terrain he had ordered troops on the ground below to occupy at whatever hazard.

At 3:10, little more than an hour after takeoff, Story turned south, over the Chosin Reservoir area. Nothing could be seen but the snow-capped spine of Korea. Relieved to be touching down soon in Tokyo, the elite GHQ reporters who traveled with the general began preparing dramatic dispatches for home. "MacArthur Shows No Fear," the AP would headline. Relman Morin quoted Major General Courtney Whitney, a MacArthur cheerleader, as boasting, "That is what I would call thumbing your nose at the Chinese." It was, said a correspondent on the flight out of MacArthur's hearing, "what I would call pushing your luck a little."

An imaginative Chinese account dramatized how General Peng and his staff supposedly learned about the showboating flight while holed up in a farmer's hut just below the Yalu:

> Xia Wen came down and stood under a big walnut tree with the others. They saw a squadron of American Shooting Star jets in formation heading north. Then came more planes, more and more. "The enemy offensive is starting," said Deputy Commander Qin Peng.
>
> "I'm afraid it has already started," said Ten Yun Han, the second deputy commander. As he was talking, a large aircraft came flying up from the south. It came slowly, leisurely, calm and unhurried. Fighters escorted the plane on all sides. Everyone gazed at this large plane in amazement. It flew north and, shortly after, circled and began to broadcast. Xia Wen, who understood English, listened carefully. It was a broadcast from General MacArthur to the American troops below. Someone in the crowd said it was really MacArthur!
>
> Xia Wen then interpreted for the others. "MacArthur said this war could have ended by Thanksgiving. The situation became complicated because of the

appearance of unidentified foreign forces. He believes, however, that there are no obstacles in front of the United Nations troops that cannot be overcome. The offensive was launched today—a general offensive to end the Korean War by Christmas. If the war ends by Christmas, all enlisted men can return home and spend Christmas with their families.

Qui Peng laughed. "Well, we'll invite them to spend Christmas in heaven."

MacArthur's alleged broadcast from his plane was a Chinese invention, as was the absurd contention that his words could be heard nearly two miles below, over the roar of the accompanying F-80 jets. Nor were any American troops as far north as Peng's headquarters hideout. In reality, Peng Dehuai learned later of radio reports from correspondents covering MacArthur about his flying visit to announce his offensive. "Liar!" Peng was quoted as scoffing. "So you plan to drive up to the Yalu by December 25th! That's a groundless tale. I think that MacArthur is too optimistic."

When the *Constellation* touched down at the Haneda airbase near Tokyo, once Japan's principal prewar airport, 5th Air Force commander Lieutenant General Stratemeyer was on the tarmac to award MacArthur the Distinguished Flying Cross. (No one else on the flight was apparently eligible.) *Time* once described a scene at the *Dai Ichi* where "bleary eyed staff officers looked up from stacks of paper [and] whispered, 'God, the man is great.'" Not to be outdone in excess, Stratemeyer enthused to newsmen, "He's the greatest man in history."

The expanse below the Yalu was not as dramatically stark as described by MacArthur. Kanggye, believed at the *Dai Ichi* to be Kim Il Sung's emergency NKPA headquaters, was still smoldering after low-level Far East Air Force raids. The Yalu dams and power plants sending up plumes of steam seemed quiet and untouched. Where spans on the Korean side of the big steel bridges were bomb damaged, it appeared in the waning daylight as if nothing moved. Yet after dark, loaded trucks and peasant-conscripted porters bearing A-frame burdens on their backs crossed the ice each day. Before the brightening of dawn a small army of villagers and farmers emerged with brooms and swept away the telltale tracks. The small blur of Hyesanjin, newly reached by U.S. troops, had been pointed out to MacArthur. As he did not know that Barr's troops had since withdrawn, he joked to Tony Story, "Flap the wings, or something."

From a height greater than the general's plane flew, northern Korea resembles an immense upside-down boot with its heel in the west and its foot in the east and the Chosin Reservoir where a buckle might be. The heel end is at Sinuiju. On the other side of the arch the foot continues from Hyesanjin to the Tumen River toe in southeastern Siberia. Story, wary of possible MIGs, had kept wary distance from Soviet airspace. The border from Sinuiju to Siberia, 570 miles long—five times that of the narrow waist of Korea—was an impossible front to defend if the Yalu and Tumen banks were held, and it was inconceivable that Stalin would permit an American presence touching Russian territory. Nevertheless, the general perused his maps contentedly as the jet escorts pulled away. He radioed to them, via Colonel Story, "Thanks for the grand ride." Lunch was served as the plane continued south over the snow-capped hills and the shoreline of the Sea of Japan. It had been a heady experience, but MacArthur saw little of what was there.

On the return flight, despite concerns even from the toadying General Willoughby that the Chinese were capable of infiltrating masses of troops under cover of darkness "in preparation for a counteroffensive," MacArthur had begun drafting a confident message to the Joint Chiefs of Staff in Washington. "My personal ren [reconnaissance] of the Yalu River line yesterday demonstrated conclusively that it would be utterly impossible for us to stop upon commanding terrain south of the river as suggested." There wasn't any alternative, he claimed, to "the natural features of the river line itself." He also had a political case to make. Failing to unify all of Korea would be "a betrayal" of its people and "the solemn undertaking entered into on their behalf." Substantial Chinese or Russian intervention was now less likely, he claimed. "We hold the initiative and have a much smaller area within which to interdict their hostile moves. Our forces are committed to seize the entire border area, and indeed in the east have already occupied a sector of the Yalu River [bank] with no noticeable political or mil[itary] Soviet or Chinese reaction."

The military response was not "noticeable" to MacArthur as he peered down nine thousand feet into the ice and snow, but it was unmistakable below. To a British observer, American soldiers had only one concern, and it was not victory: "How soon can we get the Hell out of this goddam country?" MacArthur had the answer to the unheard question. Once he consolidated positions along the length of the Yalu, he expected to withdraw American forces "as far as possible" and replace them with ROK troops. On complete victory, he would return American units to Japan and the States.

Rhetoric was often reality for MacArthur. For the press covering the *Dai Ichi* he drafted a communique announcing, "The giant UN pincer moved according to schedule today." Also, as if true, he added, "The air forces, in full strength, completely interdicted the rear areas, and air reconnaissance behind the enemy line, and along the entire length of the Yalu River border, showed little sign of hostile military activity." The Yalu reconnaissance had been his own tourist flight of fantasy. "Our losses were extraordinarily light," he imagined about the attacks in advance, having no such facts. "The logistics situation is fully geared to sustain offensive operations." Santa had apparently approved his wish list.

3

The Pincers Parlay

"Nothing but Chinamen from here to Mongolia"

Awaiting Marine orders to advance cautiously, Captain Benjamin Read's 105mm howitzer battery was holed up in the frigid north end of Hagaru. At 1:45 a.m., as the 25th became the 26th, a Sunday, Sergeant Elmer Walling awakened Read and suggested he listen in on their field telephone link between gun crews around the village. Their new equipment worked fine. Corporal Ed Mifsud recalled other radio and related gear stamped "SOLD AS SURPLUS" with a post–World War II date. In the Korean emergency these had been repurchased and pressed back into service.

As Captain Read adjusted his headset, Private Stanley Lockowitz, his portable electric generator cranked up, was announcing, in a pastiche of the Armed Force Radio Network from Tokyo, "This is broadcasting station H-O-W, deep in the wilds of cold Korea. The *Mystery Voice* program is now on the air, sponsored by Lieutenant Wilbur Herndon's Tennessee Twist Chewing Tobacco. . . . But before we hear the Mystery

Voice, Private Bergman is going to favor us with a Christmas carol."

Prompted, Siert Bergman, a Swede from Michigan, sang "Silent Night." Lockowitz followed, very likely masking the mouthpiece of his field phone, introducing the stern "Mystery Voice," and challenging the personnel in the gun pits, manned round the clock, to call in a solution. When the first guesses were declared wrong, he tried another identity, intoning, "You shall return, as *I shall return*, by Christmas."

"You have just won the grand prize," Lockowitz told the first of the Marines who called in MacArthur's name—"which is a 105mm howitzer with two rounds of white phosphorus and the opportunity to fire both rounds at a target of your choice. Good-bye and good luck." Their morale, Read realized, was still high. After another brief snowfall, the thermometer began to plunge, and the next day, Monday, November 27, the brutal weather bottomed out at twenty-five below.

On MacArthur's orders, X Corps was to commence a multipronged attack just before dawn. O. P. Smith had made no secret of his concern, but Almond insisted that the Marines were his most "battle-worthy" troops, able to negotiate the nearly impassable reservoir country to the north. Prisoner interrogations and warnings from villagers in the far north had already elicited dismaying intelligence about a massive Chinese presence above the reservoir, at least equal to X Corps' strength. Peng Dehaui's chief of staff, Xie Fang, boasted in mid-November, "We have over 150,000 men on the eastern front, the enemy over 90,000, giving us a 1.66 advantage over him. We have 250,000 men on the western front, the enemy 130,000, giving us

A 105mm from Captain Benjamin Read's battery fires from its position at Hagaru-ri. *National Archives*

a 1.75 advantage." That numerical superiority would continue to increase as more "Volunteers" crossed the Yalu.

ROK general Paek Sun Yap's soldiers patrolling to the north had captured prisoners they identified as Chinese. Skeptical, Paek interrogated them himself. "Are there many of you here?" he asked in his limited Chinese. "Many, many," they confirmed.

The alleged volunteers had been stationed earlier in the southeast of China, and "all training," according to Hu Hai Bo, "was for preparing to liberate Taiwan. Now they were deployed to this high and cold area with blowing snow. . . . They had nearly no preparation. The Korean situation was very urgent. The troops knew they were going to Korea when they were on trains heading toward the northeast. At first it was intended that the more than a hundred thousand soldiers would change to winter uniforms . . . but now they had to cross the Yalu quickly." When border guards at the northeast frontier saw "the thin clothes," they began persuading other local officials to remove their hats and quilted uniforms to give to the troops heading into winter, but "these little bits of temporary clothing for more than a hundred thousand soldiers was a drop in the ocean." By the second day across the border, thousands were suffering from hypothermia. Yet there were always thousands more to call forward.

According to Hu, the Chinese IX Army Group, ordered toward the Chosin Reservoir, "had only one of two padded [sleeping] quilts for more than ten people. At night the soldiers could only put these one or two padded quilts on the snowy ground, and more than ten soldiers embraced one another on each padded quilt to ward off the brutal-30C weather." In the deep freeze, "two-thirds of the mortars were dumb," and hand grenades "became the heavy weapons." The blowing snow seemed "as big as cotton balls." Even more desperate was the depletion of rations ("replenishments") to resupply the few days' diet of rice and gruel each man had in his pack to start. "They did not have beans and fried noodles to eat." The hardy, peasant-bred Chinese would have to forage for dried corn and other edibles from the fields and plunder from the wounded and the dead.

Japanese railway engineers had told Far East Air Force intelligence officers that Yalu River winter ice could support considerable weight. On at least one occasion during the late war the Japanese army had laid railway tracks across the surface and had moved trains over it. MacArthur had discounted that reality, authorizing FEAF, supporting the offensive, to disrupt bridge and road communications south of the Yalu.

Almond also discounted whatever he dismissed as obsolete or deliberate misinformation. Reports from villagers about the enemy crossing in flimsy gear and without heavy weapons had to be an enemy plant. He had his orders from the *Dai Ichi*. X Corps was to draw any Chinese who intervened away from Walton Walker's weak, ROK-manned, Eighth Army right flank, on the western slopes of the Taebek range, while occupying territory to the northeast up to the Yalu.

Although Smith preferred to have the Marines, with their amphibious expertise, defend the long Hungnam-Wonsan beachhead over the frigid winter, leaving the frostbite casualties up-country to the Chinese, his instructions were to coordinate inland with the unreachable Eighth Army and win the war by Christmas. Smith had not even known where elements of the Eighth Army actually were until Harry Truman's friend, Major General Frank Lowe, had turned up at Hungnam as part of his orders from the President to report on the performance in Korea of called-up reserve and National Guard units. With Lowe were map overlays of pre-offensive EUSAK troop dispositions—the first real knowledge the Marines had of the whereabouts of two-thirds or more of the Korean command. But Lowe knew little about the looming Chinese, as they had been downplayed in Tokyo.

Even if the Chinese were indeed as numerous and as close as Smith feared, to Almond the enemy was disadvantaged by weather and equipment and no more than a large guerrilla force. From the evidence of the few prisoners taken, although they wore pile-lined coats, white on one side, mustard-colored on the other, and matching caps with earflaps and a red star, they had no gloves, resorting to tucking their bare hands into their sleeves. They wore rubber-soled canvas sneakers in the snow. The Chinese seemed to have little artillery heavier than mortars, often disassembled for portability, the parts which had to be carried on their backs. There were no covering aircraft now below the Yalu. (Attacking in darkness, they evaded opposing air power.) Only top commanders could communicate by radio. Most units employed, the Chinese boasted, making a virtue of necessity, "the dazzling red signal flares" and "the elevating military trumpet." Effectively, it was technology in reverse.

As what was termed their "Second Offensive" was about to commence and scouting patrols were already in action, Chinese military commissars—political officers on the Soviet model—were urging troops on and belittling the enemy, "Soon we will meet American Marines in battle. We will destroy them. When they are defeated, the enemy will collapse and our country will be free from the threat of aggression. Kill these Marines as you would snakes in your homes."

A prisoner who identified himself as from the Chinese 66th Army had been taken into custody on Sunday the 26th, the day before the Marines were to move forward. In his possession was a "Military Lessons" paper dated November 20, encouraging troops that there was little to fear from American soldiers. On its translation, X Corps Intelligence may have interpreted the capture and the document as deliberately misleading about

Captured Chinese soldiers shown here wearing quilted coats, but little protection for their hands and feet. *National Archives*

the Chinese presence and intended to frighten an enemy that
had never engaged the Chinese. More likely it was genuine—
to bolster Red morale. And there was much truth in it.

American infantrymen, the Maoist evaluation claimed,

> are weak, afraid to die and haven't the courage to attack
> or defend. They depend on their planes, tanks, and artil-
> lery. . . . They must have proper terrain and good weather
> to transport their great amount of equipment. . . . They
> specialize in day fighting. They are not familiar with night
> fighting or hand-to-hand combat. They are afraid of our
> big knives and grenades; also of our courageous attack[s],
> regular combat, and infiltration.
>
> If defeated, they have no orderly formation[s]. . . .
> They become dazed and completely demoralized. . . . They
> are afraid when the[ir] rear is cut off. When transporta-
> tion comes to a standstill, the infantry loses the will to
> fight.

On the advice of Charles Willoughby, who evaluated intelligence at the *Dai Ichi*, MacArthur scorned such allega-
tions as planted disinformation. Lieutenant Colonel John H.
Chiles of X Corps later observed, when a general, "Anything
MacArthur wanted, Willoughby produced intelligence for."
Also downgraded were claims from the daily interrogation
of further Chinese prisoners that their orders were to go all
the way south to Pusan and eliminate the "puppet" government of Syngman Rhee. "They have been interviewed, and
they say they are regular troops," Almond reported reluctantly

to Tokyo. General Willoughby was welcome to fly over to look at them. Willoughby responded that very likely there were only a few of them, probably sent to say exactly that. The vast Chinese potential was "a Marine lie."

Very likely few American officers and the even fewer in the ranks who knew about the charge and the reality of an increasing Chinese presence saw the enemy's sneer at their fighting qualities as anything but preparatory propaganda. Yet it was very likely based upon the embarrassing inadequacies exposed by troops rushed forward from Japan during the early stages of the NKPA invasion of South Korea and the earlier inadequacies of American armies in North Africa and Western Europe, where foot soldiers often traveled in trucks rather than on their feet—in military euphemism, a "motor march."

Almond remained skeptical about further sightings of swarming Chinese. Yet Marine pilots returning from sorties to the north of Chosin who observed few visible enemies below the Yalu saw southbound traffic above the Chinese border that was "heavy, very heavy, tremendous and gigantic." Someone, somewhere to the south, was being supplemented and supplied. West of Chosin, the Marine 5th and 7th Regiments were soon taking heavy casualties at Yudam-ni, Turkey Hill and Fox Hill, and reported them to X Corps.

East of the reservoir, arriving by light plane to distribute medals, a Santa gesture borrowed from MacArthur, Almond, mustering up empty bravado, assured troops about to move, "There aren't two Chinese divisions in the whole of North Korea! The enemy who is delaying you for the moment is nothing more than the remnant of units fleeing north. We are still attacking, and we're going all the way to the Yalu. Don't let a bunch of goddamn Chinese laundrymen stop you." He reboarded his L-5 and flew off. Until the overwhelming reality fell upon him, he would continue to disparage the tough, disciplined yet often illiterate Chinese as laundrymen.

Smith kept his men moving warily north up the western slopes of the reservoir. The Marine command did not want to be ambushed or overrun or to distance itself from the support system developing at Hagaru and the reach of air cover. It was already so frigid in the higher elevations, where the Taebek passes are at 3,500 feet and the peaks at 6,500 feet, that men gasped in the first shock of exposure. Trucks lacked tire chains to negotiate the snow and ice. Even caterpillar treads froze and jammed. Motors and generators turned off to conserve fuel were restarted only with difficulty.

Colonel Homer Litzenberg's 7th Marines were expected to skirt Chosin and turn northeast, beyond the remote Fusen Reservoir into more open country and the upper Yalu. His misgivings unallayed by Almond's bluster, Smith had prepared a long, wary message to Commandant Clifton Cates in Washington before the Marines were to jump off. "I do not like the prospect," Smith warned, "of stringing out a Marine division along a single mountain road for 120 miles from Hamhung to the Manchurian border." The Chinese referred to it as a "rubble highway." No EUSAK unit was closer than eighty tough and almost impassable miles across the inhospitable Taebek range to the southwest. To the northeast, the only mountain track from Hamhung (inland from Hungnam on the coast) to the distant Yalu was narrow, icy and switchback.

Following Almond's orders meant "simply get[ting] farther out on a limb," Smith contended to Cates, hoping that an urgent voice from Korea would be heard in the Pentagon, "that a winter campaign in the mountains of North Korea is too much to ask of the American soldier or Marine, and I doubt the feasibility of supplying troops in this area during the winter or providing for the evacuation of sick and wounded." Ending his message heedless of service diplomacy, he added, "I have little confidence in the tactical judgment of X Corps or the realism of their planning."

Although Smith was attempting to influence the Joint Chiefs of Staff through Cates, the dominating aura of MacArthur and his insistence that he could end the Korean war between Thanksgiving and Christmas left the Marine commandant, whose troops were an adjunct of the Navy, with little influence in Washington. Cates did not know that one of Litzenberg's counterparts, Chesty Puller of the 1st Regiment, had marked the anniversary of the founding of the Marines by hacking at a frozen hundred-pound birthday cake, hauled in from the beachhead, with a captured North Korean sword. Following a tribute to Marine traditions, Puller had added a reminder that "raggedy-tailed North Koreans have been shipping"—dispatching—"a lot of so-called good American troops, and may do it again." His warning did not even mention the looming Chinese, with their plethora of manpower.

In the Pentagon, Lieutenant General Matthew Ridgway, deputy chief of staff and an airborne commander in France in 1944, observed with disquiet MacArthur's divided thrusts toward the Chinese frontier. The intelligence upon which

MacArthur relied was largely his own ambitions. "It is not possible," Ridgway wrote later, "to attack an enemy whose positions are not known, whose very existence has not been confirmed, and whose forces are completely out of contact with your own." The opportunistic Chinese had withdrawn—somewhere—until they chose their time and place.

The other army in Korea, EUSAK, had jumped off, a term too dramatic for the reality, on the morning of the 24th and seemed nearly as unopposed as MacArthur had declared prematurely in his complacent communique to the Pentagon from Tokyo. At first, everywhere the Eighth Army moved forward, the concealed Chinese permitted EUSAK to continue out on a limb, strictly following Mao's dicta in his *Protracted War*: "The first stage is the one of the enemy's strategic offensive. . . . The second stage may be termed the stage of strategic stalemate. . . . We say that it is easy . . . to attack an enemy on the move precisely because this is the most effective military policy for a weak army in strategic defense against a strong army."

The next stage would be a surprise counteroffensive. The home front, through a "Hate America" propaganda campaign, would be prepared for substantial manpower losses. Troops disciplined by two decades of cheaply held life accepted the Maoist doctrine that the outcome of war "is decided by the people, not by one or two new weapons." (The threat of the A-Bomb seemed dismissed.) In the Maoist contention, abetted by Hollywood films once seen widely in China, the United States was "the paradise of gangsters, swindlers, rascals, special agents, fascist germs, [financial] speculators, debauchers, and all the dregs of mankind." American soldiers, led by "the Wall Street house-dog General MacArthur," could not be any better than the "depraved" civilization that spawned them.

—⧑—

Deep into the night, battery commander Lieutenant Harold Dill of the 31st Field Artillery east of Chosin was awakened with frantic orders from 7th Division headquarters to remove his guns south as quickly as he could or to render them useless before withdrawing. "We had a message brought in," he was informed, "to our forward outpost by relays of Korean runners. It was written in Korean and it was from the headman of a village downriver from Hyesanjin. . . . He says that thousands and thousands of Chinese are crossing the Yalu near his village and heading due South." Dill checked his watch. It was 4:30 a.m.—and the thermometer read -36°F. Division commander David Barr, who had served in China in the last war, knew "that there was no terrain that Chinese troops could not cross, regardless of the weather."

Dill awakened his men and ordered them to get going— in reverse. By darkness on November 27, Almond's X Corps offensive, less than two days in motion, was dematerializing. Colonel Allan MacLean's 31st Infantry had trained in cold weather on Japan's big northern island of Hokkaido and had parkas with pile-liners and "shoe-pacs"—rubber and leather hunter's boots used in Northern France and Germany in 1944–45, but not intended for subzero temperatures. Keyes Beech of the *Chicago Daily News*, who was not yet on the scene, would learn from survivors that "it was so cold that men's feet froze to the bottom of their socks and the skin peeled off when the socks were removed."

The Chinese sufficed with even less winter gear and counted upon enemy prisoners and enemy corpses for remedying their deficiencies. When American troops began encountering masses of enemy dead from artillery and aircraft strikes, they found Navy-issue field glasses and Army Springfield rifles, Thompson machine guns and other weaponry shipped for Chiang Kai-Shek's use yet almost never employed against the Japanese. In American-made knapsacks they also found packs of Camels and Lucky Strike cigarettes, Palmolive soap, Colgate toothpaste and small entrenching picks and shovels helpful for breaking into the frozen ground. Also in the Chinese arsenal were Russian burp guns, Japanese pistols and British Lee-Enfield rifles. A Chinese account boasted that "not a few volunteer soldiers started fighting with Japanese weapons and ended the battle holding U.S. guns." American officers soon had to issue, in self-preservation, distasteful orders to extract guns, grenades and ammo from their own dead.

Before Thanksgiving, MacLean's regiment had begun moving into barren highlands housing only a few Koreans in remote villages of mud-and-thatch huts. Toward the coast was the mostly Puerto Rican 65th Infantry of the 3rd Division, which had followed Barr's 7th Division ashore. After the 65th came, the 15th Regiment and 7th Regiment arrived, their tasks to relieve the Marines moving northward—if they did. Accustomed to balmy weather, the Puerto Ricans had debarked in shock. Companies ordered to attempt a link-up with Eighth Army patrols across the Taebek ridges managed only static-punctuated radio contact. Almond complained that the 65th was not sufficiently "energetic." The gap between armies at its narrowest was fifty or more barely passable miles across cratered, boulder-strewn roads unintended for wheels. Only North Korean guerrilla bands hunkered down in the Taebek hills.

Almond had even more objections to the Marines in the north, who "delayed the execution of some orders." Smith refused to risk his troops on what seemed senseless probes beyond their covering fire and insisted methodically on stockpiling ammunition and supplies at each stage of his cautious advances. "I was told to occupy a blocking position at Yudam-ni with the 7th Marines after Thanksgiving," he recalled, "and to have the 5th Marines go up the east side of the Chosin Reservoir until it hit the Yalu. I told Litzenberg not to go too fast." Yudam-ni was well beyond the high Toktong Pass, exposing "a tremendous open flank in the west" above reservoir country.

The Marines moved out, Lieutenant Joseph Owen wrote thirty years later, in a "colorless dawn, and . . . in the subzero darkness beat their [numb] hands against their sides. . . . They were helmeted, shapeless figures in their long, hooded parkas, showing only a small patch of face to the north wind." A rifleman walking backward for shelter from the gusts muttered to Owen, anticipating the worst, "Nothing but Chinamen from here to Mongolia." Eugene Timseth, then a private, remembered in 2012, "I was raised on a farm in North Dakota where it gets cold. On the farm you get shelter out of the cold, like going into a barn where the cattle were to stay warm. But at Chosin we had no shelter. We had to live, try to sleep and survive in the snow and cold, day and night."

The Marines' winter clothing was cumbersome but effective, except for the shoe-pac. *National Archives*

Where possible, sleeping holes were dug behind fighting holes and frequently covered with ponchos. *National Archives*

Both Almond and MacArthur had persuaded themselves
that some symbolic American presence along the Yalu would
intimidate the Chinese into holding back. The comparative
lull since early November initiated by Peng had seemed a val-
idation of *Dai Ichi* thinking. Mao's strategy, however, was to
draw UN forces* forward into positions in which they could
be outflanked and trapped. Supported by Willoughby's smug
intelligence forecasts, MacArthur had misinterpreted the Chinese withdrawals earlier in November as an unwillingness to
confront mechanized firepower. Yet any moving mechanical
part was at hazard to the plunging thermometer.

What few Chinese there were, according to estimates
from Tokyo, were light infantry armed only with the weapons
they could carry. Their dispersal about the reservoir was unseen by day. Somehow also invisible were thousands of supply
bearers—*coolies* in colonial terms—balancing bales on bam-
boo shoulder poles or bearing wooden A-frame racks. Unseen
as well were the camouflaged weapons' caches and concealed
rations' dumps set up in darkness to support seven Chinese
armies. Two legs were better than four wheels, went a Maoist
saying exploiting their deficiencies.

On the basis of fanciful intelligence, MacArthur had reported to the JCS in Washington that Far East Air Force attacks had prevented enemy reinforcements from crossing the
Yalu. But the FEAF operated almost entirely in daylight. On
the EUSAK front, Walker's conglomerate was moving—if
briefly—toward the much closer border with China. As many

---

*In addition to unreliable ROK soldiers, there were British and Common-
wealth troops in the east and west, Turks in the west.

of Walker's troops in summer gear—the *Dai Ichi* expected
the war to end before winter—remained unprepared for subzero conditions, transport planes from Japan had rushed over
33,000 winter field jackets, 40,000 pairs of mittens and 33,000
mufflers. Airlift, however, could not outfit all forward troops
in time.

Operating at night on both fronts without radios and
lights and concealing themselves by day, the Chinese pushed
on with stubborn discipline. Frostbite was common. Their dead
in the numbing cold remained unceremoniously where they
lay beneath the deep snow. Food would freeze too, as it was
cooked under tarpaulins before five in the morning to eliminate the possibility of visible fire and smoke. Nothing moved
after dawn. Whistles and bugles, shepherd's pipes and flares,
eerie and unnerving in the cold, clear air to the other side, signaled a night attack. Lacking in up-to-date communications,
the substitutions for such shortcomings became unanticipated
assets. To forestall discovery of their positions, the wily Chinese remained ten to twenty miles from enemy advance posts,
an easy trek for hardy, experienced foot soldiers.

Terse message traffic to X Corps headquarters from both
banks of the Chosin on the 28th, the second day of its offensive,
beginning at 0815, revealed how badly it was going: "All available air s[u]p[por]t over area commencing day break. R[e]q[ue]st
resupply drop of Art[iller]y and small arms." At 0950: "Enemy
penetrated Art[iller]y. . . . Medical train ambushed . . . rqst
ambulances for wounded." At 1130: "all El[e]ment[s] have been
at[tac]k[e]d. Need ammo and Med Aid." At 1345: "Mar[ine]

tr[uc]k in ambush, being fired on from hill. En[emy] in excellent P[o]s[itio]n to cut supply route N & S." At 1600: "Sit[uation] is getting worse; need help badly . . . have considerable number of wounded that [we] are unable to evacuate." At 1730: "Send 2nd Bn 31st Inf fwd at once, even if they have to fight their way up." Almond's only message on record that day to the beleaguered units reporting trouble is "X Corps . . . reminds commanders of their responsibility in respect to indiscriminate firing."

MacArthur did not know how precarious the situation would quickly become when, promising his end-the-war offensives, he agreed to an interview with the Tokyo correspondent for Henry Luce's flagship magazine, *LIFE*, a mass-circulation picture platform glorifying MacArthur's views. The hawkish Luce, China-born son of a missionary and a Waldorf Towers friend and neighbor of Herbert Hoover, was a steadfast admirer of Chiang Kai-Shek and an inflexible anti-Communist. The intended focus was a British proposal, with UN member support, for a militarized buffer zone in Korea acceptable to all participants—although it was utterly unlikely that the North Koreans or the Chinese would accept anything short of removal of the Western presence from Korea.

The interview at the *Dai Ichi* was on MacArthur's cautious terms. No direct quotes permitted. Instead, an indirect pseudo-interview was concocted, probably prepared or at least vetted by Courtney Whitney, who often assumed MacArthur's voice in print. A time lag in preparation and production was inevitable, and issues of *LIFE* were dated well ahead of mailing. The result appeared in the guise of a Luce editorial, "Yardstick from Tokyo," in the issue dated December 4 but on newsstands and mailed to subscribers earlier, as events had already begun turning for the worse. (The EUSAK push, begun on the 24th, had lasted only two days before the Chinese hit.) A hasty cavil was added as the opening sentence.

It had been "a week of grave decision," the unsigned piece began. "General MacArthur is not infallible—far from it. But his estimate of the actual situation in Korea, and his attitude toward the Communist aggression, are in healthy contrast to the sick and fearful atmosphere of London, Washington, and Lake Success"—the temporary Long Island location of the UN. What followed, in question-and-answer form, seemed unrelated to the worsening situation south of the Yalu. The bellicose *Dai Ichi* spin was already obsolete when *LIFE* reached its readers.

Q. How bad is our situation in Korea? Is it "impossible" as Washington thinks?

A. General MacArthur would not agree with the view . . . that we are even in a bad situation in North Korea. . . .

Q. If General MacArthur were completely free to dictate his own course, how would he try to resolve the military situation on the Korea-Manchuria border?

A. He would do exactly what he is doing—that is, seek a military decision through the destruction of the opposing forces, whether North Korean or Chinese, or mixed.

Q. Is some concession indicated in order to avoid a major war?

A. History demonstrates unmistakably that yielding to un-
justified international pressure leads inevitably to war.

Q. Must the United Nations forces go all the way to the Yalu
border? Is there anything good in the idea of offering the
Chinese Communists a "buffer zone"?

A. General MacArthur believes that to give up any portion
of North Korea to the Chinese Communists would be
the greatest defeat of the free world in modern times. To
yield to so immoral a proposal would bankrupt our leadership and influence in Asia.

Q. If the Chinese Communists were calling on General
MacArthur in Tokyo . . . , how would he receive them
and deal with them?

A. His reply would be characteristically terse. "Get out of
Korea and stay out. Those who persist in practicing international banditry . . . will be destroyed."

From Tokyo, a British official writing to the Foreign Office in London reported that American officers and GIs alike
were characterizing MacArthur as overplaying his hand at
their expense, in "ribaldries which conveyed, in picturesque but
unmistakable terms, their opinion that he was either a dangerous dotard, or an egomaniac determined to be Commander-
in-Chief of a world crusade against Communism."

MacArthur would have to employ more of his public relations resources than *LIFE* alone, as the rapidly deteriorating
situation made the buffer zone proposal for disengagement a
political and military nonissue. Over a long career, he had cultivated many friends in the media. But as always, the bad news

and frustrated strategies would be interpreted as resulting from someone else's miscalculation. "The greatest defeat of the free world in modern times" had become empty hyperbole, a futile call to enlarge the war into more of the Asian mainland and perhaps beyond.

4

Mission Impossible: The Offensive Short-Circuits

"The whiplash of MacArthur's known wishes"

On Sunday morning, November 26, General Smith had visited Yudam-ni, the northernmost village along the reservoir reached by the Marines. His forebodings were already becoming fact. On the 24th, he had helicoptered up from Hamhung as his command post was being moved forward to Hagaru-ri. Its airstrip was unfinished but already becoming crucial. The motor convoy with his staff and equipment was attacked en route north at Koto-ri, cut off by the Chinese, who seemed to swarm everywhere. The Marines had to fight their way up to Hagaru, which itself confronted Chinese from every direction.

The outlook was even worse on the EUSAK front. During the night, Smith had learned that the ROK II Corps on the right flank of the Eighth Army, across the Taebek ridges from X Corps in the east, had been ambushed and thrown back from the Tokchon area, about seventy miles southwest of Yudam-ni. Ignoring instructions, the marginally trained ROKs had built bonfires to keep warm, leaving them visible and vulnerable. Unlike the Marines, who nevertheless shivered beneath their winter garb, many in the Eighth Army, despite the airlifting of warmer coats, remained unprepared for the raw weather. William F. Pounder, a civilian employee of the Quartermaster General in Korea, had been sent to prepare the command for "the proper issue, fitting, and maintenance of wet-cold and dry-cold climate clothing," as South Korean weather in early winter "is comparable to that of Washington or Baltimore, and at best the region two hundred miles into the mountains farther north was more like Maine." He was told "that at this time, ammunition, POL [petroleum products] and rations had number one priority, and that when cold weather came the supply of overcoats would be taken care of in due course. The supply of overcoats is not all that is concerned in issuing cold weather clothing." Besides, the war would be over by Christmas.

By the second morning of the home-by-Christmas offensive in the west, the EUSAK advances, about eight miles northward from jump-off, had seemed almost unopposed. Mao's strategy remained entrapment. The Chinese would emerge before daybreak, heaving grenades and spraying rifle fire. The trackless hills, ridges and valleys made movement on wheels and treads difficult, but the Chinese relied on sneakers. Troops dependent on radios and telephones found their frozen equipment failing, and some panicked. At night the Chinese employed flares to expose the enemy to mortar fire. Their newly unleashed six armies in the west alone were equivalent to eighteen American divisions, many more than in all of Korea and Japan. MacArthur's divided commands, divided also by language, included Koreans, Turks, Thais, Ethiopians, British Commonwealth troops and a brigade from the Philippines.

As the Chinese heaved their wooden-handled grenades at the retreating enemy, they shouted in what may have been the only English many knew, "Come on back, GI! Afraid, GI?"

To the right of the American 2nd, 24th and 25th Divisions in the Eighth Army, the three divisions of the ROK II Corps collapsed and fled, abandoning their trucks, tanks and jeeps. The Turkish Brigade, on its way to assist the floundering South Koreans, met a Chinese roadblock and was ambushed. Turning toward the right flank of the 2nd Division, the Turks encountered ROK troops fleeing south and mistakenly killed or captured about two hundred. Knowing neither Korean nor Chinese and receiving confused orders in minimally understood English, the Turks lost all of their vehicles and abandoned many of their weapons. The 300-man forward Turkish unit suffered 255 casualties. In all, 770 Turks would be buried in Korea. After years of self-imposed isolation, sitting out World War II, it was, through little fault on their own but failed leadership in Tokyo and failed coordination in Korea, Turkey's inglorious military reappearance.

From Pyongyang to the south, still in American hands, IX Corps had received a message on November 29 that ten truckloads of Turks had arrived there with an American officer as interpreter. "What shall I do with them?" he asked. The dissolving front was moving in their direction. In the post-Thanksgiving panic that did not even require contact with the Chinese, the Eighth Army's end-the-war offensive was becoming a disorderly withdrawal.

Unaware of the extent of the debacle as he got his manipulated news of the other front from the distant *Dai Ichi*, Almond belatedly brought O. P. Smith the updated but already obsolete X Corps offensive plan designed and approved in Tokyo by MacArthur. Tokyo utilized maps hastily printed for use in Korea from old Japanese stock dating from 1916. The terrain hadn't changed, but populations had increased and new villages had sprung up, and some inhabited places on the maps had all but disappeared. Hydroelectric power and coal mining had prompted industrial growth and rail trackage. Place names were a confusion of Korean and Japanese, and the Chinese would have their own even more puzzling names for them. Hagaru-ri in Chinese was Xia Ye Yu Li and Koto-ri was Gu Tao Li.

Before GHQ's bulletins came, the bad news from the west first reached the east by radio. Lieutenant Colonel Leith Crue of the Canadian Military Mission in distant Pusan was playing cribbage with American colleagues that evening when hit tunes broadcast from the Armed Forces Radio Network in Tokyo ended abruptly shortly before eight. General MacArthur, an announcer advised, would be making an important statement. "Guess he's gonna tell us we'll all be home for Christmas for sure," an officer predicted, reaching to turn up the volume. On the hour, the general's resonant voice came through without his usual reassurance, reporting the Eighth Army disaster-in-the-making at the hands of the Chinese. "All United Nations Forces in Korea," MacArthur intoned, "are facing annihilation." The two engineering officers in the billet silently tugged on their jackets to go out into the night to lay demolition charges, in case of need, in the port's huge supply depots.

At home in New York, popular radio pundit Walter Winchell ended his rapid-fire Sunday broadcast melodramatically with, "If you have a son overseas, write to him. If you have a son in the 2nd Division, pray for him."

Even after Almond learned from Tokyo about the dismaying EUSAK debacle, he and his staff delayed informing Smith, as the X Corps offensive was officially still on. General Ridgway would contend that Almond "was under the whiplash of MacArthur's known wishes." Drew Pearson, writing his column in Washington, reminded readers wryly that at Wake Island in mid-October, MacArthur had told the President that "he was thoroughly familiar with Chinese psychology and that they were only bluffing."*

Just after noon on the day of the X Corps push, which would be spearheaded by the Marines, Eighth Army chief of staff Colonel Eugene M. Landrum had telephoned MacArthur's deputy at the *Dai Ichi*, Major General Doyle Hickey, with an urgent message from Walton Walker. He was not requesting approval to withdraw south; it was too late for that. Rather, Walker was confessing that his troops were in retreat. "Indications are that [the] en[emy] is no longer on defensive but taking action in str[ength]. Main effort at the moment is

---

*He had visited China for two months during a family Grand Tour of Asia in 1906.

against IX Corps (center) and II ROK Corps on our right. . . .
We are consolidating positions of I Corps until situation clar-
ifies." Hickey's terse note-taking for MacArthur conveyed the
language of desperation. "Consolidating positions" was the
cautious euphemism for withdrawal. EUSAK troops were
buckling under attack. The Christmas offensive had imploded.

Although the catastrophe of rout and retreat had its origins in the *Dai Ichi*, where decisions were made distant from
the reality, heads had to roll closer to the collapsing front. First
to go was the 2nd Division's Laurence Keiser, who received a
message via Walker's HQ informing him that as he was desperately ill with pneumonia, he would be evacuated to Tokyo
Army Hospital. Confronting Walker's chief of staff, Major
General Leven Allen, the irate Keiser exploded, "I don't have
pneumonia, so cut out the bunk." (Very likely a stronger exple-
tive than *bunk* was used.) Well, Allen said, the diagnosis was
a direct order. The general would be taken care of discreetly
with a desk job somewhere. "You tell Walker," Keiser shouted,
"to shove his job up his ass!" But Keiser would depart for the
Infantry Replacement Center at Indiantown Gap, Pennsylvania. His successor would be Major General Robert McClure,
whose fixation was to have his disheartened troops grow beards
in order to look tough. He would last only thirty-seven days,
after which the warrior beards, and McClure, were gone.

What Colonel Landrum, speaking for Walker, did not
confide to the *Dai Ichi* about the ongoing EUSAK disaster was
that the chain of command, from top to bottom, was buckling. Despite the bitter cold, some troops were discarding their
stocks of food and fuel, vehicles, helmets, bayonets, grenades,

guns and even boots in order to unburden themselves for flight. The lightly armed and insufficiently clad Chinese would be the eager beneficiaries.

Although the X Corps operation would also become mission impossible had it not already been that, in theory, before Thanksgiving, the Marines were ordered to advance on the west beyond the icy reservoir to the frozen Yalu. Barr's 7ᵗʰ Division was supposed to follow, and units of Major General Robert Soule's 3ʳᵈ Division were to move northwest to establish contact with the Eighth Army, although, realistically, EUSAK was already retreating in collapse to the south. General Baik Kil's ROK I Corps was to move northeast toward the Tumen River, which continued the long frontier with Manchuria, but no moves north were now feasible. General Ridgway would deplore the failed strategy as "like a pure map exercise put on by amateurs, appealing in theory but utterly ignoring the reality of a huge mountainous terrain largely devoid of lateral communication, and ordered for execution in the face of a fast-approaching sub-arctic winter."

Almond would defend his orders from General Mac-Arthur as merely reconnaissance—intended "to determine whether the enemy . . . would threaten either the front of X Corps or the front and right flank of the Eighth Army. . . . What General Smith was really complaining about was . . . that his division happened to be the division that would determine the strength of that [unknown] force." MacArthur, however, was not ordering, as he would claim later, merely a probe in force but smugly proclaiming an end-the-war operation in the face of extreme weather and daunting geography.

Realizing the hazards, Smith insisted on coordinating both his regiments at Chosin on the western side of the reservoir, with the 1st Regiment below at Hagaru, the Marine collection point and airstrip. Separation was a recipe for trouble.

Reluctantly, Almond shifted the boundaries. Ordered to hold the eastern edges of the reservoir were battalions from the 7th Division's 31st and 32nd Regiments commanded by Colonel MacLean and Lieutenant Colonel Faith. Both had staff backgrounds and had never led units in combat. To assist in coordination of air support, Captain Ed Stamford, a Marine air controller, was assigned to them. Employed mostly over EUSAK territory, the FEAF had F-84 Thunderjets and soon obsolescent F-80 Shooting Stars. The Marines and Navy, operating largely from offshore carriers, had F4U-5 prop-drive, gull-wing Corsairs, first used over Guadalcanal in 1943. The newest version was armed with four 20mm cannons and carried four thousand pounds of bombs—or napalm canisters—and rockets. The Corsairs would prove crucial.

Under darkening winter skies, Marine units had jumped off as scheduled. The reservoir highlands were more frigid and mountainous than the EUSAK west. Elements of Walker's army that were theoretically to link up across the Taebek were already in retreat far below the Yalu, often without exchanging any fire with the Chinese, who were also infiltrating X Corps' positions in the Chosin area. At Yudam-ni, to the west of the reservoir, it had been seventeen below when Marines occupied the mud-and-thatch village, unaware of the Chinese lurking nearby. From a helicopter, O. P. Smith could see no evidence of the enemy, yet he knew they were there.

Never shirking risk, Ned Almond also flew forward to inspect dispositions and, at the Yudam-ni command post of Homer Litzenberg's 7th Marines, summoned the regimental intelligence officer. "What's your latest information?" he asked Captain Donald France.

"General," said France, hardly masking the contempt Marines felt for Almond, "there's a shitload of Chinamen in those mountains." Almond later denied that the Marines were reporting substantial Chinese forces to their north. Still, when Marines captured fifty prisoners and Almond duly reported it to Tokyo, Charles Willoughby offered his expected response that any Chinese in the vicinity had to be volunteers. Almond radioed back, "They have been interviewed, and they say they are regular troops." Come to Korea and look at them, Almond challenged. "That's a Marine lie," retorted MacArthur's intelligence guru once more.

A wounded veteran of Makin Atoll in 1943, 1st Lieutenant John Yancey had been confronting the Chinese since early November. At Yudam-ni, the Marines were using frozen enemy bodies in lieu of sandbags to protect their machine guns. "Sure, they'll be back," Yancey told his men, exhorting them to be ready for live Chinese. But he did not expect a sniper shot at long range which grazed his cheek and lodged in his nose. He removed a stiffly freezing glove and plucked the bullet out. In the extreme cold, the bleeding froze.

As night fell on the 28th, the Chinese, as a light snow came down, attacked Hagaru, fourteen miles below Yudam-ni, from all sides. Marine foxholes on the perimeter had been blasted from the frozen ground by dynamite charges stuffed into empty rations tins. Engineers, as they would do again, continued working on extending the airstrip under floodlights and falling snow, dropping their tools for rifles when the shooting got too close. Through the night, before the surviving Chinese melted away at daybreak, defenders took nearly five hundred casualties, many of them frostbite cases who would recover in warming tents. The Chinese abandoned hundreds of dead and wounded, and Hagaru held. "All our clerks were out with weapons," O. P. Smith would write to his wife a few days later, although he knew that Esther might not read his letter for months, if at all. "All hands have done a splendid job and will continue to do so."

Later, Smith told *The New York Times*, "They knew all about us, all right, where we were and what we had, but I can't understand their tactics. Instead of hitting us with everything at one place, they kept hitting us a different places." The Marines were strung out from Yudam-ni to Koto-ri to the south, just above the steep Funchilin chasm. He had little idea how rough the going was to the north other than by radio. The Chinese hurled potato masher (wood-handled) grenades, carrying baskets of them and heaving them in clusters at Yudam-ni through the night. A piece of shrapnel from one pierced the roof of Yancey's mouth, costing him his front teeth. In the flickering lights of firing, another plopped in the snow in front of Sergeant Robert Kennemore's assistant gunner. Kennemore scooped it up and heaved it back before it exploded. Two more potato mashers landed nearby. To protect his men, he pushed one deep into the snow to smother the blast, dropping his knee on the other. He lost both lower legs but survived as the

Marines on the firing line. *Naval Historical Center*

bleeding froze. Dragged to an aid tent below the action and still alert, he asked Navy surgeon Robert Wedemeyer about the state of his genitals. The lieutenant had a morphine syrette handy, kept thawed in his mouth. "You wouldn't worry about half a tank of gas, would you?" said Wedemeyer. Flown to Japan and then to the States once his company got through to Hagaru, Kennemore long after Christmas would be patched up enough to father a family.

General Peng complained to the distant Chairman Mao, who never crossed the Yalu to Korea, about the conditions in which his troops were fighting. Although the snow fell on both sides, thousands of poorly garbed, sneaker-footed Chinese were dying in the arctic conditions of Chosin. Incessant attacks from the air limited their movements to darkness, and troops froze in their foxholes. "We have no freedom of action during the daytime," Peng explained. "Even though we have several times the armed strength to surround them on four sides, fighting cannot end in a night."

Chosin was long, narrow and frozen hard, with its two longest, frigid arms to the far north. Litzenberg's 7th Marines were digging in under fire on the western bank of the reservoir. On the other side, Lieutenant Colonel Don C. Faith's 1st Battalion, 32nd Infantry, had reached two-thirds the distance toward the upper eastern arm—the Pungnyuri inlet which fed into Chosin. Because Faith's battalion had moved the farthest up the reservoir, for coordination General Barr had ordered it merged with Colonel Allan MacLean's 31st, and MacLean moved his headquarters close to Faith's position—Hill 1221, just above the village of Twiggae. (Hills were identified by their height in meters.) MacLean and Faith would soon share a hut in the below-zero cold.

Son of a brigadier general, Faith, thirty-two, had been with the 82nd Airborne Division in Europe, on Ridgway's staff, and then with Barr in China before Mao's takeover. Ray Murray's three battalions of the 5th Marines were being held back cautiously on the west bank as they had encountered infiltrating Chinese. Faith had determined to go ahead on the east with 715 Americans and his unreliable burden of 300 South Koreans. Most Army units were augmented by KATUSAs—Korean Army Troops with the U.S. Army—who were short on weapons training and in comprehending English.

Faith had trucks, but icy surfaces and failed batteries made their movement difficult. All army units traveled via "motor march" as best they could. It was the American way, however ineffective it had been in the European war, when, after

Normandy, road-bound units in France were bogged down by fuel shortages, maintenance problems, and mud or snow. General Almond often chanced light plane flights to embattled positions, risking deadly rifle fire.

As usual, in MacArthur fashion, Almond found, wherever he touched down, recipients for medals he stashed in his pockets, offering Silver Stars to a junior officer at Hagaru and two to enlisted Marines. After Captain Alexander Haig, his newly promoted twenty-six-year-old aide, wrote down their names on his pad, the pair returned, with difficulty, to Hamhung. Ambitious and close to Almond since *Dai Ichi* days, Haig had been "the coffee and tea man" at headquarters in Tokyo. According to Haig, when the war began late that June, "I sat in on the telecom [in the *Dai Ichi*] between MacArthur and Harry Truman [in Washington]." Yet according to Ed Rowny, then a lieutenant colonel and GHQ planner, Haig was too junior to be permitted into high-level meetings but had used Almond's coattails to move up from lieutenant and join his X Corps staff. Haig would keep moving up.

Almond did not let on to the men everywhere out on a limb how uneasy he was. He radioed to MacArthur that field reports indicated that enemy strength—he meant the encroaching Chinese—was increasing nearby. The positions of forward units, he urged the *Dai Ichi*, had to be reexamined—a cautious way to suggest that they were already too far forward. Nevertheless, to X Corps troops he remained upbeat—"full of beans," O. P. Smith recalled—wherever Almond flew in.

The 5th and 7th Marines were intermixed and stretched out as they occupied new locations. In several cases, a motor march up from Hagaru-ri and its marginally operational air-strip failed, as vehicles broke down in the arctic weather and troops left them to continue on foot. Where batteries of big guns could be moved, the below-zero freeze affected the recoil systems of the 105mm howitzers, reducing the reach of their ordnance. Even hand-held bazooka rocket launchers became ineffective, some tubes and shells cracking in the cold.

In the quiet of the night in Faith's sector, Captain Stamford, the air controller, awakened to gunfire and chattering that did not seem English. A poncho hung at the entrance to his bunker swung alarmingly, and the swaddled face of a Chinese soldier appeared. He leaned in to heave a grenade. Stamford leaped aside before it exploded. Others in nearby bunkers were less fortunate. The Chinese quickly melted away, forming hidden roadblocks that isolated troops from Hagaru to the south.

The next afternoon Almond returned to the reservoir area as if nothing significant had occurred. Colonel MacLean had set up his 31st Infantry command post in an abandoned schoolhouse below Faith's CP on Hill 1221. In the early hours of the 28th, Faith's forward units had been under fire and a company commander killed. Below Chosin and unaware of the deteriorating situation to the north, Almond met with Smith at Hagaru, arriving with Captain Haig in an L-17. As there was no strip beyond Hagaru to land a prop plane, Almond borrowed Smith's helicopter to go north to consult with MacLean and Faith. MacLean was gone, having left for his own endangered CP, which would be combined with Faith's command post. With galoshes over his combat boots, as Faith found that standard issue shoe-pacs held in moisture and hastened frostbite, he watched the chopper descend. After it touched down in the snow, Faith came over to greet the general, and Almond assured him that there were only scattered Chinese in the area and that he would be able to retake the high ground from which he had withdrawn. Faith knew better. The Chinese concealed themselves in daylight, and the prisoners his men had interrogated identified themselves not as "volunteers" but as regulars from the 80th Division. The Medical Company of the 31st had already been ambushed, with its few survivors, Faith guessed, fleeing south.

Pulling a map from a leather case which Haig held, Almond unfolded it on the hood of a jeep. The Manchurian frontier was seventy-five miles above them. The enemy, Almond claimed in a familiar mantra, was "nothing more than remnants of Chinese divisions fleeing north. We're still attacking," he asserted, "and we're going all the way to the Yalu." Pulling three Silver Stars from a capacious pocket, he presented one to Faith and asked him to designate two other recipients: a wounded platoon leader, Lieutenant Everett Smalley, who was sitting on a water can, watching, was summoned, and a surprised mess sergeant, George Stanley. "Stanley, step over here for a minute," Faith called. Then he rounded up some clerks, drivers and walking wounded nearby as witnesses. Almond pinned on the medals while Haig dutifully wrote the recipients' names in his notebook.*

---

*MacArthur and Almond did not invent the proliferation of unearned medals and ribbons. A World War I British officer and minor poet, Owen Rutter, in his mock-epic "The Song of Tiadatha" (1919), describes a visiting general pinning the Military Cross on the surprised Tiadatha (a pun on Longfellow's Hiawatha), who "Very nearly asked the General / What on earth he'd done to get it." World War II continued the practice.

Once the chopper was airborne and whirling away, Staff Sergeant Chester Barr watched as Faith and Smalley ripped the baubles from their parkas and tossed them into the snow.

At his next stop, Almond had no medals left for MacLean but descended to tell him absurdly that the "advance"—already aborted—would be resumed as soon as the 2nd Battalion, 31st Infantry and Battery C of the 57th Field Artillery had caught up. Stuck in the snow and ice and blocked by stalled vehicles, the promised reinforcements would never make it.

Fox Company of the 7th Marines, as units moved toward Yudam-ni, was to protect the MSR—the icy main supply route—over the Toktong Pass, which curved southwest toward Hagaru and its airstrip below. (Despite Chinese infiltration and sniper fire, the town sawmill remained in round-the-clock operation, cutting local timber for protective bulwarks and to fuel potbelly stoves.) The attacks east of Chosin continued as the numbing night of the 27th under a gleaming full moon became dawn on the 28th. As Captain Barber's men ran out of ammunition, they substituted abandoned Chinese arms, test-firing them to determine whether each worked. Some re-captured weapons had also been appropriated from the GI wounded and dead. Fifty-four men had been in Barber's 3rd Platoon. Sixteen were dead, nine wounded and three miss-ing—taken prisoner.

All three taken captive were stripped of their watches, and the two unwounded men were ordered to carry the wounded Private Daniel Yesko to a Chinese command post—a farm-house and shed on the far slope of 5,454-foot Toktong-san. In the early morning light, as the prisoners were allowed to relieve themselves at a slit trench, Australian World War II vintage P-51 Mustangs flew over and rocketed the enemy site. The flimsy buildings were obliterated, but the call of nature saved the Marines' lives.

The surviving Chinese ordered the POWs to carry Yesko four miles north to another farmhouse, where Marines captured at Yudam-ni were huddled. One, Corporal Wayne Pickett, veteran of a Shanghai tour in 1947 when he was eighteen, would survive 999 days in a Chinese prison camp in North Korea, enduring starvation (often only one rice ball a day), brutality and bouts of dysentery, and assisting in the burial of many of his mates.

The few days of the aborted offensive cost UN forces uncounted numbers of prisoners—uncounted because many starved to death or were frozen to death while marching to prison camps, and unidentified others would starve more slowly, especially under North Korean captivity. Treated differently at Camp No. 10 at Kanggye, just above the reservoir, few of the 250 POWs were dying, as the Chinese were experimenting upon them with "brainwashing"—behavior modification based upon the Soviet system of psychological pressure. Somewhat better food and other benefits were dangled as rewards for "students" who spoke at prisoner assemblages about being duped by their governments and docilely wrote essays on the evils of capitalism. For the compliant, it seemed better than death.

Fox Company's remnants remained surrounded. One of them, Private Charles Parker, had been in a sick bay tent in Hagaru-ri with the flu but refused to remain a casualty. He worried that he might be evacuated to Japan while his Fox Company buddies in Korea went directly home for Christmas. Back with Fox on their rocky knoll, Parker took a bullet in the stomach from a sniper and would not get to Japan, or home. Private Jerry Triggs, seventeen, an ammo carrier with a machine gun unit, heard Private Bob Ezell gibe that "the smart guys back at Division" had no idea that the Chinese were crossing the Yalu. Yet the Marine command knew and could do nothing. It was, rather, the X Corps leadership, and above, that had fudged intelligence about the intervention and put the Leathernecks in jeopardy.

"Home for Christmas, my ass," said Triggs. His pal Ezell would be wounded and would lose all the toes on his left foot to frostbite but would make it home. Triggs would take a Chinese grenade and end in a shallow grave. Private Hector Cafferata sensed the aroma of garlic before he and Private Ken Benson, who had been dozing, saw white-clad Chinese flash past their foxhole. Benson was still struggling awake when a satchel charge was thrown at them. He picked it up and heaved it back before it exploded, shaking them both. "Home for Christmas, Hec?" Benson shouted, reaching for his BAR and emptying a clip of his Browning at the fleeing figures in white. Still the Chinese returned in force, with unspoken commands in bugle blasts and shrill whistles. Sergeant Meredith Keirn, crew leader of a machine gun platoon, opened up, as did Corporal Hobart Ladner, with the dead piling up so close to Ladner as to impede his field of fire. Two of Ladner's three-man crew were killed, as was Ladner, and the third was left for dead as two Chinese infantrymen dragged the abandoned machine gun down into a ravine. It was not a good night, but a typical one as the Chosin operation crumbled.

Air drops called in were soon the only source of Marine replenishment, but many parachutes fell out of reach. Other loads broke apart on the icy terrain. "Retrieving them was difficult," Private Don McAlister of the embattled 32nd Infantry recalled, "because the Chinese wanted them as much as we did." In the tumult near the reservoir he had already lost his pack and sleeping bag, which was the most vital item of gear he possessed other than his Browning automatic rifle (BAR). The sleeping bag wasn't only for sleeping; in a foxhole one stood in it for warmth.

Cargo on the big C-119 "Flying Boxcars" included ammunition, blankets, medical supplies and rations. Aboard one mission, as Private Robert A. Foelske of Waterloo, Iowa, watched over the eleven thousand pounds of provisions near the open rear hatch being released on rollers, two guidance ropes snapped in the frigid winds. Foelske was blown out of the plane. He was wearing a parachute and harness but was knocked unconscious. When the chill air cleared his head as he fell, he reached for his ripcord. "It's quite a shock," he recalled, "coming to while falling from an airplane. I tried to keep from landing in a tree, but I didn't do it. All that country—and I had to land in a tree."

Neither friend nor enemy spotted him, and he had no idea where he was, although he knew that the C-119 had been in the reservoir area. He saw nothing of the cargo that had fallen with him. As night came, Foelske extricated himself and searched in darkness for a route back. He evaded two Chinese soldiers and continued walking, discovered a road and kept going—south, he hoped—into the next morning. Luckily he spotted an Army truck, which took him to a jeep. Ferried back to his airbase two days after he dropped from his plane, he reached an airstrip where a C-119, its props turning, was preparing for another flight to the Chosin area. Startled crew members stared at him like a returned ghost. It was his plane. When it took off for another cargo run, Foelske was aboard as crew, going all the way—and, this time, back.

"Everything was frozen," Navy Lieutenant Commander Chester M. Lessenden, with the 5ᵗʰ Marines, later told Keyes Beech. Lessenden ran the hospital tent at Yudam-ni, where rifle fire had punched holes in the canvas, and the overflow wounded were placed outside under tarpaulins. "Plasma froze and the bottles broke. We couldn't use plasma because it wouldn't go into solution and the tubes would clog up with particles. We couldn't change dressings because we had to work with gloves on to keep our hands from freezing. We couldn't cut a man's clothes off to get to a wound because he would freeze to death. Actually a man was often better off if we left him alone. Did you ever try to stuff a wounded man into a sleeping bag?"

Marine corporal Alan Herrington, a veteran of Guadalcanal, where the temperature had been more than a hundred degrees warmer, recalled of Chosin, "I can still see the icicles of blood." Wounds at minus twenty-four Fahrenheit remained pink and red rather than turning brown because blood froze before it could coagulate, icing wounds shut. One of the unforgettable memories of war in normal temperatures is the fetid stench of the putrefying, unburied dead. In the frigid north, corpses in the open only stiffened. The medical facts on the ground did not suggest a happy outcome. Nor did a progress now in reverse.

5

An "Entirely New War"

"There can be no retreat when there's no rear."

Messages to the *Dai Ichi* from the EUSAK front early on the 28th established that the "end the war by Christmas" offensive had failed after its first day. It would not take much longer in the east. The amateur air reconnaissance along the Yalu about which MacArthur had boasted had seemed on the money when the Eighth Army, innocent of Maoist deception, had made unopposed advances of eight miles. Then, as Air Force general George Stratemeyer conceded to a Senate subcommittee later, "Lo and behold, the whole mountainside turned out to be Chinese." On site, Private Jack Wright remembered, "the guy on watch" woke up his platoon with "Man, the hills all around on both sides are lit up like Christmas trees." A "How Able" (Haul Ass) order from Major General Laurence "Dutch" Keiser on the EUSAK front had come too late, as his troops, in peril of being outflanked, were already in disorderly withdrawal, abandoning weapons and equipment never used against the enemy. And he was gone.

MacArthur described the bad tidings to the Pentagon not as a miscalculation but shrewd strategy to expose enemy intentions. He was never wrong. "The developments resulting from our assault movements," he radioed, have now assumed a clear definition. All hope of localization of the Korean conflict to . . . NK troops with alien token elements can now be completely abandoned. The Chinese military forces are committed . . . in great and ever-increasing strength." He went on to describe an unanticipated attack on the order of Pearl Harbor, yet he had been warned for more than a month. Even the loyal Almond had interrogated Chinese prisoners and warned of the potential for trouble. Although MacArthur would consult his embattled commanding generals for updates, he planned to forget his allusions to Christmas as quickly as possible.

At the Pentagon, the Army duty officer before dawn, Washington time, was Colonel John R. Beishline. He awakened General Ridgway, who asked that MacArthur's frantic message about the Chinese be brought to his quarters at Fort Myer. While he awaited delivery, he telephoned the chief of staff, General J. Lawton Collins. After studying MacArthur's lengthy appeal, Ridgway suggested in a second call to Collins that he thought the President and the JCS should be informed right away. Harry Truman would learn of the disaster in the making through JCS chairman, General Omar Bradley. "A terrible message has come in from General MacArthur," Bradley began, and described the general as "rather hysterical." Uncensored press dispatches from Korea about the deteriorating situation were already in early editions that morning, but the unexcitable Bradley doubted, so he told the President, that it was "as much of a catastrophe as our newspapers were leading us to believe." Or MacArthur. Still, Bradley confirmed that the Chinese had "come in with both feet."

Downplaying the looming disaster did not persuade the President. Although neither he nor Bradley trusted MacArthur, it was evident that Red China, without heavy artillery, armor or an air force, had emerged suddenly and surprisingly as a world power, threatening the entire UN position in Korea and American illusions of military supremacy. At a hastily summoned Pentagon conference, Ridgway urged Lieutenant General Wade H. Haislip, the Army vice chief of staff, to begin planning for a possible evacuation and to issue contingency instructions to MacArthur, although he had a record of ignoring instructions. Anticipating the worst, Vice Admiral C. Turner Joy in Japan quietly began to assemble ships for withdrawing X Corps from Hungnam and Wonsan. No other alternative seemed possible. Unlike Almond's divisions, Eighth Army had a land route for withdrawal.

After a conference in Tokyo with MacArthur, Admiral Joy would fly to Hungnam, assuring Almond that the Navy could send transports quickly to evacuate troops—if they could get to the coast—but that it might take several weeks to assemble enough shipping to extricate supplies and equipment. Almond claimed that he wanted to bring everything possible out, although tanks and artillery upcountry were icebound, nearly without ammunition and, worse, short of fuel. Joy recoiled at Almond's show of confidence. "If the enemy breaks your perimeter while you are trying to outload your gear," he warned, "the American people will never forgive you for the loss of lives."

Although Almond soon suggested to O. P. Smith that abandoned equipment could be replaced from Japan, he was having it both ways, depending upon whom he was talking to. He assured Joy, "I came in like a soldier; I'm going out as a soldier." Dignity, Almond declared, required rescuing every bit of gear as well as every man.

At the *Dai Ichi*, MacArthur put his panic aside long enough to draft an exculpatory communique for the world press, which was already headlining the ongoing disaster. From his first sentence, he brushed aside personal responsibility for the gravity of the situation. Little more than two hours after his frantic message to Washington, he confirmed to the media that Chinese ground forces were now committed to an undeclared war. "This has shattered the high hopes we entertained that the intervention of the Chinese was only of a token nature on a volunteer and individual basis as publicly announced."

Curiously, for someone who often claimed he understood the Asian mind, he had finally come to a belated understanding of Mao's long-published strategy:

> It now appears to have been the enemy's intent in breaking off contact with our forces some two weeks ago, to secure the time necessary surreptitiously to build up for a later surprise assault upon our lines in overwhelming force, taking advantage of the freezing of all rivers and roadbeds which would have materially reduced the effectiveness of our air interdiction and permitted a greatly accelerated forward movement of enemy reinforcements and supplies.

Evasively, MacArthur then twisted the looming catastrophe into a cunning strategic initiative of his own making. Despite having admitted being outfoxed, he contended that the long-planned Chinese attacks had been "disrupted by our own offensive action which forced upon the enemy a premature engagement." In a cable to Arthur Krock of *The New York Times*, always friendly toward him in hopes of soliciting a scoop, he claimed that "every major step" in his Korean operations had been approved in advance by Washington. To Hugh Baillie of the United Press, an old friend, he cabled, covering his posterior, "It is historically inaccurate to attribute any degree of responsibility for the onslaught of the Chinese . . . to the strategic course of the campaign itself." To the supportive *U.S. News & World Report* he claimed, "The tactical course taken was the only one which the situation permitted." The restrictions placed on him by Washington—such as the refusal to permit the bombing of Chinese targets in Manchuria—were "an enormous handicap, without precedent in military history." In still another press release, ignoring that as Supreme Commander, Far East, he had forbidden the CIA from operating in his theater, he blamed the Pentagon, the State Department, and the CIA for faulty intelligence about the Chinese. He only needed the all-knowing Charles Willoughby.

Since MacArthur knew the realities, he desperately ordered a secret emergency council in Tokyo, an arrangement that would look better than his rushing personally, in humiliation, to two fronts, in what could no longer be his usual grand style. He had touched down in Korea only six times since the war began, five of them flying visits of only a few hours. (For the Inchon operation, he spent time on the ground but returned to dine and sleep on his command ship, the *Mt. McKinley*.)

Almond discovered MacArthur's summons after a day of urgent conferences with Army and Marine commands. On the afternoon of November 28, he met with the harried regimental officers of the 31st and 32nd Infantry, with David Barr of the 7th Division, and visiting Australian general Sir Horace Robertson, who was inspecting Commonwealth troops. On leaving MacLean and Faith at their forward CP east of the reservoir, a chancy undertaking, Almond helicoptered to his posh compound at Hamhung. There he found a message urgently ordering him to Tokyo for a meeting that evening.

With a few staff, he flew out of Yonpo, south of Hamhung on the Sea of Japan, on a four-engine C-54, and arrived at Haneda at about nine. A Far East Command colonel was on the tarmac to escort the X Corps party to MacArthur's residence in the park-like American Embassy grounds. A late-night meeting at the *Dai Ichi* would have attracted unwelcome notice.

The conference convened at 9:30, a late hour for the aging Supreme Commander. Walton Walker had already arrived. It was his sector that was in disarray—in headlong retreat, with heavy losses and abandonment of equipment and supplies. Walker claimed that two hundred thousand Chinese were bearing down on his troops. The ROK II Corps had been decimated, exposing his right flank, and his IX Corps was struggling to close the gap. The American dimension of the debacle belied, in part, General Peng's earlier view that "the South Korean forces are no good at fighting but [it is] difficult to catch [them when they retreat]; the U.S. forces are good at fighting, and that is why more American soldiers are killed than captured alive." Without conviction Walker contended that he could slow down and arrest EUSAK's flight at the narrow waist of the Korean peninsula and establish a defensive line north and east of Pyongyang. "Deep withdrawal," he called it, prior to resuming the offensive, although that seemed now impossible. Almond proposed extricating his X Corps into Hungnam and having the Navy ferry troops to Wonsan, where they had first gone ashore in the north, yet Wonsan was obviously an unrealistic enclave. There was no viable route further south by land. The *Dai Ichi* ambience seemed to encourage fantasy.

Buoyed by events, Kim Il Sung, who had fled his capital, Pyongyang, and was in hiding near the Yalu in northwest Korea, telegraphed a plea to Mao, "We should not give the enemy breathing time. We ought to advance in the crest of the victory to seize Pyongyang and Seoul and to press the enemy to withdraw from [all of] Korea." Mao would wire his commanders on December 4, "It is possible that the war may be resolved quickly; it is also possible the war will be protracted. We are prepared to fight for at least one year. . . . It is most advantageous that we shall not only seize Pyongyang but also capture Seoul. . . . [If we] wipe out all the ROK forces we will be in a stronger position to compel United States Imperialists to withdraw from Korea."

Mao did not mention the Chosin sector, perhaps implying that X Corps would become outflanked and its position untenable with victory in the west. The Americans, he told Kim, "have a lot of steel but little spirit." His Chinese had the spirit. "Our forces are absolutely capable of defeating the U.S. forces no matter how superior their equipment and air power are." Rescuing the rump state of North Korea seemed to Mao, because of Chinese initial successes and MacArthur's miscalculations, the initial stage of expelling the Americans from the peninsula and establishing a turning-point victory over imperialism.

Despite the empty confidence of his generals, MacArthur realized that the Humpty Dumpty of a unified Korea was beyond repair. And Washington understood without specific warnings to Tokyo that the grandiose aspirations MacArthur once embodied about undoing Red China put the entire Pacific Rim at risk. No notes were formally taken at the Tokyo meeting. Walker was vaguely encouraged to hold at Pyongyang, yet if the enemy threatened him there, he was to withdraw further. That backpedaling was already happening. Almond's situation was no better; he was to withdraw, if he could.

MacArthur suggested the expedient of wheedling reinforcements out of the Pentagon, but he knew there were none available. Divisions being readied could not be anywhere near Japan, or Korea, for months—too late to resuscitate EUSAK above the 38th parallel. With the Christmas offensive thwarted, contingency plans were already being initiated beyond the *Dai Ichi* to evacuate X Corps and, at last resort, all of Korea thereafter. Ships of all kinds were being gathered, with crews, some of them Japanese, being readied at the sprawling naval station at Sasebo in southern Kyushu.

As if he were really running what was happening, MacArthur directed Almond to cease offensive action and concentrate his forces in the area well below the reservoir highlands, from Hamhung to the harbor at Hungnam. As a generalissimo whose experience of Korea, other than at In-chon, consisted largely of photo-ops, he had little idea of the dilemmas which had to be resolved. Flying to big airbases in a big plane, being jeeped about nearby and going home for din-ner was being little more than a war tourist.

The postage-stamp airstrip at Hagaru-ri, for example, sev-enty tough road miles above Hungnam, with hairpin turns, had to be kept open, although under fire, to resupply units and to withdraw casualties from Chosin. Four Marine bulldozers from D Company, 1st Engineer Battalion, with tank escorts, had scaled the slopes on November 18, blasting and leveling the hard, icy soil on the edge of the village into a primitive runway. Lieutenant Colonel Ed Rowny, commanding an ad-vance party of Army engineers, recalled that at first

> the ground was so frozen that we couldn't use the bull-dozers to do much, so . . . we set off charges and we set up a warming tent in each end and then a bulldozer would go one way and smooth that out and then sit in the other end and get warm and . . . come back the other way. Now the problem was [that] warm blades when they hit the cold earth, the earth stuck to the blades and they couldn't work. I had a brilliant executive officer . . . down in Ham-hung and he said try ski wax, so I had them air drop 100 lbs of ski wax and it worked like a charm. The ski wax didn't allow the earth to congeal and the *Stars and Stripes* [which had a reporter in Hamhung] said there was a war

going on and there is a crazy officer in charge of the Engineers who is having us drop in ski wax for recreational purposes.

F Company of the 7th Marines remained to guard the strip when the rest of the regiment moved northwest to Yudam-ni. When F Company followed, I and H Companies, two platoons of heavy weapons and two batteries of 105mm howitzers moved in. The goal was a longer runway to permit the landing and takeoff of cargo planes as well as light liaison aircraft. By November 27, when Chinese attacks intensified above Hagaru-ri, only one-fourth of the planned 3,400-foot runway was complete. Despite the threat of attacks from Chosin and infiltration from everywhere, work continued day and night in below-zero winds and snow under floodlights and tractor headlights.

At MacArthur's conference in Tokyo, Brigadier General Edwin "Pinky" Wright, FEC operations chief, had proposed that Almond send troops from the 3rd Division westward to Tokchon, across the Taebek spine separating EUSAK from X Corps, to help protect Walker's collapsing right flank. The road existed on paper on Wright's prewar Japanese map, Almond explained, but in reality it was only a dirt path unable to handle military traffic and now was frozen over. The armies could link up only in deep withdrawal below the 38th parallel. Once again. the Taebek strategy proved to be tinkering with unreality.

At 12:40 a.m., after Almond agreed to withdrawals already underway on his front, the conference broke up. At noon on the 29th, he departed from Haneda for Yonpo to prepare orders for immediate withdrawal to a perimeter around Hungnam. *Immediate* would not be easy. Marine units, some isolated in the west at Yudam-ni, were breaking out of entrapment. The battered remnants of Army battalions along the east coast of the frozen reservoir had to be collected and marched south. One narrow MSR existed, and it was subject to infiltration and harassment.

The necessary heroics around Chosin would not be limited to one side. A Chinese account describes—or invents—an officer with the 20th Army near Yudam-ni, Yang Gan Si, "embracing a bag of dynamite and being killed together with ten U.S. soldiers rushing towards him."

Shrunken by casualties and continuing firefights at roadblocks, the American withdrawals were covered when the skies cleared by low-flying Marine aircraft at risk from Chinese guns below. Support also came from the FEAF Combat Cargo Command in Tokyo, run by Major General William H. Tunner, only forty-four, who had commanded the risky India-China "Hump" operations in the Pacific war and the brilliant, clockwork Berlin airlift in 1948–49. He began employing quartermaster packers at Ashiya in Japan to prepare drops of supplies by C-119 air freighters to troops cut off in the Chosin area. Soon he added C-46 cargo planes and workhorse twin-engine C-47s (the civilian DC-3). Not easy to work with, the demanding Tunner was characterized as "a great guy if you were a cold infantryman on the main battle position."

Working with Tunner from Almond's headquarters to propose drop sites was Colonel Aubrey Smith, the staff logistics officer. Planes would deliver 565 tons of supplies and munitions by parachute and 202 tons to airstrips, largely at Hagaru.

At Almond's CP in Hamhung, Major General Clark L. Ruffner, his chief of staff, wondered to Major General Robert Soule of the 3rd Army, its ranks bolstered by inadequate KATUSA draftees from the streets of Seoul and Pusan, "I don't know whether we will be able to save the Old Man's corps." Soule responded loyally, "Yes, we will be able to do it." But first the battalions upcountry had to fight their way down.

In Washington, the Joint Chiefs of Staff convened. Earlier, it had accepted the hard line of General Charles Bolté, the Army's operations chief, who had visited the persuasive MacArthur and come away agreeing with the up-to-the-Yalu strategy. "A show of strength," he argued, "will discourage further aggression while weakness would encourage it." With little knowledge of what policy reversal had now occurred at the *Dai Ichi*, only Admiral Forrest Sherman, responsible for the Marines, proposed sending MacArthur tactical orders. Sherman wanted both armies withdrawn to the waist of Korea to hold a shortened line. Omar Bradley felt that the theater commander needed his own options, which left the JCS only able to radio MacArthur weakly, "What are your plans regarding the coordination of the Eighth Army and X Corps and the positioning of X Corps, the units of which to us appear to be exposed?"

When MacArthur cautiously referred to the situation as "fluid," Truman told his National Security Council, "That's a public relations man's way of saying he can't figure out what's going on." General George C. Marshall, the Secretary of

Defense recalled from retirement, refused to offer any strategic opinions, observing that the Chinese had more manpower than firepower. Wartime Army Chief of Staff, then Secretary of State and finally Secretary of Defense, Marshall was the nation's finest soldier-statesman since Washington. But he conceded that he did not know the facts on the ground in Korea, for MacArthur had been grandstanding rather than forthcoming. Marshall's successor as Secretary of State, Dean Acheson, who was sitting next to him, recalled the general's position. "No military judgment from me. What can we do? We are eight thousand miles away from the battle. We don't know the terrain except that it's bad. There are only two things we *can* do. One is the way we've operated since the Spanish-American War, which is to trust the commander in the field, say to him, 'Go to it, brother.' You don't say, 'Send this division here, or use these supplies and movements there.' Churchill tried to do that and got everything bolloxed up. The second way is to relieve him—and who wants to do that?"

Very likely everyone at the table wanted to do exactly that, but the political costs at home would have been enormous. Marshall read a memorandum to him from the service chiefs urging that American diplomatic responses to China proceed through the United Nations. He added that the United States should not get "sewed up" in Korea and that if complete withdrawal became necessary, it had to be accomplished without loss of prestige. Hopefully but unrealistically, General Collins believed that MacArthur could hold the disintegrating line above the 38th parallel. General Bradley agreed without much confidence that it was possible. Secretary Acheson worried that attacking Chinese targets across its Manchurian borders might bring in Russia, prompting a world war. MacArthur had criticized such constraints from Washington as "an enormous handicap, without precedent in history." Narrowly taking his side, Admiral Sherman proposed that if the Chinese mounted air strikes from Manchuria, "We must hit back or we cannot stay there [in Korea]." Air Force secretary Thomas Finletter also warned of open intervention by China and Russia, but the Chinese had few air resources, and within Stalin's cautious limits, the Soviets were already flying covert missions for North Korea and China along the Yalu.

Concerned that further strategic confrontation with Stalin was inevitable, Marshall recommended that Truman propose to Congress and the nation a comprehensive plan for vigilant military mobilization against Communist adventurism worldwide, just as NATO was about to initiate in Europe. Painfully, that would add billions more to the budget. Under the umbrella of a national emergency, which the Chinese intervention had already created, Truman hoped for reluctant cooperation from hawkish conservatives and their promoters in the newsprint empires.

A further cable from MacArthur had warned that the Chinese objective was "the complete destruction of United Nations forces and the securing of all Korea." His urging the importation of Chiang Kai-Shek's troops from Taiwan, which appealed to the press barons, was dismissed by the JCS as wholly unacceptable. MacArthur exploited alarm. Not only did Truman intend to keep the war localized and limited, involving the discredited Chiang in Korea would disrupt cooperation from UN-affiliated countries. Besides, the aging Nationalist remnants had proven hopelessly ineffective against Mao's forces on the Asian mainland.

Everyone agreed that MacArthur had to go on the defensive, but that reversal had already occurred, and not by choice. Truman would direct General Collins to fly out and consult with MacArthur and, if possible, with the commanders in the field. Consultation was cheap and put off hard decisions.

In *The New York Times*, James Reston would write, "There is no doubt that confidence in General Douglas MacArthur, even on Capitol Hill, has been shaken badly by the events of the last few days. Similarly, there is no doubt that United States leadership in the Western world has been damaged by President Truman's [passive] acceptance of the bold MacArthur offensive." After the Inchon success, MacArthur had seemed too formidable to fail. Ordered to use only Korean troops in the far north, to avoid antagonizing the Chinese, he ignored all restrictions. And, indeed, ROK forces in the northwest, manning a third of the front, had shown what Richard J. B. Johnston of *The New York Times* reported as "flagging morale" and "a general lack of will to fight Chinese troops." Outflanked and on the run, the inadequate South Koreans endangered the entire Eighth Army.

Bold was the word the general might have employed to characterize his "home for Christmas" brag, but *brazen* fit the dismaying results. MacArthur's troops, Homer Bigart of *The New York Herald Tribune* explained from Korea, were "paying the initial price for the unsound decision to launch an offensive north of the peninsula's narrow neck. . . . It was taken with forces far too small to secure the long Korean frontier . . . even without the open intervention of Red China."

"I should have relieved MacArthur then and there," Truman later conceded in his memoirs. He had not wanted it to appear, he claimed, that the general was being sacked "because the offensive failed. I have never believed in going back on people when luck is against them." Yet he knew that the ongoing debacle had nothing to do with luck and everything to do with arrogance. The President understood that the bleak outlook left him with no options against the political Right at home other than keeping MacArthur on to save face in resurgent postcolonial Asia.

Despite editorial-page sarcasm about MacArthur's "home for Christmas" boasts, the calls across the country for a guilty head to roll rarely brought up the general's name. Warding that off in advance, MacArthur publicly blamed the disaster on the far-off Truman administration, which had allegedly licensed his risky moves up to the Yalu. The media as well as MacArthur's claque in Congress called for the resignation of Secretary of State Acheson, who had once observed that the Asian mainland, which included Korea, was not an American responsibility. (MacArthur, on the other hand, had assured Koreans on his one prewar visit that he would defend Korea as he would California.) Acheson was also charged with weakness in confronting supposedly monolithic world Communism, especially the Soviet Union and its satellites. Rabble-rousing Senator Joseph McCarthy of Wisconsin, later thoroughly discredited, blamed "the Korea deathtrap" on both Stalin and Acheson, and another Senate demagogue, William

Jenner of Indiana, charged Secretary of Defense George Marshall with being "a front man for traitors." The increasingly heated Cold War was not a good time to be associated with the Truman administration.

One of the State Department's most trusted advisers, especially on Communism, was George Kennan. After conferring with Acheson, he wrote a follow-up memorandum to the Secretary, urging firmness as policy and, by inference, referring to MacArthur: "In international, as in private, life what counts most is not really what happens to someone, but how he bears what happens to him. For this reason almost everything depends from here on out on the manner in which we Americans bear what is unquestionably a major failure and disaster to our national fortunes. If we accept it with candor, with dignity, with a resolve to absorb its lessons and to make good by redoubled and determined effort—starting all over again, if necessary along the pattern of Pearl Harbor—we need lose neither our self-confidence nor our power for bargaining, eventually, with the Russians."

That meant, also, getting over another disaster nearer home. In an embarrassingly misspoken press conference on November 30, broadcast and published across a nation numb with Korea shock, Truman had declared that the government would take "whatever steps are necessary to meet the military situation, just as we always have done." Asked by a reporter whether that included the atomic bomb, the President added, too hastily, "That includes every weapon we have." Reporters did not know, as Truman certainly did, that in September, Lieutenant General James Gavin had been charged with investigating "the possible employment of nuclear weapons" and, on returning from Korea, had proposed forming a study group to examine the possibility of using tactical nuclear rockets. The likelihood of exposing American troops to radioactive fallout and the questionable ethics of again using atomic devices would close the matter, but nuclear intervention remained an ongoing, if secret, issue.

Rattled by continued questioning about using the Bomb, Truman responded, forgetting that by law only the President could authorize its employment, "The military commander in the field will have charge of the use of the weapons, as he always has." MacArthur, it appeared, had been handed the Bomb by Truman.

Fourteen minutes after the press conference closed, the presidential gaffe was on the wire. It would take days to quiet the worldwide furor. And it would never quiet MacArthur, who would keep appealing for the Bomb until his last days in Tokyo. Yet there would be no nuclear alternative, and, indeed, if the war were to remain confined to Korea, there were no useful targets anyway.

The global fuss over the faux pas would prompt Prime Minister Clement Attlee to fly to Washington to confer with Truman on what was conceded to be "the military disaster in Korea." It was described in *The New York Times* as "an atmosphere reminiscent of the grim Roosevelt-Churchill meetings after Pearl Harbor," but the long conferences by many principals over two weeks were, in 1941, about planning for ultimate victory. The brief and largely one-on-one meetings between

Truman and Attlee would be about finding a respectable opportunity for closure in Korea short of defeat.

Acheson would take Kennan to meet with Truman, but only after sharing ideas with George Marshall, who agreed that withdrawal from Korea would be a disaster. What was needed was a military response, somewhere in Korea, to hold the line and fight the Chinese to a standstill at a strategic point where negotiation became possible. Acheson and Kennan then lunched with Truman, who agreed that MacArthur's cut-and-run hysteria was as misguided as misusing the Bomb.

The Bomb could not have extricated the Marines outflanked at the Chosin Reservoir. Even dismayed Washingtonians understood from the early days of the thwarted offensives that the key to withdrawal to a secure defensive perimeter required the breakout of O. P. Smith's regiments. At Yudam-ni, west of one of the northernmost arms of the reservoir and well above Fox Hill, Lieutenant Colonel Robert D. Taplett's 3ʳᵈ Battalion, 5ᵗʰ Marines and Lieutenant Colonel Raymond G. Davis's 1ˢᵗ Battalion, 7ᵗʰ Marines, appeared trapped but were battling their way out. Having infiltrated in darkness, the Chinese seemed everywhere about them.

Before the X Corps offensive stalled, a secured mess tent at Hagaru had been stocked with canned delicacies and choice liquors flown in from Tokyo and intended for Ned Almond's use. Hagaru, he planned, would be his next command post as the Corps moved up toward the Yalu. Yet suddenly the rosy situation had turned. In the unanticipated circumstances, there would be no forward CP. Transports too formidable to land at the Hagaru runway released, via gaily colored parachutes, color-coded supplies in red, green, blue and yellow hues toward a drop zone two hundred yards from the airstrip. In the gale-driven snow, the drops were less than accurate, and some were plucked by the Chinese.

The earlier confidence of tall, lean 5th Marines commander Ray Murray had been sapped by the perils of entrapment. His slow Texas delivery belied the urgency of his message. "Gentlemen," he said to officers within range, "we are going out of here. And we are going out like Marines. We are sticking together and we are taking out our dead and wounded and our equipment. Are there any questions?" There were no questions.

That afternoon, the correspondents still at Hagaru, to the south, the most forward location permitted to the press, listened as General Smith explained that his battalions had to attack their way out. A British reporter questioned whether that meant retreat. "Certainly not," fudged Smith, citing the swarming infiltration of the Chinese. "There can be no retreat when there's no rear. You can't retreat, or even withdraw, when you're surrounded. The only thing you can do is break out, and in order to do that you have to attack, and that's what we're about to do."

In the fluid fighting, the lines shifted, usually rearward, and more so in the retrograde EUSAK west. Don Huth wrote for the AP that correspondents would head for the front toward a town and then were told at advance command posts, "Hell, the town fell to the enemy an hour ago, and there are a couple of road blocks [now] on the road you used." Correspondent

Tom Lambert visited one command post, according to Huth, "and left before dark to write and send out [dispatches]. . . . When he returned the next morning he found that the Chinese had broken into the CP perimeter, killing the officers and men in their tents. The [command] post had been removed to the rear during the night." Reporters, he wired, "shiver by the fire, eating a can of cold beans and swearing they won't go back. Then they write their stories and catch a few hours of fitful sleep in a freezing room. In the morning they crawl slowly out of their sleeping bags, rub up a little circulation in aching limbs, pull on as many garments as they can carry, and ask: 'Well, where are we going now?'"

Huth's wry humor hardly concealed the desperation, which, without censorship, traveled home to newspapers and a very worried public and put agonizing pressure on Washington—and on Tokyo. Hal Boyle wrote of the vanished home-for-Christmas mirage that the miles which troops "had bled to win" were being lost. "The roads no longer led to home. They were only roads going back to more stubborn stands against an outnumbering foe, more winter wounds, more death in the snow."

Panic mode pervaded GHQ in Tokyo. MacArthur had no reserves in Japan which he could commit, and two fronts in retrograde. General Soule's 3rd Division, which had landed with little interference above Hungnam, at first was directed to move further north, to the Manchurian frontier. With the Chosin offensive in reverse, Soule's new orders were to back up the Marines as they fought out of entrapment toward the sea, with his division deploying a defensive perimeter on the coastal plain to enable the evacuation.

On December 1, contrary orders for Almond arrived from the *Dai Ichi* that Soule was to reassemble his division at Wonsan, south of Hungnam, for immediate shipment around South Korea to bolster the beleaguered Eighth Army. It would have been the maddening reverse of the flawed win-the-war-by-Christmas diversion of X Corps from Inchon around Korea to Wonsan and Hungnam. The misdirection seemed useless to Almond, if not completely insane, but he dutifully began to carry it out. Then, realizing its impossibility to stem the retreat in the west as well as its disastrous impact upon his own front, he ordered Colonel Edward H. Forney, the senior Marine officer on his staff, and Lieutenant Colonel William W. Quinn, his intelligence deputy, to fly to Tokyo to appeal the decision.

Forney was an expert on amphibious operations who had been instrumental in the success at Inchon. Even before the pair left for Japan, MacArthur began ordering shipping to Wonsan to implement his orders, an operation that would prove useful but not as he intended. Cancellation of the absurd instructions made it possible for the 3rd Division to concentrate at Hamhung, which made more strategic sense. Troops and their gear also moved up by road and rail, emptying the Wonsan harbor area but for one Victory ship, which took on Korean refugees fleeing the Chinese. Agents for Syngman Rhee's Home Minister Cho Pyong-ok were frightening Koreans in the north with tales of Communist atrocities and lied that the regime in the south would give them grants of land. Soon there would be other reasons to flee.

The 3rd Division's perimeter defense based at Hamhung would be in place and in time for reassembly of the Marines, although it was not what MacArthur had intended. He had appealed to Washington that he faced an entirely new war. He did.

6

Beginning the Breakout

"The place looked like one gigantic Christmas card, except most of it was on fire."

Ned Almond flew into Hagaru once more to appeal to O. P. Smith about rescuing "Task Force Faith." Earlier, on November 28, before it had been overrun by white-clad Chinese wearing the inside-out liners of their mustard-hued parkas, Almond had been at Don Faith's command post on an eastern fork of the reservoir. In the subzero cold, in a hut on a lower slope of Hill 1221, Faith had halted his RCT-31, the augmented 31st Regiment of the 7th Division. Warning signals were obvious. The 3rd Battalion of the 5th Marines, above Faith on the western bank of the reservoir, had almost reached the northern end when it encountered a Chinese patrol, portending trouble. The 5th Marines commander, Ray Murray, warned Faith by radio link not to go farther. Reception was crackling and inconsistent, as the highlands between units and the deep freeze impeded communication and batteries faded or failed. But Faith already knew he was in a desperate situation.

At about noon on the 26th, Brigadier General Henry Hodes, assistant commander of the 7th Division, had reached Hill 1221 to survey matters with Faith and then jeeped to O. P. Smith, who had received ominous reports about the other front from Johnnie Walker's staff. The ROK II Corps, on the Eighth Army's right flank, the edge of EUSAK's perimeter near Tokchon, about seventy miles over the Taebek ridges southeast of the reservoir, had been outflanked and routed by the Chinese. The EUSAK offensive and Eighth Army itself were in sudden jeopardy.

Smith had already helicoptered to Yudam-ni, the closest command post to the Taebek ridges west of his troops, that of Ray Davis's 1st Battalion of the 7th Marines. Smith's chopper pilot could not touch down, slipping backward on the ice. "After 4 or 5 tries we went down to the floor of the valley to land. The elevation here was about 4,000 feet. At this altitude the helicopter does not have much hovering capability. . . . For the last ten feet we simply dropped." Almond still then expected to continue the X Corps advance. "Litzenberg's role [for the 5th Marines]," Smith noted in his log, "is to hold the Yudam-ni area while Murray [with his 7th Marines] passes through him to continue the advance to the westward. Litzenberg indicated he would like to keep going." Without cautionary intelligence from X Corps, "Litz" was chancing the ice, snow and subzero conditions.

Afterward, Ray Murray confessed, "It was unbelievable. The more you think about it, the more unreal it becomes. Well, anyhow, those were [Almond's] orders and that's what we started to do." By darkness, the 2nd and 3rd Battalions, 5th

Marines, were in attack position at Yudam-ni, and two Marine Corsair aircraft were due over at daylight for close support. Also a weapons company from Hagaru-ri was promised, and Marines awaited trucks for their heavy batteries. In the ice and snow, the trucks would never arrive.

Leathernecks knew they were close to the Chinese when they could sniff them as well as hear them. Each carried a three-day supply of rations, and in the clear, cold air, a sergeant recalled, "We could smell the garlic and hear them talking." Before nightfall, a patrol of the 7th Marines reported the capture of three Chinese soldiers, learning from them that three divisions were approaching. During the night, the 79th and 81st CCF Divisions, with submachine guns and grenades, came close to surrounding Yudam-ni, and the 59th Division moved south toward the Toktong Pass, held only by Captain Barber's Fox Company, 7th Marines. Only the firepower at the ridgelines of howitzer batteries from the 3rd and 4th Battalions, 11th Marines, in twenty-below cold, kept the Chinese almost at bay. Almost. Several hill positions were lost, and overpowered units were battered. Companies were reduced to the size of platoons. In the crisis, Murray met with Litzenberg at the 7th Marines CP at dawn on the 28th and agreed that, whatever Almond's orders, they had to go on the defensive and backtrack. By evening, the home-for-Christmas offensive was history.

General Sung Zhi Lun, who commanded the 9th Army Group, equivalent to three American corps, had received a challenging message from Chairman Mao, "It is said that the American Marine First Division has the highest combat effectiveness in the American armed forces." It was more than a hint about Sung's offensive priorities. Despite his good intelligence from patrols, he may not have known that the positions vacated by the 5th Marines were occupied by Faith's ragtag army column, which, stretched thin over ten miles, lacked the manpower and weapons of a Marine regiment.

Corsairs flown in for close support strikes had little effect on disciplined columns of white-clad Chinese. Their wounded died quickly in the intense cold, and the survivors proceeded over and around them. "There were dead Chinese lying all around us," Lieutenant Jerome McCabe recalled fifty years later, "and they were frozen in place." His right arm and leg bled from a mortar round that exploded near him. He lay unconscious for several hours until he was lifted into in the rear of a truck heading, under fire, south toward Hagaru-ri. When the truck stalled, he would "slither out" and "hobbled and crawled."

As the Chinese were effective at infiltration during the long nights, even Hagaru to the south seemed threatened. The Marine division's operations officer, Lieutenant Colonel Thomas L. Ridge, seeking more riflemen, ordered Company D, 10th Combat Engineer Battalion, to pick up arms and fill a gap in his perimeter. Captain Philip A. Kulbes protested. His seventy-seven Americans and ninety South Koreans were constructing an advance command post for Almond, who still expected the advance toward the Yalu to continue somehow.

"Pulling rank," Ridge reassigned the engineers, although untrained in infantry tactics, to Captain John C. Shelnutt of the 3rd Battalion's weapons company. Reluctantly, his new troops took their time about moving out trucks and equipment. Ordered to man another roadblock was a platoon from the Army's 4th Signal Battalion, sent to Hagaru to install communications for the new X Corps CP. Lieutenant John A. Colborn complained that his signalmen, picking up rifles, also had no infantry training. At a higher level, confusion persisted. While X Corps headquarters, remote from the action, continued to plan offensive action all the way to the Yalu, forward units, defending themselves, were withdrawing under fire.

Chinese infiltrators seemed everywhere along the Marines' perimeter, striking southwest of the reservoir at East Hill, just above Hagaru, where H and I companies of the 3rd Battalion, 1st Marines, protecting the escape route from Yudam-ni, were stretched thin. Snow continued. Close to midnight, three red flares and three shrieks of whistles signaled the onrush of the Chinese. Mortar shells mixed with deadly white phosphorus began falling. Some Chinese broke through How Company's lines and reached the edge of the Hagaru airstrip, where armed engineers, alerted to danger and their working lights darkened, fired at them.

More Chinese came, driven off by a mixed Army and Marine platoon led by Lieutenant Grady P. Mitchell, Jr. who was killed. "They would come at us like fire ants," Marine Sergeant Joe Quick remembered, "wave after wave. . . . You'd burn the rifling out of your M-1 shooting at them. Our machine guns would overheat from all the firing. . . . We were stacking up dead Chinese soldiers in front of us and using them as shields to fire behind. We'd work in relays."

Soon the Chinese, with men to spare, were back, and Quick, a veteran, when seventeen, of Okinawa in 1945, was wounded by mortar shrapnel. He only remembered "leaving the ground" when the incoming round hit. Awakening in a rear area hospital tent, he heard a Catholic chaplain giving last rites to a Marine. Then the chaplain came to him. "Father," Quick murmured, "I'm not a Catholic; I'm a Baptist." If he believed in God, said the chaplain, they could pray together anyway. A week later, Quick answered a call for walking wounded who could still hold a rifle and returned to action.

Rather than render the airstrip useless, their primary mission, the cold and hungry Chinese had gone after the cooking and supply tents. One stripped a parka from a Marine who survived by stiffening and feigning death. By 0130 on the 29th, the Chinese had vanished northward toward East Hill, where they occupied its summit. The shaken engineers put down their rifles, relit their floodlights and went back to work on the airstrip.

At a ridge on East Hill, the Chinese attacked the 3rd Battalion's Weapons Company, which answered with machine gun fire. At the crest of the hill, Captain Shellnut was radioed about the enemy column. His operator, Private Bruno Podolak, replied that Shellnut was dead. "There's nobody up here except me and a couple of doggies."* Soon after, another radio message brought no response. A bullet had penetrated the radio, then, having lost force, lodged in Podolak's back. The radio had saved his life.

Military radio and telephonic frequencies in Korea required an encyclopedic mental directory. A Corsair pilot radioed below, "This is Lovelace." Lieutenant Neal Heffernan,

---

*In World War II usage, ordinary soldiers were *dogfaces*.

a forward air controller, radioed, "Secure the mission, Blueberry!" Captain Edward Stamford, another fire controller, radioed, "Boyhood One Four, this is Fireball One. Acknowledge. Over." Koto-ri was "Whiskey One." From Fox Company came "Delegate Six, this is Fox Six. Message understood." A field hospital to the south was, realistically, "Ragbag."

After first light, Marine Corsairs radioed for by Major Reginald Myers, Ridge's executive officer, flew thirty-one sorties low over Hagaru and East Hill once the morning fog lifted, one plane taking hits from Chinese small arms fire. The pilot, Lieutenant Harry W. Colmery, crash landed inside the Marines' perimeter and survived. Myers pulled together the half-frozen remnants of his unit, but he had so many wounded that not enough medics were available to retrieve them. Some lay where they fell. The Marines, now too thin to keep the crest of the hill, hung on below.

East of Chosin, the plight of embattled GIs was worsening as more Chinese came down. Seventh Division assistant commander Henry Hodes reported helplessly to Oliver Smith that RCT-31 had taken four hundred more casualties, had only half of its three thousand–man force left and was falling back toward Hagaru. Don Faith was taking fire from all directions, and his shattered remnants seemed unlikely to make the thirteen tough miles. Smith asked Hodes to draft a message to Faith that circumstances required his command to come under the orders of the Marine HQ below him at Hagaru. Unable to assist and unaware of Don Faith's plight, Smith wrote in his log, "I have nothing now with which to lend a hand except the battalion at Hagaru-ri and it has its hands full. I cannot see why the cut-off battalions cannot at least improve the situation by moving toward us."

By radio link, Faith appealed desperately to Hagaru for what would be the last time. "Unless someone can help us, I don't have much hope that anybody's going to get out of this." He was assured, unhopefully, "We are bringing in a lot of air support, but that's all we can give you. We just don't have enough people here to risk losing our hold on the foot of the reservoir."

"I understand," Faith said hopelessly. All his depleted units were encumbered with casualties and running low on everything. His medical supplies were exhausted. The frozen dead were laid out in four-foot-high rows, stacked upon each other. If he failed to execute his new orders, Almond insisted blindly by radio to the 7th Division's command post, well out of danger, as was Almond, Faith should be replaced.

Lieutenant James G. Campbell, who was too badly wounded to walk, crawled in darkness along a railroad track and found a carbine with one round in it. Crawling further, he fell into a foxhole. Someone helped him to the embattled aid station, which had run out of bandages and morphine. By noon, after eighty hours of siege, Faith ordered Lieutenant James Mortrude's Company C, least hurt, to slip out as advance guard, supported by a dual 40mm half-track. Hobbled by a knee wound, Mortrude planned to ride in the half-track, and as the company began to move out under fire, four Marine planes, in too-close support, dropped napalm on the lead elements, setting the half-track ablaze and burning horrified GIs to death. Others, clothes afire, frantically tried to beat out the flames as they fled. In the disorganization, as Mortrude's company encountered Chinese troops, they fired wildly, screaming obscenities and scattering them. But Faith's men in every direction, hobbled by wounds from "friendly fire," sleepless and running out of ammunition and supplies, could not get past enemy roadblocks toward Hagaru and hunkered down to await the inevitable. Shot up again, Mortrude, now with a head wound, somehow made it alone to the airstrip at Hagaru at 3:30 a.m. on December 2.

At Toktong Pass, halfway to Hagaru, Captain Barber's Fox Company, radioing for resupply and down to 237 Marines, was parachuted medical supplies and ammunition from a twin-boom C-119. Strong winds deposited the cargo at the base of the icy hill. In the recovery process, not altogether successful, two Marines were wounded, and much of the drop left to the Chinese. At two in the morning, a voice, in stilted English, was heard in the dark at Toktong, calling out, "Fox Company, you are surrounded. I am a lieutenant from the 11th Marines. The Chinese will give you warm clothes and good treatment. Surrender now!" Obviously the Chinese had a prisoner who had identified Barber's company, but someone else was doing the talking. Marines sent up 81mm illumination shells, then mortar and machine gun fire. Many of the surprised Chinese were struck; coming closer, others lofted hand grenades, then slipped away. Dug in, Fox Company gathered in another wounded Marine.

Potato masher grenades and mortar rounds were the Chinese chief weapons as they closed in. Unable to tug on his shoe-pacs over ice-encrusted socks and frost-bitten feet,

Private Hector Cafferata seized a fallen grenade and heaved it back to protect wounded men unable to move. It went off before it traveled far, damaging his right hand and arm, but he fired back with his other hand until a sniper got him in his riddled shoulder, the bullet ricocheting off a rib to puncture a lung. He too would survive, not losing his feet, but never afterward was he able to write right-handed. A big man, his feet hung over his stretcher as he was later carried to safety.

East of the reservoir, troops had not awaited orders from Almond to go on the defensive. The swarming Chinese forced the reversal. Allan MacLean and Don Faith had merged their command posts at Faith's hut. It was near dawn and snowing heavily on the 29th when Faith ordered a breakout to the south. Abandoned vehicles were to be disabled, and usable ones loaded with wounded. Without a clue to the ongoing disaster, Almond had returned from Tokyo with MacArthur's orders for a "strategic withdrawal." Any withdrawal whatever would have been strategic if successful.

A queue of sixty trucks and jeeps was slowly crawling downhill over the ice when MacLean jumped off his jeep to survey progress and, in blowing snow, ran into an ambush. Although Corsairs were flying overhead, pilots could not identify friend from enemy. A column of troops was seen coming up the road as the GIs approached a bridge over a reservoir inlet. "Those are my boys!" shouted MacLean as he ran toward them. But it was the Chinese in white who held the lower end of the bridge. A crackle of fire was heard from Faith's vantage as MacLean was hit several times. Each time he picked himself up and pitched forward. Soon, several Chinese pulled him out of sight.

After an exchange of sick and wounded POWs in 1953, a released prisoner reported that Colonel MacLean had died of his wounds on the fourth day of an agonized march of captives in the ice and snow toward a prison camp. What remained of Task Force MacLean was inherited by Don Faith, who struggled toward a roadblock above Hagaru, four and a half miles distant. A helicopter sent riskily by General Hodes extricated two wounded battalion commanders. The task force was nearly leaderless.

Air drops failed. Parachuted ammunition and materiel hastily called in often landed outside the shrinking perimeters and were hazardous to retrieve. Some, prepackaged in Japan, often by civilian workers with limited English and under little oversight, contained the wrong ammunition or useless supplies. (One drop to beleaguered Marines consisted of thousands of condoms.) Cases of 40mm shells parachuted in successfully but where no artillery existed to employ them had to be destroyed. Tanks requiring 105mm shells did not receive any, and eleven tanks sent forward failed to find fuel.

Although General Barr, Faith's division commander, helicoptered into Hagaru on the morning of November 30, he was nearly useless. He promised Faith some air support and pressed O. P. Smith for Marine planes, which came in on December 1 in relays, covering Faith's rear and sweeping the breakout route with rockets and bombs. Those able to walk found an escape route, but the wounded needed trucks, and some who did not

require wheels tried to slip aboard anyway to their later cost, for
the trucks were hit. When relieved and back in the States, Barr
conceded that the situation had been far worse than he realized.

Faith's final orders by radio from Almond were to expend
all possible ammunition in support of his breakout, then to
destroy everything that remained. All unusable vehicles were
to be disabled. All supplies and clothing to be abandoned were
to be burned. Under continuing enemy fire and the disabling
cold, rule-book instructions became increasingly impossible.
Dwindling under fire, Faith's men disintegrated as relentless
grenade and mortar attacks continued during the macabre,
subzero hours. It was difficult to induce exhausted, half-frozen
troops to fight, even to stand up. Muscles would cease working; eyelids would freeze over. Few had much sleep over three
days and nights of attacks, compounding their confusion.

As early dusk came again, beginning sixteen hours of darkness when supporting aircraft could not fly, Captain Erwin Bigger and several others saw Faith railing at men huddled against
trucks and shaking his Colt .45 at them. In fear, two Korean
soldiers seemed to be waiting for Faith to pass before they attempted to crawl into the undercarriage of a truck. He ordered
them toward him. "I'm hurt," a KATUSA appealed coweringly
in Japanese—their language learned in school during the occupation. Seeing no injury and overcome in dismay, Faith raised
his pistol and pulled the trigger. One crumpled; then he shot
the other. "Shoot anyone who runs away!" he shouted at no one
in particular. Some panicked Americans who had tried to climb
into trucks with the freezing wounded drifted warily away.

The big trucks were the primary targets for Chinese mortar crews. Crippling the vehicles blocked the MSR and paralyzed the withdrawal. Badly wounded by mortar fire, Major Hugh Robbins was loaded into a truck, heightening his hazards. A group was clustered near their command post when a shell landed, wounding three officers and a truck driver. Captain Bigger was struck in the face by shell fragments. One eye was blown from its socket. A medic placed it back and, in futility, put a patch over it. Half-frozen, Bigger was added to a truckload of casualties, but the truck did not move, and he soon struggled out to lead a group of walking wounded. Hobbling under fire on a patched-up leg, Captain Dale Seaver, C Company commander who had learned two weeks before that his wife had been delivered of their son, commented then to Major Wesley Curtis, "I feel like I am a thousand years old." By three that afternoon, he was dead.

The drivers of the first two trucks in Faith's column struggling toward Hagaru-ri were shot by Chinese infiltrators and their vehicles disabled, closing the narrow road in yet another place. More Chinese emerged from the hills, spraying submachine gun fire. Struck in the chest by grenade fragments, Faith went down. A mortar officer, Lieutenant Fields E. Shelton, tried to pull Faith into his jeep, but, weakened by his own wounds, he could not. Shelton lay him at the roadside and searched for help in the darkness. Private Louis J. Grappo and several others heard Faith's failing voice, found him and lifted him into the cab of a truck next to the dead driver. Limping by, using a fallen tree limb as a crutch, was Major Curtis, 1st

Battalion operations officer. In the tumult he heard Faith's voice. "How are you doing, Colonel?" Curtis asked, peering in.

Not realizing that the truck was inoperable and the driver dead, Faith murmured, "Let's get going." Then his voice faded out. Technically, Curtis now inherited the command, but he hobbled on. "There was no resistance left in the column. . . . Motors in the trucks were not running—drivers were not in the cabs of the trucks. The only sound was the moaning of the wounded and dying."*

Faith would be awarded another decoration, one he could not reject, as it was posthumous—a Medal of Honor. The citation was dramatic but wide of the reality. "Lieutenant Colonel Faith," it reads, "reconnoitered the route for, and personally directed, the first elements of his command across the ice-covered reservoir and then directed the movement of his vehicles which were loaded with wounded until all of his command had passed through the enemy fire. Having completed this he crossed the reservoir himself. . . . In the face of direct enemy fire [he] led an attack on the enemy roadblock, firing his pistol and throwing grenades. . . . [He] was mortally wounded but continued to direct the attack until the roadblock was overrun." Only 1,050 of the original MacLean-Faith force of 2,500 would be recovered alive. Not a single RCT vehicle made it through.

---

*Conflicting recollections of Faith's end exist. Private Russell Barney told General David Barr in January 1951 that he had driven the truck in which Faith was wounded a second time by rifle fire while in the cab next to him and that when he abandoned the truck, Faith was dead. His remains were buried in April 2013.

Although Faith's remains were repatriated in 2004, only in 2012 were they identified through DNA. Of the 101 bone samples extricated from the recovery site, twelve were those of Don Faith—among the last physical evidence to come out of North Korea. MIA recovery teams have since been barred. The North Koreans, said Michael Mee, chief of the identifications branch, rarely let American retrieval teams "go to a primary burial site. They would take remains from a primary . . . location and re-bury them somewhere else." As a result, the site and cause of death were only recalled by surviving eyewitnesses.

Among the survivors was a platoon led by Private Glenn J. Finrock, who had tried to get the disabled truck in which Faith's body was found started again. After failing and trudging away, his squad was seized on the ice. Rather than shoot them to be rid of the burden of prisoners, Chinese soldiers bandaged their wounds, gave them shots of morphine, held them a few days until they were mobile, then released them to walk, if they could, toward Hagaru. It was a rare act of apparent chivalry in a mean climate and a mean war.

More than three hundred of the frozen dead, including Faith, were left in the abandoned vehicles in the darkness of early December. The Chinese considered truck drivers special targets, as they knew that GIs moved on wheels. Foot soldiers aware of the realities considered volunteering to drive a two-and-a-half-ton "six-by-six" as a form of suicide. In subzero Korea, stalled vehicles became coffins.

Emboldened that the Americans were disintegrating, the Chinese began materializing by day as well as by night, partly camouflaged by their quilted white uniforms and headgear. Their discipline, whether under fire from the ground or the air, seemed hypnotic to observers. A tactical air controller on the ground was heard asking a Corsair pilot by radio, when it was difficult in swirling snow to see anything, "What 'n hell [are] you guys shooting at?"

"You won't believe this," the pilot radioed back. "We've got Chinese walking five abreast. We're throwing everything we've got . . . at them and they won't break ranks. Almost out of fuel, but we'll be back." The gull-winged, napalm-bearing Corsairs from the carrier *Leyte* were almost the only source of heat in the icy reservoir region. "One of the craziest sights," Private Francis Killeen remembered, "was to stand on a mountaintop and look down at Corsairs making strikes. . . . The place looked like one gigantic Christmas card, except most of it was on fire. You could watch this speck nose down, then the orange glow of a napalm bomb. . . . Often we led them in with tracers."

Gingerly, Killeen's unit passed "all these dead Chinese—I mean hundreds—and their quilted uniforms were still smoldering." Yet sometimes the canisters of jellied gasoline fell too close. Bob Hammond "could tell immediately" that a Corsair attempting to blast a path for trapped Americans was "coming down short" as the napalm cargo was disgorged. "There were only seconds to react, and when the stuff hit, there was a tremendous ball of fire. . . . I saw about ten guys running away, their whole bodies engulfed in flames. . . . I think that some of them were shot by their buddies, for there was no saving any of them." Major Hugh Robbins, lying wounded in the bed of a truck, was jolted, then peered through the slats at soldiers aflame. "Looking back up I could see the terrible sight of men ablaze from head to foot, staggering back or rolling on the ground screaming." Private James Ransone, Jr. of Task Force Faith barely evaded incineration. "Men all around me were burned. They lay rolling in the snow. Men I knew, marched and fought with, begged me to shoot them. It was terrible. Where the napalm had burned the skin to a crisp, it would be peeled back from the face, arms, legs. It looked as though the skin was curled like fried potato chips." In evasive military euphemism—but literal in such episodes—they were casualties of "friendly fire."

The narrow, contested road to Hagaru, the destination for withdrawing troops, was the stem of the "Y" made by positions coming together from both sides of the Chosin. In the deep darkness, it seemed so close from the mountaintops overlooking the reservoir that when engineers frantically continued work on the runways by floodlights, it appeared to an awed officer like New York at night. It continued to draw Chinese infiltrators with submachine guns and mortars, but it was safe from the air and from heavier artillery fire as the enemy had no way to bring in long-range guns.

The Hagaru airstrip had to be held at all costs. Carved from the frozen loam by five bulldozers, the operation first required explosive charges tamped into emptied ration cans to loosen the soil. Welding claws to the dozer blades to bite into the icy earth, engineers found unforeseen consequences. When the grader pans were filled, the earth froze to them, requiring removal by jackhammer. Blinding snow also delayed the work crews. At 2,900 feet in length and 50 feet in width, the runway was still less than half what guidelines decreed for its elevation. Yet there was neither more space between hills nor more time, and Smith's fighting complement defending the strip was being thinned by casualties.

During the last days of November, Ridge's battalion defending the precious airstrip would lose a third of its strength in killed, wounded and weather-related injuries. (A soldier on sentry duty was found in his foxhole, frozen to death.) In the early afternoon of the 30th, Almond flew up to Hagaru in an L-17 from Hamhung for a conference ostensibly of commanders in the Chosin area. None of the officers fighting to escape the reservoir ridges could get to Hagaru, but the meeting went on with less embattled brass. Almond would order the resupply of units by air to give them the wherewithal to get out to Hagaru, and they would have to destroy anything usable left behind. Smith reminded him of the burden of the sick, wounded and dead. Except in extraordinary circumstances, Marines did not leave their dead behind—and there were very many dead. At 3:40, Almond flew back to Hungnam, and commanders at Hagaru radioed orders to units within contact to do what they were already doing. Troops on both banks of the reservoir had to funnel, if they could, through the main supply route to Hagaru. *Main* was a misnomer—there was only one narrow MSR.

East of Chosin, troops had reached as far as the northernmost Pungnyori Inlet and now were winding southbound down the frozen reservoir shore, by vehicle, if any, and on foot, toward Hill 1221 and the blasted village of Twiggae. Those on the icy ridges above Yudam-ni had to weave south through the Toktong Pass. Only five miles above Hagaru, the road at the pass was penetrated by Chinese squads, which even slipped below the village, setting up a roadblock cutting it off from Koto-ri to the south. Colonel Puller assembled a relief force to open the narrow road above Koto, soon labeled Hell Fire Valley—a company of the 1st Marines with a divisional headquarters complement of 70 men and a signal battalion, a company from the 7th Division, and the 235 newly arrived officers and men of the 41st Commando, British Royal Marines. The task force of 942 men was under Royal Marines Lieutenant Colonel Douglas B. Drysdale. Puller realized that Chinese might block the road, but he gave the go-ahead, counting on the spearhead of 29 tanks leading 141 other vehicles.

About four miles north of Koto-ri, fire from ambushing Chinese halted seventeen Pershing tanks at the head of the column. To flush out enemy emplacements, tankers fired their 90mm cannon and followed up with machine guns. The Chinese responded with mortar rounds, setting a truck ablaze and blocking movement behind it with flurries of potato masher grenades. Drysdale radioed General Smith, who ill-advisedly told him to push ahead rather than return under fire, as Hagaru crucially needed bolstering if the airstrip was to function. "Very well," said Drysdale, "we'll give them a show."

Smith had underestimated the Chinese, who, adept at roadblocks, had infiltrated the valley in force from every direction, hidden along a frozen creek and wooded rises, making up for their lack of heavy armament with punishing small arms and mortar fire. White phosphorus grenades were the most vicious weapons in the Chinese arsenal. Thrown into vehicles, they burned to death men not already incapacitated by wounds or weather. Lieutenant Colonel Arthur Chichester, the 1st Marines senior officer in the stalled tail of the column, ordered the blocked vehicles, including twelve tanks at the rear of the column, to turn around toward Koto. He was wounded and captured, dying in the valley.

Corsairs called in for support from the air had to return as early darkness fell, leaving isolated segments of the column running the Chinese gauntlet backed by ineffective artillery fire from Koto. In a northern pocket, Major John M. McLaughlin and his Marines as well as Associated Press photographer Frank Noel were ambushed. Known to troops by the single Private First Class stripe glued to his Speed Graphic, Noel had run into trouble before. To escape the Japanese invasion of Singapore early in 1942, he had boarded a freighter bound for Rangoon. It was sunk by a Japanese submarine, and he was adrift for five days, yet he kept his camera, and a picture taken from his lifeboat won a Pulitzer Prize. This time he was not so lucky. The Chinese sent the prisoners to a holdout unit of forty with a surrender demand. No holdout had more than eight rounds of ammunition left.

McLaughlin agreed to surrender if the Chinese would permit the seriously wounded men to be evacuated south. The parley stretched out in what would have been a comic pause had lives not been at stake. Private William Spain, twenty-two, had been jeeping Noel. "I was behind the wheel. The Chinese told me to drive back to my commanding officer and tell him if he would surrender, the Chinese would treat us OK.

I went back and came across Major James K. Eagan, who told me, 'You go back and tell them they ought to surrender and we will feed them good and take good care of them.'"

Spain drove back over the icy road and explained Eagan's unrealistic offer. "They told me in pretty good English to go back and tell my superiors that if we didn't surrender in 10 minutes that they would attack us. This time the officers went back by themselves to talk things over with the Chinese. They stayed up there about 30 or 40 minutes. Pretty soon they came back and said, 'Let's fight it out.'" In the interim, a Marine in one of the three smaller pockets then trapped suggested, while the Chinese were distracted and darkness had come, "Let's make a break for it."

Spain was captured a second time while others were able to escape in darkness. "They took me and some others up a canyon. As we walked up there I spotted three Marines up a draw"—a gully. "The Chinese dropped back like they weren't following us anymore. So I ran and made it back okay." Still, they would not release the casualties but instead moved them to a nearby house, where they were found by Marines when the Chinese, taking Noel with them, slipped into the hills in daylight.

Noel would spend thirty-two months in prison camps. So would the Marines with him. In the snow, a Leatherneck who got away found a lens from a camera. "This is Frank Noel's," he guessed.

"Hold on to it for him," said another Marine.

Also ambushed as the Chinese broke through, Task Force Drysdale was in deeper trouble. Surrounded, exhausted and freezing, troops were too numb to fire back and huddled in icy gullies and behind snow-covered boulders. Robert Tyack, a British Marine, remembered a desperate moment when his mate succumbed to sleep as they attempted to scrape a shelter from the frozen ground with their bayonets. As Tyack tried to rouse him, he mumbled, "Leave me! If I don't wake, what the hell!" The MIA statistics in frozen Chosin include some choosing such oblivion.

Commandos and Marines in enemy hands were gathered together near a disabled truck. The Chinese were not going to burn the truck before looting its contents. The prisoners watched in tears as the soldiers in padded uniforms ripped open what were mail sacks. On their way to Hagaru were early Christmas packages from home. Wind gusts blew the holiday wrappings into the snowy ridges as the Chinese extracted watches, fountain pens, ski socks and other gifts. Another marooned truck was en route to the Hagaru PX. From it the Chinese looted Tootsie Rolls, Hershey bars, chewing gum, toothbrushes and cigarette cartons.

Badly wounded little more than a mile from Hagaru but out of range of Chinese grenades, Drysdale relinquished his battered and diminishing command to 1st Marines captain Carl Sitter, who led the remnant into the village. In Hagaru and in Koto, the casualties in the three-day ordeal were tallied—61 Commandos, 141 Marines and 119 Army men—321 out of the original 922 who set out from Koto-ri. Seventy-five vehicles were lost—one tank and weapons carriers, trucks and jeeps. The survivors bulked up the defenses of the critical airstrip. "You were grateful," Robert Tyack recalled unsentimentally, for what the cold had done to the dead. "You were looking at a chunk of frozen meat, rather than a messy, stinking corpse."

After the war the hidebound British Admiralty attempted to deny Drysdale and others in his 41st Commando the ribbon of the Presidential Unit Citation awarded to the Marine division because the honor hadn't been recommended by a British officer. *He* was the ranking British officer attached to the division, Drysdale insisted. The Admiralty relented.

—⁂—

Bearded and frostbitten, Bill Barber's beleaguered Marines descending from the Toktong Pass would hold on for three days at Fox Hill. Coming down from Yudam-ni, Sergeant Aguirre of 3rd Battalion, 7th Regiment, compared the fireworks from the direction of Fox to the Fourth of July. Gravely wounded, Barber led his men with a board strapped to a leg, then while prone on a stretcher. Eighty-six men remained from Fox Company's original 237. Only one officer, Lieutenant John Dunne of the 1st Platoon, remained unhurt. When the company withdrew from the hill as Homer Litzenberg's 5th Marines came through, Dunne would be the effective commander, although Barber continued to shout directions.

Pushing through high drifts and frozen ridges, Davis's 1st Battalion, 7th Marines numbered in all companies eight hundred walking wounded still carrying weapons and more than a thousand wounded and weather-disabled men in trucks and lashed to anything else on wheels. Among the uncomplaining casualties surviving in a frigid tent for two days before withdrawal on December 1 was John Yancey, who would be attended by a corpsman regularly to dig coagulated blood out of his mouth to prevent him from choking. Yancey would make it, but his Easy Company was in remnants, now combined with the diminished Dog Company. Listening to an attack nearby that was driven off without him, he "felt naked" without a rifle he could not shoulder. Exiting in the frigid gloom, Corpsman James Claypool recalled, the morale of "Dog Easy" was low. "When Yancey was with us, his people had a kind of Valhalla complex, but once he was gone, [the] death [of others] was just stark and ugly and final."

Ray Aguirre considered the breakout downhill

the roughest battle we had ever encountered since we landed in Korea. The 5th Regiment was in front and the 7th was acting as rear echelon. They had jeeps, meat wagons,* everything that could roll with one purpose, to make it out as fast as possible. How far we walked we did not know and I guess we did not care to find out as long as we could make it out alive. The Chinks had us surrounded from all sides. They had the road blocked off, so it was slow going. We would move about 200 yards and we would stop to clear the road and to fight our way forward. . . . As soon as it became dark it got worse. The gooks would try to stop us in any way possible . . . , even suicide teams, but we still would fight them off and keep going. Our casualties kept

---

*Ambulances or their equivalent. Not to be confused with John Bishop's metaphor.

mounting up. We would put our wounded in anything that had wheels. When we did not have room anymore we would pile one [casualty] on top of the other, but we were not leaving any Marine behind. Homer Litzenberg's 5th Marines were largely walking or immobile wounded. It meant little to them that thousands of Chinese, frozen and shot up, lay lifeless behind them, other than that they were no longer in pursuit. Litzenberg ordered his operations officer, Captain John Grove, to halt each truck at the base of Fox Hill in order to squeeze more wounded onto them. Private John Bishop recalled seeing "a six-by-six truck full of frozen bodies waiting to move out. It looked like a load of meat going to market. I saw a Marine strapped over the barrel of a howitzer. He was covered by a poncho, all but his stiff legs. It reminded me of a deer carcass tied to the top of a car." Typically, Private Doug Michaud of the 5th Marines recalled the dead "stacked in trucks like so many cords of wood. When they ran out of truck-bed space they laid the dead on fenders, across hoods, tied on the barrels of artillery pieces. God, there were a lot of them."

Marines took saddened pride in leaving no dead behind, but there was no space for some of the dead other than in the frozen ground. Living casualties had priority. As Lieutenant Colonel Frederick Dowsett, Litzenberg's executive officer recalled, "We already had bodies on fenders and tied to howitzer barrels and anywhere else we could think of. We would collect the dead man's identification and personal effects and make some sort of grave for him, even if it was only a matter of covering him with rocks. In *The Marine Manual* it's called a hasty field burial. Sometimes you can only do so much."

There were always more dead. During the final fire fight to break out of Yudam-ni toward Hagaru, Lieutenant Colonel Robert Taplett of Murray's 5th Marines radioed for the evacuation of a critically wounded casualty by helicopter. Lieutenant Robert Longstaff flew in and was shot down. Taplett sent out a patrol to recover his body.

While Corsairs strafed and rocketed Chinese positions on the icy ridges, the Marine columns moved south, company by company. At constant hazard, Ray Davis of Homer Litzenberg's 7th Marines had set up outposts along the route to cover the long train with rifle fire. The only personnel to ride were the badly frozen and seriously wounded. When his jeep filled with casualties, Litzenberg, keeping pace with it, walked. Of their 1,500 wounded, 600 seemed beyond walking, even very slowly and with sticks made from limbs easily broken off ice-glazed trees. It would take the 5th and 7th Marines four days and three nearly sleepless nights to push the fourteen miles through seven roadblocks to Hagaru.

At each long pause, as firefights broke up Chinese ambushes, vehicles kept motors running to avoid freezing up. They began to run low on fuel. A radioed appeal led to airdrops of gasoline at the head of the column, but when no diesel came, several tractors towing 155mm guns could go no further. The rest of the train continued around them, and at 7:35 in the evening on December 3, the advance group of 7th Marines,

A Marine helicopter brings in a casualty. *Naval Historical Center*

shepherded by Frederick Dowsett, came within sight of the Hagaru perimeter, itself under intermittent assault.

When word spread that the 5th and 7th Marines had fought through, those in Hagaru who could be spared came to observe the arrival in the increasing darkness. Vehicle headlights beamed ahead, and dozens of flashlights cut through the shadows. Navy Lieutenant Robert Harvey, who had been a battalion surgeon earlier with the 5th Marines, began looking for surviving friends as men trudged forward. Corporal Selwyn Handler of the 2nd Battalion, 1st Marines, searched without success for his brother Irwin, eighteen, among the weather-beaten men of B Company, 5th Marines. He had not seen him since landing at Wonsan, and would not see him again.

About six hundred yards from the perimeter, the column halted, and its trucks braked to a stop. Those wounded and frostbitten yet could manage to walk crawled out and formed on the frozen road. Then they began, in silence, to march, picking up the cadence as their boots pounded ahead in the falling snow. They were haggard, stubbled and crusted with ice. Hu Hai Bo, from the vantage of the other side, wrote in admiration, "Those slightly wounded helped one another, grinding their teeth and advancing in heavy steps, their M-1 rifles hanging disorderly on them. The accompanying vehicles were fully loaded with seriously wounded unconscious soldiers. Some were simply tied to the radiators of the vehicles. They were frozen like pieces of hard wood. Their bodies were covered by fragments of pink frozen blood."

As the marchers came close they began singing, unbidden and in frost-cracked voices, "The Marines Hymn." The "halls of Montezuma" and "the shores of Tripoli" had been a hundred degrees warmer, but to recall the lyrics was a matter of pride. Those who watched and listened were too overcome with tears to cheer. Robert Harvey wept and whispered to another onlooker, "Look at those bastards, those magnificent bastards."

7

Hagaru to Koto-ri

"No, sir; his eyes are moving."

As bleak as Hagaru-ri was, the village seemed the pot of gold at end of the rainbow to men who had been cut off in Chosin Reservoir inlets like Yudam-ni. Even air cover had been no guarantee of survival. Napalm could fall short. Guns could misfire. A Corsair mistakenly machine gunned Marines held prisoner by the Chinese, the pilot seeing only what appeared to be white-uniformed enemy. Corporal Wayne A. Pickett felt his knee swell after he crashed into a rock to evade unfriendly fire.

Captivity was worse. A Chinese political commissar—each unit, as in the Soviet system, had one—demanded that American prisoners sign a prepared statement, obviously composed in China weeks before the Yalu crossing, and written in English, attesting that each was being treated in accordance with the updated Geneva Convention on Prisoners of War, which Red China had not ratified. (Nor had the United States.) Pickett, only twenty-one, knew a little Chinese to chatter with, as he had served as a teenager in Shanghai in 1947. He saw no alternative, and after watching two officers put down their names, he also signed.

On the American side there were no papers for signature. Sergeant John Audas made Chinese prisoners carry the Fox Company wounded down the hill in thirty-below cold. The Marine casualties, Bob Drury and Tom Clavin would write, were "swaddled in the blue, yellow, and red silk of the supply-drop parachutes, [which] resembled bulky, oddly wrapped, Christmas presents." (The suggestive image would be repeated by others as they saw the promise of Christmas vanishing.) On occasion, the parachutes were the only elements of the packaging that survived, as the breakage rate of equipment drops on the hard-frozen ground remained disappointingly high.

The FEAF Combat Cargo Command had been geared to deliver only seventy tons a day, assembling and loading airborne supplies at Ashiya in northern Kyushu, the closest airbase to Korea. Augmenting its staff with Japanese employees, Cargo Command began round-the-clock packaging. Deploying a C-119 Flying Boxcar detachment to Yonpo, FEAF brought airlift capacity to a daily 250 tons, parachute dropped and, by C-47s, ground delivered to the crude airstrip at Hagaru-ri. Also in the supply chain were C-47s of the Royal Hellenic Air Force. The Greeks flew thirty sorties to Hagaru.

Below Chosin, ringed by Chinese and risky of access by land, was the Hagaru airfield. Although the airstrip construction site may have set a wartime record for brevity of use, O. P. Smith's decision, in the face of Ned Almond's belittling, to build the strip on the southern edge of the town proved crucial. It enabled the flying out of wounded even before it was finished. In fact, it was never completed.

The first C-47 to come in, on December 1, had replacement supplies and ferried Marines returning to duty. "But the fourth plane to come in was loaded with ammunition," Smith recalled, "and it collapsed its landing gear; and that finished the strip for the day, because the plane was so heavy you couldn't move it." Once the cargo was offloaded, the waning day proved too dim for incoming flights. The next morning, Navy pilot B. J. Miller, who had flown his four-engine R5D (the civilian DC-4, the Air Force's C-54) to Yonpo from Japan, offered to airlift casualties from Hagaru and was authorized by the field air controller, who didn't realize the size of the plane. Miller's volunteer crew loaded stretchers and medical supplies and, after a few minutes, circled the Hagaru strip and, to the astonishment of onlookers, came in "hot," braking hard on the short runway. Miller took on thirty-nine wounded and their caregivers, taxied to the extreme end of the strip, gave his engines full throttle and cleared the ridge line by thirty feet. No R5D would chance Hagaru again.

With sturdy C-47s and combat-retired vintage torpedo planes from offshore carriers and from Yonpo, Smith recalled, "We got operating at full speed, and [that day, December 2] I think we got out over 900.* . . . Here was accumulated the wherewithal to support the subsequent breakout from Hagaru-ri. Here was a defended perimeter where the 5th and 7th Marines could reorganize, resupply, reequip, and evacuate

---

*The actual count was 919.

their casualties." In five days, 4,312 casualties would be flown out [via Yonpo], with one C-47 lost to a power failure on take-off. No one was injured, but the plane had to be destroyed at the edge of the runway. By December 10, 240 sorties had landed cargo at Hagaru, flying out sick and wounded evacuees who might otherwise have died in the frigid weather.

"What we were working on first were . . . casualties from over-run Task Force Faith. . . . The outfit just fell apart," said Smith. "They moved down toward the Reservoir which was frozen to a depth of 18 inches. It could take a jeep. . . . For some reason or other the Chinese didn't shoot at the troops on the ice; I don't know why, but they didn't." According to a Chinese claim, "Many attempted to break through [to Hagaru] from the frozen Chosin Reservoir. As a result the ice collapsed and the soldiers were drowned or frozen to death." No evidence exists for an ice break. It would have been unlikely at minus-twenty or minus-thirty.

On December 2, Smith recalled, Lieutenant Colonel Olin Beall, who commanded the division's Motor Transport Battalion, "drove up on the ice to see what was going on. . . . Some of these men were dragging themselves on the ice; some had gone crazy and were walking in circles. He began rescuing them. He devised sleds and hauled the sleds up there, and in one day he rescued 250 of them. . . . The young Marine who was up there with the air liaison party, [also] got out."

The "young Marine" was Captain Edward P. Stamford, Faith's Marine air controller, who had lost his crew to the Chinese and been taken prisoner. Escaping alone, he had turned up at Benjamin Read's 105mm battery position at 0230 on the morning of December 2. Also escaping prison camp or worse was Private Don McAlister. Wounded, he managed to crawl out of a stalled truck just before the Chinese set the vehicles, with casualties still aboard, afire. "I will never forget the smell of human flesh after that," he said. After an enemy guard hit him twice on the head, already bloody from shrapnel wounds, McAlister passed out and was left for dead. "When I came to, I was alone. I stumbled around for what seemed hours, and finally got to the [Chosin] lake. I could only walk for a few minutes before falling down. My feet were frozen. . . . Somehow I got started towards Hagaru-ri. At last I met a big ole Marine colonel who carried me to a truck." It was Olin Beall. As McAlister's frostbitten right wrist was almost severed, he was flown on an evac plane to Japan, remaining in the hospital more than a year, until late May 1952.

The night before, Beall had observed Ben Read's H Battery, firing at swarms of unseen but not unheard Chinese. "Pouring everything they had," Sergeant Vincent Fosco remembered—"mortar rounds, rifle and machine-gun fire, grenades, and [anti-tank] rifle grenades fell like hail." Because his 105mm howitzer could not be dug into the frozen ground to reduce recoil, Fosco's battery began using a lower charge and resumed firing. "Our casualties grew. My crew was reduced to three. Someone grabbed my arm and shouted in my ear to use a charge-seven." Fosco turned to explain that the gun would recoil too fast to secure it. It was not attached to its tractor to weigh it down. "I don't give a damn about the difficulties," said the unidentifiable Marine. "I want you to use a charge-seven."

Fosco yelled back, "Who 'n hell d'ya think you are?" And he asked to see the Marine's "horsepower." Beall flipped up the visor of his fur-lined cap to show his silver oak leaf and identified himself. Not intimidated, Fosco asked amid the incoming fire whether Beall would take responsibility for the damage an oversized charge might cause.

"Hell, yes," shouted Beall. "Fire away."

Fosco reloaded; Private Bender pulled the lanyard, and the howitzer roared and jumped, hitting the radiator of a truck and bouncing to a stop. "Sorry about the truck," said Beall, and pitched in to shift the gun back into firing position.

Even when there was no volley to return, Marine artillery poured out shells. N. Harry Smith, a reporter with the troops, asked about the fusillades. "We have more shells with us than we can possibly find vehicles to carry [them] when we start marching out of here," a colonel explained. "Instead of blowing up all those shells, we decided to give the Chinese a bellyful of them. . . . This is the best way to dispose of it: give it to the enemy in the manner they like least."

When daylight came, Beall's jeep driver, Private Ralph Milton, and a Navy corpsman, Oscar Biebinger, found dozens of "doggies" both alive and dead sprawled on the windswept ice. (Of the original 3,200-man task forces, 2,815 were either KIA, WIA, or MIA.) Braking to a sliding stop in view of the Chinese on the shoreline, the crew placed Beall's sniper rifle, Milton's Garand, and Biebinger's .45 on the ice to demonstrate peaceful intent. Some of the GIs were beyond rescue—"like human vegetables," said Milton. One, seemingly so, who had crawled out on elbows and knees, was Private Edward Reeves, an Illinois farm boy of nineteen who had thought only days before that nothing could have been worse than his stomach cramps at Thanksgiving from an allergy to shrimp. He had been one of thirty-two remaining in his 3rd Battalion, 31st

Infantry. Playing dead while the Chinese had searched his broken body for boots and gloves had been easy. He was barely conscious but had somehow extricated himself from a stalled and burning truck loaded with corpses. Reeves would make it to Tokyo Army Hospital, where his scalp was sewn up and he became a quadruple amputee. If he survived for three more days, he was told, he would be flown to the States in time for Christmas. When he returned, in a wheelchair, to Korea, it would be as a spectator—for the 1988 Olympics in Seoul.

In each mission, Beall's crew ferried six or seven casualties who seemed responsive, lashed to their jeep and on its hood, to a collection point on the southern perimeter of the reservoir where onlookers had built a bonfire of ammunition crates to thaw out survivors. A second jeep joined them and, with crude sleds made of blankets and boards, they loaded men in shock from wounds and exposure and hauled them off the ice. After the Chinese fired a few shots but hit no one, Beall warned that it was getting too dark for safety. "We better get out of here."

In an AP dispatch filed by Tom Stone, he watched "a medic with a hunting knife . . . cutting clothes off a GI, assuring him, 'You'll be warm in a minute.'" They had been trapped, the GI told him—"the same continuous pounding . . . day and night. The Chinese had plenty of mortar, grenades and Thompson guns. I don't know where in the hell they got those tommy guns but they really had them. They came running at us, yelling and shouting. We made for the last lake [inlet] that was frozen over. Some of us crawled and some of us ran. I wasn't going to get killed there. But something hit me. Those of us that got away finally got back on ground and to some railroad tracks. We knew if we followed them we would reach the Marines. You don't know how happy we were to see them this morning."

The next morning, Beall's crew returned to the reservoir with more assistance, left their weapons in the jeeps at the shoreline and, dragging parkas to use as stretchers, trudged over the ice in a bitter wind toward GIs who seemed alive. Their numbers had grown overnight to an estimated two hundred. A lone Chinese soldier, out to loot the bodies of the dead, was kneeling by a prostrate soldier, offering him a cigarette and lighting it from a Zippo, both smokes and lighter very likely lifted off a corpse. Four GIs were huddled under two blankets in a derelict fishing boat frozen in the ice, and as Milton approached, one shouted, "Go back! They'll kill you!" As the Chinese fled and a jeep driver pulled the GIs out, they complained to him of abandonment by their officers. Yet most of their missing officers were casualties.

Not all morale problems were from "doggies." Fortitude and vitality will fade under frustration and stress, which stemmed from service issues to domestic or personal ones. Fear of death was not as widespread as the fear of mutilation or prolonged agony. In the below-zero Korean winter, the urge to escape what seemed inevitable, even for men with high career expectations, must have been formidable. Yet even then, there were exceptions. Corporal C. V. Irwin, Smith's stenographer, the general observed,

> an awkward, red-headed reserve, . . . was one of those; he
> was wounded in the hip, and he dragged himself into a
> hut. . . . A little North Korean boy took care of him, gave
> him water and what not . . . and we didn't come back on

that road until the 6th of December, and when Litzenberg came back down . . . he heard this faint call, "American, American!" or his patrols did. They thought it might be a trap, and they cautiously surrounded this hut, and found Corporal Irwin in there. He had on his parka and his shoe-pacs and everything, but he'd been wounded and had lost blood, and had lost circulation, and his legs were frozen. We got him to Koto-ri and flew him out to Japan. They had to amputate both [lower] legs. . . . I wrote him a letter in the hospital in Japan and he wrote back, "It was too cold up north to take shorthand anyway. I did have an 8 day vacation with pay while visiting the Chinese."

He had good spirits. He said, "After all, I'm a stenographer and I don't need my legs to be a stenographer." Then he went to Oak Knoll Hospital in Oakland, and when I came out of Korea I went around to Oak Knoll to see him, but the nurses said they couldn't keep him under control. He'd taken his furlough and shoved off before his artificial limbs had arrived. They said he was a ball of fire, and his spirit must have impressed people because he was made marshal of the football parade of the University of California [at Berkeley] while he was there. . . . Then I lost track of him. . . . He sent me a picture of himself and with what I assumed to be his wife and child. . . . They were standing by an automobile and he looked perfectly natural.

Most men were more fragile. Being pinned down and fired at and watching one's companions being maimed and dying was not a recipe for stability. Even for rather senior officers, such as Lieutenant Colonel William F. Harris, 3rd Battalion,

7th Marines, and son of Major General Field Harris, who was directing the superbly effective 1st Marine Air Wing. Sometime before dawn, after two of his companies, hit hard, with men fallen in the snow, had pushed the Chinese out of grenade range between Hagaru and Koto-ri, he was seen walking down the road alone with two rifles slung over his shoulder. Was Harris looking for nothingness? To have the enemy turn his own lights out? He was not identified as having been taken prisoner. His body was never found. The executive officer of the 1st Battalion, a major next in command, took over the 3rd Battalion. For all troops in encircled Hagaru, it would take thirty-nine hours and six hundred more casualties to fight the eleven miles southward to Koto-ri.

On December 4, Almond made another helicopter visit to what remained of battered Hagaru to award Distinguished Service Crosses to Smith, Litzenberg, Murray and Beall. A group of grimy Marines gathered to watch. "Well, men, how are you today?" Almond began in failed lightheartedness. "Pretty cold, isn't it? Do you know I wear a [dental] plate? When I got up this morning there was a film of ice on the glass by my bed."

"That's too f——bad, General," said an onlooker long without the experience of a bed.

Despite his jaunty pose, when Almond arrived, his eyes were in tears. "I could never figure out whether it was the cold or his emotions," Smith recalled, "but he was weeping when he came to see me. He came up to me and asked me if I'd line up Murray and Litzenberg and myself and Beall. He had [only] one Distinguished Service Cross with him. We suggested that he give the cross to Beall, who was the junior. Let him have the cross and we'd get ours some time later. I never did get a citation for that because that's the way they operate. . . . I supposed I would have to write my own."*

Almond actually held a second bauble in his pocket. An hour later in Koto-ri, he pinned a DSC on Lieutenant Colonel William Reidy, whose 2nd Battalion, 31st Infantry had been chewed up in what Martin Russ, then a Marine corporal, described as "disarray." In the award citation, a cliché written later, possibly by Captain Haig, Reid is described as having "distinguished himself by extraordinary heroism . . . in keeping with the highest traditions of military service." Reidy, summoned unsuccessfully to the aid of the trapped Colonel MacLean, had been far to the south, at Hamhung. When MacLean, already shot several times, thought he had seen Reidy coming to his rescue, it was an armed Chinese, and MacLean was taken prisoner, dying of his wounds. But Reidy had a ribbon.

At about noon at the southern edge of the reservoir on December 3, the day before, Beall had seen a stranger, clearly not Korean, standing by his jeep. "I'm the Red Cross field director in this area," he explained. "Name's LeFevre." Since somehow he was left alone by the North Koreans and presumably the Chinese, Beall was suspicious. It seemed impossible. Buck LeFevre nevertheless was put to work collecting the walking wounded on the ice while, as the Chinese watched,

---

*That was not merely a jibe. The writer of this narrative was ordered, before departing Korea, to write his own citation for a Bronze Star.

Beall, unarmed, walked toward them to examine, for survivors, the blackened hulks of Task Force Faith's vehicles. "It was the bravest act I ever saw," said Milton, watching Beall from their jeep. "I watched him climb the slope and walk up to the line of trucks, inspecting every one of them." Returning unscathed, he confirmed, "They're all dead." About three hundred bodies, Beall estimated.

After bringing in 319 GIs still alive, the Marines turned toward the guttering bonfire and then to Hagaru, where clusters of Task Force Faith soldiers had arrived on their own and were being organized by Lieutenant Colonel Thomas L. Ridge into a provisional battalion and furnished Marine equipment. Fewer than half of the 672 survivors of Task Force Faith seemed capable of being rearmed and utilized. Although Ridge's intent was to instill discipline and bolster his perimeter, the demoralized GIs would fail the uniform. "I attached them to Litzenberg," Smith said, "and they were pitiful. Litzenberg gave them the job of guarding the left flank . . . , and when the Chinese opened up, they simply went through the column to the other side and took off."

Lieutenant Colonel Berry Anderson had been gifted with the loftily titled Provisional Army Battalion, collecting both Korean and American personnel orphaned from their units. Soon he reported to Frederick Dowsett of the 7th Marines that the refitted troops were less than useless. "The ROKs wouldn't move, weren't organized and there wasn't any way to move them." Exasperated, Dowsett growled that he would "get a Marine unit to chase them there. If they still didn't move, we would open fire on them." It was an empty threat. He soon realized that the best solution for them and also for the "doggies" in shock was "to get them the hell out of the way."

What the reclaimed personnel openly wanted was to get far out of the way. Until the divisional surgeon, Navy captain Eugene Hering, Jr., and the 5th Marines' regimental surgeon, Chester Lessenden, intervened with the Air Force's imperceptive loading officer, some stragglers would fake their way on C-47 evacuation flights to Yonpo and then Japan. "They would go down to the strip and get a blanket and a stretcher and then groan a bit; the corpsmen would come along and put them on a plane." Despite painfully frostbitten feet, Lessenden took over the medical tagging of casualties for evacuation—a "ticket," Smith called it—with "You fly . . . you walk . . . you ride. . . ." At Yonpo, triage would determine which casualties might recover in thirty days or less. These would go the Marine field hospital in Hungnam or the Army's tent in Hamhung, both to be wound up, or to the hospital ship *Consolation* in Hungnam harbor. More seriously wounded were flown to Japan.

General MacArthur would issue a directive from the *Dai Ichi* that frostbite casualties too light for evacuation constituted a failure of command and that disciplinary action should ensue. Admiral Turner Joy intercepted the message. Seeing it months later, Smith was indignant, writing acidly to the Marine deputy commandant that the indictments should go to those responsible for ordering troops into a Siberian winter. Even Genghis Khan, Smith contended, would not have done so.

Marine disgust with Army performance at Chosin (yet some Leathernecks malingered too) reached all the way to Navy Secretary Francis P. Matthews, a politically connected

A casualty arrives at a field hospital. *Naval Historical Center*

Nebraskan known as "the rowboat secretary" because that accurately delineated his nautical experience. He found it necessary to send a message, ALNAV 26, to unit commanders, directing that "no member of the naval service utter any comment reflecting adversely upon or belittling any other branch of service." Matthews was worried about potentially embarrassing "interviews with press and radio." A poor fit himself for a seafaring office, Matthews would be removed from the Pentagon by Truman to become ambassador to Ireland.

Before dark on December 3, alerted by Beall to the burned-out vehicles, General Almond ordered a flight of Corsairs to napalm the blackened RCT column, incinerating the tanks, trucks, and the dead they carried. It was Almond at his most efficient.

Realizing from the newspapers what withdrawal under fire meant, Esther Smith, on December 4, wrote a letter to her husband which she knew would be obsolete on arrival. She quoted Exodus 23:20: "Behold I send an angel before thee to keep thee in the way, and to bring thee into the place which I have prepared."

Much of the bad news was reported and published at home, where there was further disconcerting news. As two Puerto Rican pro-independence radicals had traded shots on November 1 with White House police in an attempt to assassinate the President, Harry Truman went to the annual Army-Navy football game on December 2 under a heavy guard. While wartime prices continued to rise, more labor unions struck for higher wages. Taxes would go up after Truman and Marshall called on Congress to add $18 billion to military appropriations. Draft calls were increased, and the thin, bespectacled Alfred Bergdoll, twenty-three year-old son of Grover Bergdoll, the most notorious draft dodger of World War I (who had fled the country to avoid Army service), was arrested in early December after writing his draft board refusing induction. On December 5, Truman's press secretary and boyhood chum, Charles Ross, a Pulitzer Prize–winning former newspaperman, collapsed and died of a heart attack in the White House.

The next day, just when the impulsive and harried President needed Ross's staying hand, he picked up his morning edition of *The Washington Post*, looking for reaction to his daughter Margaret's vocal recital at Constitution Hall the evening before. Shaken by so many untoward events of the past week, including his own atomic misadventure with the press, he went nuclear after reading Paul Hume's review. "She is very attractive on stage, yet Miss Truman cannot sing very well," Hume wrote. "She is flat a good deal of the time . . . and cannot sing with anything approaching professional finish." George Marshall noted wryly that Hume criticized everything about the performance but the varnish on the piano.

Harry Truman had held his fire about criticizing General MacArthur, but his patience had now been further tried. Reaching for two sheets of White House paper and his pen, he admonished Hume, "I've just read your lousy review of Margaret's concert. . . . It seems to me that you are a frustrated old man"—Hume was thirty-four, Margaret twenty-six—"who wished he could have been successful. . . . Someday I hope to meet you. When that happens you'll need a new nose, a lot of beef steak for black eyes, and perhaps a supporter below!" As it was a private screed, he stamped the envelope and mailed it himself.

Hume showed the two pages of vitriol to his editor. Both agreed that it was unfit for print. But Hume made the mistake of telling a friend, and by Saturday, December 9, reports of the screed had surfaced in the national press. Letters, pro and con, flowed in every direction, and Hume was suddenly famous—or notorious. One irate newspaper reader, William Banning, wrote heatedly,

> Mr. Truman:
>   As you have been directly responsible for the loss of our son's life in Korea, you might just as well keep this

emblem on display in your trophy room, as a memory of your historic deeds.

Our major regret at this time is that your daughter was not there to receive the same treatment as our son received in Korea.

Banning enclosed the "emblem"—his son's posthumous Purple Heart. Then, anger appeased, he decided not to mail it and put the invective in his desk.

Paul Hume did not respond to Truman's condemnation and merely filed the letter. Some years later, he visited the retired President at his home in Missouri. Truman was delighted to see him and played the piano for Hume, who did not review the concert-for-one. After Hume died at eighty-five in 2001, the Truman letter, still filed, sold for $193,000.

The press circus about Margaret Truman reinforced the adage that no publicity is negative. She received a contract from NBC television for appearances on such of its offerings as its popular variety program "The Big Show," and would soon exceed her father's presidential salary.

—⁂—

As the evacuation from Hungnam by sea and air began, General Ridgway sat in on an hours-long discussion at the Pentagon, a dreary meeting on a dismal Sunday morning. MacArthur had violated a JCS directive of September 27 that he was to use only Korean forces in the areas bordering the Manchurian and Siberian frontiers. He claimed military necessity, yet his orders had furnished the Chinese an excuse for their already-planned intervention. Ridgway told colleagues that the JCS needed to furnish explicit instructions to MacArthur, as the debacle was worsening. "My only answer, from the twenty men who sat around the wide table, and the twenty others who sat around the walls in the rear, was complete silence." The hesitant conferees had looked for guidance to Secretary of Defense Marshall. Worn by four wartime years as chief of staff, by his long postwar mission to China in civil war, and by exhaustion as Secretary of State and now failing with kidney malfunction requiring surgery he was postponing, he had reluctantly accepted President Truman's plea to take over Defense "for six months to a year." He had offered his cautious views, which did not yet include relieving the domineering eminence at the *Dai Ichi*.

Marshall's only peer in prestige remained the distant Douglas MacArthur, a personal burden for decades and boss at West Point when many around the table were plebes. However uneasy, Marshall had no quick fixes. Sacking or even merely admonishing MacArthur would serve no purpose other than outraging key congressmen who saw him at his own estimation.

As some lingered and others left, Ridgway had approached Air Force chief Hoyt Vandenberg, whom he had known since "Van" was a cadet at West Point and Ridgway an instructor. "Why," asked Ridgway, "don't the Joint Chiefs send orders to MacArthur and *tell* him what to do?"

"What good would that do?" said Vandenberg. "He wouldn't obey the orders. What *can* we do?"

"You can relieve any commander who won't obey orders, can't you?"

Astonished at the idea of giving God instructions, Vandenberg "walked away without saying a word."

—◇◇◇—

At the *Dai Ichi*, General Collins would meet twice with MacArthur, who had prepared for him a draft of the dire, sweeping CINCFE Plan No. 203 (December 6, 1950), thirty-eight sheets proposing "the orderly withdrawal" of all UN forces and gear from Korea to Japan, including ROK troops and even enemy prisoners of war, "due to pressure from superior forces." To MacArthur, the only alternative to pulling out of Korea was authority for him to strike at Manchuria, to blockade the China coast, to use tens of thousands of Chiang Kai-Shek's troops from Taiwan and to employ ("if technically appropriate") atomic bombs. It was dramatic overkill, and Washington would not let any of it happen. Still, in the west, the prize of Pyongyang was about to be abandoned to the Chinese without a fight. At Kimpo airbase near Seoul, soon to be evacuated as EUSAK retreated in disorder, Walton Walker, shaken by events, asked that "specific places in Japan [be] set aside for the Eighth Army if it evacuated Korea."

After visiting two command posts for briefings, Collins met with reporters at Kimpo and announced, with more confidence than he felt, "I think the Eighth Army can take care of itself." Flying east to Yonpo, Collins spent Wednesday, December 6, with Ned Almond and visited at Hamhung the

CPs of the 7ᵗʰ and 3ʳᵈ Infantry Divisions. Barr's 7ᵗʰ had been partially chewed up east of Chosin after a token reaching of the Yalu; Robert Soule's 3ʳᵈ, last to land, had been given backup duties in the east and was to reinforce the Marines as they came down from Koto-ri to board ships already arriving at Hungnam. Almond's diary noted that "weather precluded flying to Koto-ri" for a conference with O. P. Smith—a relief for the X Corps commander, as Smith looked through a different lens.

The closest Collins got to the real action was an abbreviated flight north from Hamhung which turned about in a swirling snowstorm over Sudong, well below the Funchilin Pass and the Marine collecting point at Hagaru. When Almond had proposed that the Marines abandon vehicles and weapons if conditions rendered them unusable, Smith saw the practice as dishonorable unless urgent and contrary to good order, as already proven by the headlong flight of EUSAK in the west. Earlier, Almond had asserted that "dignity" required extricating whatever gear could be withdrawn. "Don't worry about your equipment," Almond now barked impatiently on his final flying trip to Hagaru. "Once you get back we'll replace it all." Resources were apparently bottomless, somewhere.

"I'm not going to do that," the usually imperturbable Smith snapped. "This is the equipment we fight with." Once Almond was again airborne, Smith observed to Colonel Alpha Bowser, his operations officer, "This guy is a maniac. He's nuts. I can't believe he is saying these things." Even more beyond logic was the empty boast to Collins, about which Smith did not learn, that if ordered, Almond could retain a substantial perimeter in the Hamhung-Hungnam area. Hanging in would have been a personal triumph but a sinkhole of men and materiel.

Boarding his C-54 at Yonpo, having seen nothing of the fighting withdrawal from Chosin yet realizing that no troops should have been ordered into the forbidding reservoir area in the first place, let alone in winter, Collins asked why they had been sent there. Almond said frankly that MacArthur had planned the thrust to take enemy pressure off the Eighth Army's drive to the Manchurian border. Following the briefing, Almond noted confidently in his diary, "Gen. Collins seemed completely satisfied with the operation of X Corps and apparently relieved in finding the situation well in hand."

Back in Washington, MacArthur's "home for Christmas" boast quietly forgotten, Collins told Truman that conditions were not "critical" and that a defensible line could be maintained well below the 38th parallel—which implied relinquishing a portion of South Korea. JCS chief Omar Bradley called Collins's evaluation a "ray of sunshine." Now there were "options to discuss other than catastrophe." Yet, below Chosin, there was no sunshine, and the Marine division which Collins had not seen remained endangered in the below-zero snow, still unable to break out into its evacuation route to the sea.

—⁂—

At Hagaru, casualties continued to be flown out as fast as planes could land, load and take off, pilots gunning engines on the short runway to get airborne. The "control tower" was a manned, radio-equipped jeep. The wounded bore makeshift bandages, and arm and leg splints and crutches that were once tree limbs. Corporal Martin Russ, in his memoir, described, "the smell of fresh and dried blood, filthy combat dunga-rees, unwashed bodies, spent gunpowder, and vehicle exhaust fumes, all combined into one pervasive stench." One seriously wounded Marine, carried to a hospital tent, still clutched his submachine gun. Another casualty arrived in Osaka with a live grenade in one of his pockets. Also flown to Japan, Ser-geant Aguirre was found by a corpsman to have two grenades tucked into his pockets. Shaking hands with a buddy left be-hind, he said, "If I don't see any of you guys again, Merry Christmas!" The grenades could have seriously spoiled the hol-iday. For Private George Crotts, who choked back tears as he left his buddies behind, arrival at the Yokosuka Naval Hospital was like premature Christmas. "We were treated like royalty, with officers' wives handing out coffee and donuts from wel-come wagons. They gave each of us a [sleeping] rack in a huge auditorium that had been turned into a hospital ward; there were racks on the stage and in the balconies."

Recovering Marines kept returning from Hungnam and Yonpo on the planes evacuating the wounded. About six hun-dred men, again able-bodied, were reassigned, recognizing unit loyalty when possible, to the outfits they had served. At Hagaru, O. P. Smith spotted a young Marine who appeared in good shape but seemed very dejected and asked him what was wrong. "I belong to the 1st Marines," he explained.

"You're in the 3rd Battalion of the 1st Marines," Smith said.

"But I belong to the 2nd Battalion," the returnee insisted, eager to get back to his own outfit.

Attacks on Hagaru had temporarily slowed. Chinese divisions had suffered crippling casualties. They needed to regroup and be reprovisioned—or be replaced. Their human supply train was increasingly inadequate and further reduced by exposure. Many Chinese were weak from hunger and extreme cold. Moving primarily by dark to evade American aircraft and artillery, they had suffered massive losses when fighting into daylight. Their quilted uniforms retained moisture as well as heat and could freeze disastrously to the body. Lieutenant Colonel Ray Davis encountered an enemy example when a Marine sergeant called to him on an icy ridge. "Come with me, Colonel, I wanna show you something." The sergeant tugged out of a cavity in the snow "a solid chunk of ice that was a Chinese soldier." Davis asked, "Is he dead?"

"No, sir, his eyes are moving."

Around the dying infantryman, in other hollows filling up with snow, were other bodies, frozen solid and very dead. Davis's 1st Battalion of the 7th Marines had pushed eight miles over three snow-drifted ridges. Unlike the Chinese, they wore gloves and boots. "We had to climb on our hands and knees, hold on to roots and twigs to keep from sliding back down." He recalled "manhandling" unresponsive men collapsed and insensible in the arctic conditions to keep them moving and alive.

For both sides, staying alive was a full-time task. Bob Hammond called the extreme cold "unbearable" and, on painfully removing his boots to massage his swollen feet, could not get the left boot back on. "So Clyde McElroy and Doyle Smith, of my squad, take me to where we've got all the [Marine] bodies lined up in the snow. We pick out the bodies with the biggest pairs of feet and the three of us spend twenty minutes trying to get their boots off." Their frozen fingers failed them, and further frostbite loomed. "We finally tie a C-ration box around the three socks I've got on, and let it go at that. It lasts a couple of days." (Another alternative was to wrap a sandbag, or part of one, around a foot. It impeded mobility but may have saved frozen toes or, as a young Marine, Conrad Johnson, described the dreaded outcome, forestalled "elephant feet.")

C-119 freighters continued to air drop more ammunition, gasoline, medical supplies and rations—"the margin necessary," said O. P. Smith—and whenever the weather lifted for a few daylight hours, carrier-based fighters helped shepherd the tottering Marines, many of them walking wounded, from Yudam-ni and below toward Hagaru-ri and then Koto-ri. They had to fight their way past roadblocks, the hounded units of the 5th and 7th Marines leapfrogging each other and clearing every contested yard on the MSR with machine gun and mortar fire. Reluctantly, Litzenberg had left eighty-five dead behind at Yudam-ni in a "field burial." Anything on wheels or tracks was needed for live casualties.

When Henry "Doc" Litvin made it into the Hagaru perimeter after the difficult trek from Yudam-ni, he reported to Division Surgeon Hering to assist with the 1,800 casualties from Litzenberg's and Murray's battalions, many of them frostbite cases. "Good to see you, Lieutenant!" said Hering, looking up—but Litvin, who had learned to doze while walking half-frozen, his congealed clothing keeping him upright, was too exhausted to help. He dropped into sleep. On coming to in a warming tent, he wrote a lightheartedly false letter to his parents. At home, the Litvins

A unit from Colonel Litzenberg's 7th Marines on the march south watches from a roadblock as napalm is dropped on a Chinese position. *Department of Defense*

had been reading the Philadelphia *Evening Bulletin* and knew the reality of the situation . . . but I didn't know they knew. The letter I wrote them from Hagaru while half awake was the usual cheery travelogue. . . . Many weeks later I learned that local newspapers all over America were spelling it out: the 1st Marine Division was surrounded and in danger of annihilation. One of the Philadelphia columnists used the phrase "sliced to ribbons," and I was told later that my mother collapsed when she read that. That wasn't the worst of it, though. I gave one of my upbeat letters home to a wounded Marine to mail from Japan, where he was about to be medevacked. It turned out that he had an undetected wound—a wound other than the one I had treated—and the letter delivered to the little mailbox beside the front door of the Litvin household was actually stained with blood.

Early on Tuesday, December 5, when withdrawal was well underway toward the village of Koto-ri, correspondent Marguerite Higgins had turned up with the Marines' Pacific chief Lemuel Shepherd, having hitched a flight from Hungnam, where a flotilla was beginning to gather to evacuate X Corps. Shepherd, an old friend of MacArthur loyally guarding his reputation and a schoolmate of Almond at VMI, aspired to be the next commandant of Marines (as he would be) and was not going to badmouth anyone under MacArthur's influential wing. "O. P.," he advised Smith, "play the game; don't get mad with Almond. He's trying to do the right thing." Later, Shepherd wrote, "Smith wanted everything done right by the book. And in battle you can't always do things by the book. You've got to . . . take chances when the opportunity to gain a victory appears probable." Yet it would be Smith's "book" that would rescue the Marines and, perhaps, the American presence in Korea.

Maggie Higgins reported that she had heard on Chinese radio the prediction that "the annihilation of the . . . 1st Marine Division is only a matter of time." She had not seen Ray Murray since the heady days of the Inchon landing. The new operation, he explained to those who hadn't heard it before, including a skeptical British reporter, was not a retreat, because when surrounded, there is no rear. "This an assault in another direction [for] there are . . . Chinese blocking our path to the sea. . . . But we're going to get out of here." There were no Marines who would not fight, he said. He had offered any who wanted air evacuation to apply by faking "going lame"—and he expected no takers. Higgins would write that many "had the dazed look of men who have accepted death and then found themselves alive after all." And for a *Saturday Evening Post* article she wondered unkindly whether the ragged Marines, their stubbled faces bruised raw by the frigid winds, would have the will to make the final push to the sea.

Some resented her know-it-all recklessness. Others openly gawked at the only comely correspondent in Korea, who— despite layers of winter gear—was clearly a blonde, authentic woman. "My god!" thought Corporal Roy Pearl. "I hadn't seen one of those in months." She had covered the *Dai Ichi* and had been in Korea after Pusan and Inchon. Only thirty, Maggie Higgins of *The New York Herald Tribune* had reported the war in Europe when barely out of college.

Aggressively interviewing those she could, she took her notepad to a stretcher case awaiting evacuation. He was in obvious pain from shrapnel wounds in the stomach. What was the toughest thing, Maggie asked, that he had to contend with so far? Since the answer was obvious, the Marine answered gamely, "The toughest thing is getting three inches of dick out of six inches of clothing when I have to take a leak." Maggie moved over to the next casualty for something more printable.

Also with Shepherd was *The Chicago Daily News*'s Keyes Beech, thirty-seven and a former Marine combat correspondent in the Pacific. In Korea, he shared a jeep with Higgins.

Shepherd wanted to remain overnight to observe the with-drawal and did, although O. P. Smith had tried persuading him, "'Look, you can do more good down at Corps Head-quarters than you can here—to see that planes keep coming up.' . . . And he didn't have a sleeping bag. He went to Lewie [Puller]. . . . Then Keyes Beech made the mistake of asking Lewie where he got the sleeping bag [for him]. 'Off a corpse.' And Keyes Beech didn't sleep very well that night! But that's the only way you could get an extra sleeping bag."

With difficulty, the division was assembling at Koto-ri, a few miles to the south, where some of Puller's battalion had come together. "Lewie wanted to know," Smith remembered, "why she was there and told her it was no place for a woman." Higgins told Smith when she arrived that she was "like any other correspondent, and she wanted to march down the hill with the troops." Puller detailed a lieutenant to follow her around and see that she was on the next plane going out.

Putting aside the possibility that Maggie Higgins might be wounded or killed, Smith referred only to her being an unnecessary inconvenience as they struggled down. "There are a lot of good Marines who are getting frostbite," he explained unconvincingly, "and if you march down with these Marines you will probably get frostbitten, and then somebody is going to have to take care of you. I am sure these Marines will see that you're taken care of, and we haven't got time for that kind of business." Maggie objected that evicting her was sex dis-crimination. "Nevertheless," said Smith, "that's it. You have to get on the plane." At first, she evaded the order. After the burial of the last dead, wrapped in ponchos, because there was no outgoing aircraft space for them, she slipped into the trek down the snow-swept slopes until Smith, "in a strong sense of chivalry," as she put it, arranged that she flew out of the Koto-ri strip with Lem Shepherd. As their plane took off at twilight, the Chinese had the end of the airfield under fire. "My, God, Maggie," said the general as they watched tracer bullets reach out toward them, "won't it be awful if the two of us are found crashed together?"

Maggie Higgins was relentless. When Shepherd's plane landed at the Hungnam airstrip, she managed, recalled Smith, "to come back up to Chinghung-ni and then up the road to meet the Marines when they came down." Chinghung-ni was a village forty-five road miles from Hagaru, below the dramatic twists and turns of the Funchilin Pass and its deep gorge. The Chinese 20th Army had twice blown the span over the reservoir conduits, to them the "Watergate Bridge," leaving the breakout at extreme hazard. Reconnecting the outbound route was crucial. Maggie had been deprived of the most spectacular operation of the breakout.

"Then she wrote an article for the *Saturday Evening Post*, and she took me apart. Ben Hibbs [the editor] wouldn't publish it as she wrote it. . . . But she did put something in. She said I had ideas of chivalry that didn't agree with her ideas. . . . She wrote to [Marine commandant] Gen. Cates that I was given to discrimination. Gen. Cates wrote her a letter and kidded her along, and sent me a copy."

"It's now an open secret," she would write, hardly cautiously, in a book published early the next year, "that the Marines believe that faulty generalship was partly responsible for the extent of their entrapment. The Marines were . . . subject to . . . army orders." Without naming names, it was obvious that she was identifying Almond. As a favorite of MacArthur, who had permitted her to cover Korea early in the war, a first for a woman there, she seemed firmly protective of him while disparaging his subordinates. "I have the highest respect and a deep sense of loyalty toward General MacArthur," she wrote—and she alleged his "selflessness," which went "beyond personal ambition." She ascribed his "miscalculations" in the "home-by-Christmas" operation to the legend of infallibility "built up assiduously by his aides." Even so, she claimed, "No amount of military genius could have prevented the Chinese from hurling us back a considerable distance . . . once they chose to strike." Some underlings had given bad advice to the Supreme Commander.

Bad advice was as endemic in war as good intentions. Supporting the move from Hagaru to Koto-ri, early on the evening of December 5, an Air Force B-26 pilot, misunderstanding his radio signals, dropped six five hundred–pound bombs close to Lieutenant Colonel Ridge's command post. The result did not assist the withdrawal.

Like Higgins, O. P. Smith wanted to march out with his men, but General Shepherd, his Marine boss, did not want to risk Smith's life—or, worse, his capture as a propaganda prize. As snow fell, he would fly the contested miles in falling snow, a risk itself.

8

A Bridge Apart

"I got you an airfield and I will get you a bridge."

At the *Dai Ichi*, the grim prospects on both fronts in Korea could no longer be fudged. One of MacArthur's junior intelligence officers, Lieutenant Colonel James H. Polk, wrote to his wife, "The whole of GHQ . . . has a bad case of the blues. . . . The old man, MacA I mean, is really one hell of a gambler. . . . Well, this time he gambled it a little too hard and really pressed his luck a bit too far and the whole house fell in on him." He had chanced "staking it all on one big throw, and for once the great MacA's luck ran out on him. He just didn't believe that the whole CCF would be thrown against him. I really admire him in defeat but it sorta looks like the end of an era."

Polk typically blamed the catastrophe on old (but cautiously unidentified) loyalists. In a follow-up letter he added, "Why oh why does MacA put up with some of the people that he does? Why does he keep people around him that will lead him into pitfalls?" At a press conference, General Willoughby, long as incompetent as he was loyal, had told correspondents with more than usual frankness that his chief's strategy had been based on the premise that large-scale Chinese intervention had been only a "potential." MacArthur had been "gambling" that Mao's troops would remain on their own side of the border. The blindness of the Bataan clique, few of whom had ever set foot on Bataan, left Polk (who would soon be promoted and transferred to Korea) and his fellow underlings feeling quietly helpless. The advisers MacArthur listened to were often holdovers from the pre-Pearl Harbor Philippines.

The botched Eighth Army advance had been followed by the even more botched retreat south toward the 38th parallel. The confusion was compounded by fear that the Chinese, who did not move on wheels, would swarm around fleeing troops with mobile weapons like mortars, grenades and submachine guns. Although opportunity existed to withdraw military hardware and supplies, little was done but concede materiel to the enemy, often before actual contact. The 25th Division G-4 (Logistics) report for December described the EUSAK collapse with unbureaucratic frankness. "The apparent careless abandon and indifference with which troops were observed to burn and destroy equipment with the slightest excuse is almost criminal. . . . It is almost impossible to name [examples] . . . since they range from abandoning individual clothing and equipment to burning [needed] vehicles and [weapons] trailers, but it is clearly indicated that positive command action is called for in this matter." Little command response followed.

The eastern campaign, disciplined on the Marines side, was in more calculated reverse. "I finally decided," said Smith, "to leave to the Chinese the decision as to whether a vehicle was to be destroyed or not, but we were going to start with all our vehicles." That judgment would bolster the confidence of the division that it would prevail. The march from Hagaru-ri and then Koto-ri, anxious nevertheless, began at daybreak on December 6 in a frozen fog. On his final medevac flight from Hagaru, Captain Paul Fritz's C-47 hauled out more dead than live casualties. Bound together for stability, the bodies were not a pretty sight. "I wanted to make this particular flight with dignity," Fritz explained, "but how do you do that? I just tried to fly as smoothly as possible." Almond's chief of staff, Clark Ruffner, had objected to airlifting the dead. Smith intended to extract as many as he could. "The Marines," he contended, "have a particular reverence for comrades killed in action. They will make every effort, even risking casualties, to bring in the bodies for a proper burial. We felt it was an obligation, so that men would not be buried in some desolate North Korean village. It wasn't asking too much of the pilots and it didn't interfere with the evacuation of the remaining wounded. The extreme cold eliminated any problem we might have had in regard to the preservation of the bodies."

Even to the last of the four days of disengagement, clean, freshly shaven replacements as well as recovered returnees came in on the otherwise empty C-47s. "After I got off the plane," Private Richard Suarez recalled, "they assigned me to Item Company, 7th Marines, which had maybe fifty guys left out of a hundred and eighty. . . . I was shocked when I found out how many didn't think they would survive. . . . As for me, I had no doubt I'd get out."

A night of saturation shelling by Marine 155s had softened the Chinese attack while disposing of surplus ordnance. The 7th Marines were in the lead from Hagaru. The 5th Marines had retaken the East Ridge below, furnishing cover. Corsair flights rocketed any Chinese concentrations they spotted. Smith's "poor old helicopter had only a 5,000 foot ceiling and the road was 4,000 feet up, so we were pretty low, and what concerned me was not the Chinese. . . . And we got down to Koto-ri. Litzenberg and Murray came on down the road. They had some knock down, drag out fights. . . . [When] the Chinese closed in . . . they had to use the artillery at point blank range with fuzes cut down to practically nothing. But we didn't lose many vehicles."

The remnants of Captain Robert E. Drake's 31st Tank Company were among the last units out of Hagaru. What was left of the town was set ablaze. Through the billowing smoke they watched hungry Chinese soldiers far less interested in the Marine rear guard and the miles-long column stretching southward than in burrowing into the burning debris for undestroyed food. The Chinese interest in prisoners was largely to pick them clean of rations and winter gear. What surprised the Americans, according to Hu Hai Bo, who acknowledged that "supplies for the Volunteer Army were cut off long ago," was that the Chinese "in bare feet [were] rushing toward them across the snowy ground." Troops from the 60th Division, Hu wrote, "about 300 officers and soldiers, were resisting with their food supplies cut off and they were nearly frozen. All were sacrificed gloriously. . . . Not a single one survived."

Marshal Nie Rongzhen, who was responsible for supply, conceded that "preparations had not been sufficient." In

Marines move out of Yudam-ni area, heading south. *National Archives*

the west, the Chinese advance had slowed down despite the Eighth Army's retreat out of contact "because we couldn't transport the required amounts of rations to the front, and we were forced to cancel the [deployment of] two extra divisions." Confronting fewer numbers but more severe weather

in the eastern sector, the troops which entered Korea had not made sufficient preparations and faced even greater difficulties. Not only did these troops not have enough to eat, their winter uniforms were too thin and could not protect their bodies from the cold. As a result there were a large number of non-combat casualties. If we hadn't had these logistical problems as well as certain other problems,* the soldiers would have wiped out the U.S. 1st Marine Division.

Although taking fire all along the route to Koto-ri, the 2nd Battalion, 7th Marines, retrieved twenty-two Royal Marine survivors huddled in an empty wooden house. The Chinese had taken their parkas and abandoned them. A carrier pilot had spotted the letters H-E-L-P they had stamped into the snow and had dropped foodstuffs for them. Not far off was "Hell-Fire Valley," as Task Force Drysdale had called the road above Koto-ri where their convoy was ambushed. The Chinese had looted the vehicles but had made no attempt to salvage them. Some abandoned trucks were found overturned and buried in the snow. Others, the Marines discovered, needed nothing more than a push downhill to start them. A bullet-riddled Army ambulance, its Red Cross logo intact, was still operable. It joined the motor-march south.

The only airstrip remaining above the Funchilin gap was the postage-stamp site at Koto-ri. Marine engineers had hastily improved it to handle small aircraft, even stripped-down World War II Grumman TBMs, no longer torpedo bombers but now improvised utility planes that could lift out as many as nine casualties each. Despite swirling snow, the TBM *Avengers* along with liaison planes and helicopters extricated 200 seriously wounded on December 7 and 225 on the next day. Most small planes were piloted by volunteer deskbound aviators. However

---

*Marshal Nie cautiously did not identify the "other problems."

hazardous, the flights reduced the number of casualties who would have to wait for the Funchilin chasm to be bridged.

—〰—

Few small-scale episodes in the "Home for Christmas" misadventure exemplified the waste of war more dramatically than the downing of a Corsair as the withdrawal proceeded late on December 4. Scouting potential targets in support of the breakout from Hagaru-ri, Ensign Jesse Brown's plane was hit by Chinese fire at too low an altitude for him to bail out. He was the Navy's first black pilot, son of a Mississippi sharecropper. Looking down from his accompanying Corsair, Lieutenant Thomas Hudner, Jr. could see that Brown was still alive, one of his legs caught in the twisted wreckage. Hudner had first met Brown in December 1949 and introduced himself, but Brown then "made no gesture to shake hands. I think he did not want to embarrass me. . . . I forced my hand into his." President Truman's military desegregation order had come into effect but had been accepted belatedly and reluctantly, and the Army still fielded the black 24th Regiment of the 25th Division in Korea. Some smaller units were also still segregated, with white, often southern officers.

Although the flight of six Corsairs was above enemy territory, Hudner radioed for a rescue helicopter. Then, concerned that Brown's smoking aircraft might explode, he cost his carrier a second plane by crash landing nearby in the deep snow. Brown's leg was mangled; he was drifting in and out of consciousness. Wedged in the crushed fuselage, he could not be extricated by a single pair of frostbitten hands. Darkness loomed; the temperature dipped well below zero as Hudner worked frantically to peel away what he could of the wreckage from Brown's legs, yet he could get no footing in the deep drifts. A Marine helicopter from Hagaru with an ax and a fire extinguisher finally arrived in the deepening dusk and clattered down. The pilot, Lieutenant Charles Ward, struggled to help Hudner for nearly an hour, but Brown was near death, and removing him seemed hopeless. Finally, Hudner conceded to Ward that whether or not the Chinese on the ridges came down, if the chopper didn't get airborne soon, its primitive night navigational equipment would be worthless, and there would be three bodies and another aircraft left to the enemy.

Hudner comforted Brown, who was slipping out of consciousness, that more help was on the way but realized there would be none. "I'm sure," Hudner recalled in an interview in 1990, "that he died within a few moments of the time we left." The futile reconnaissance had cost a pilot and two planes. Hudner would be one of seven Navy and Marine pilots to earn a Medal of Honor in the Korean War.*

Medals of Honor were tough to earn in a military culture if one were from a minority group—an omission only rectified early in 2014 after a restudy of hundreds of cases from

---

*Late in July 2013, Hudner, at eighty-eight, a frail and long-retired Navy captain, flew into North Korea to try to retrieve the remains of Ensign Brown. With him was Dick Bonelli, eighty-two, a Marine veteran of Chosin. They failed. Authorities in Pyongyang claimed that heavy rains had washed out roads and bridges in the crash area, five hours away.

World War II, Korea and Vietnam. By then, twenty-one of the twenty-four belated honorees were dead. One Marine whose valor seemed to earn the honor but did not receive it even then was Lieutenant (later Major) Chew-Een Lee, who once under fire almost in sight of the enemy called out riskily in Mandarin to confuse the Chinese. The tactic worked, and although wounded, he repositioned his 7th Marines platoon and drove the enemy back. Learning in a field hospital that he was to be evacuated to Japan, Lee, with a wounded sergeant, commandeered a jeep and, unauthorized, left for the line, an arm still in a cast. On December 2, he was ordered, with his Baker Company, to relieve outnumbered and surrounded Fox Company. Evading roadblocks, he led heavily loaded troops single-file uphill in heavy snow at night with only a compass as a guide. Firing at the Chinese despite his cast and driving them from their foxholes, he kept going, reestablishing contact with Fox Hill but taking another bullet into his wounded arm. Regrouping under constant fire, Lee's company secured the road into the Toktong Pass and held on until, on December 8, closing in on the Funchilin gap, he was struck down by a machine gun blast, ending his war. He was flown to Hamhung and then Japan. Lee died in March 2014 at eighty-eight, having been awarded the Navy Cross and the Silver Star.

—⁂—

With Hagaru-ri emptied and the Chinese closely behind and also on the Marine flanks, Koto-ri, eleven miles south, could only be a brief stopover. As daylight faded, several C-47s squeezed down to evacuate the burgeoning wounded. The fight toward Koto-ri had cost five hundred casualties. Private Paul Martin of the 1st Marines recalled overhearing a major in his battalion observe, mocking Ned Almond, "I have over fifty Medals of Honor to recommend. I don't know anyone's name, though." (Fourteen were awarded for the Chosin operation, seven of them posthumously. Almond had no role in them.)

Although a heavy snowstorm blanketed the strip, the next day a C-47 from Yonpo managed to land and take off additional wounded, but no other planes could find the field in the swirling flakes. As the storm had inhibited infiltration and ambushes, by the night of the 7th and the morning of the 8th, most units had reassembled safely. When the transports and utility aircraft returned after the skies cleared, some of the newer casualties lined up with evacuation tags were labeled as suffering from internal disorders caused by eating frozen C-rations. A parachute that failed to open had crashed crates of rations. "We roamed in groups," Private Ernest Gonzalez of the 7th Marines remembered. "My favorite was wieners and beans. I didn't find any. My least favorite was pork and beans. I found plenty of those." A Marine with chronic, freezing diarrhea from gorging on icy rations was good for nothing, as he had six layers of clothing to disassemble, after which frostbite was added to his medical tag.

More than 14,000 troops, mostly Marines but including 2,300 GIs and 125 Royal Commandos, were tented in the Koto-ri area until the gap over the Funchilin chasm was closed. In the biting cold, their vehicles barely operated—motors were kept running—and weapons of every sort jammed at times.

Where possible, men huddled around sputtering exhaust pipes to seek some precarious warmth. Wounded and in sick bay, Ray Aguirre found he could not open his mouth until he could thaw out his mustache. The haggard men, David Halberstam wrote vividly, "came to look like Ancient Mariners who had sailed too close to the North Pole, all of them bearded; their beards, filled with ice shavings, told the story." With a Marine company was *LIFE* photojournalist David Douglas Duncan, gaunt, hollow-eyed and bearded, embedded with them since their breakout from the Pusan perimeter in September. Duncan had been a combat cameraman in the Pacific war. A photo he took as troops moved south from Hagaru to Koto-ri depicted a snow-covered jumble of wrecked vehicles on a steep hill where Task Force Drysdale had been ambushed. Engineers had to make the road passable, pushing the wreckage aside.

Dawn was materializing just over the hills on December 9 as Duncan watched a Marine in Puller's 1st Regiment "prodding with his spoon, trying to break loose a single, frost-coated bean from the others in his can. He could neither move it nor long continue holding the spoon between his gloved but almost rigid fingers." At last he loosened the bean and slowly raised it to his mouth and waited for it to thaw.

"If I were God and it was Christmas," Duncan intruded, "what would you ask for?"

The Marine "continued to stand motionless, with empty eyes." Then he said, "Give me tomorrow."

There would still be a continuing toll of men for whom there would be no tomorrow. Infiltrators and snipers exploited

A unit of Litzenberg's 7th Marines were the first to leave Koto-ri in the early hours of December 8. *National Archives*

the falling snow as cover to harass the gathering convoy. A platoon leader in Baker Company, 7th Marines, Lieutenant Woodrow Wilson Taylor, flattening himself on the ground as hot lead flew south of Koto-ri, warned his company commander Lieutenant Joe Kurcaba, who had been at "Turkey Hill" on Thanksgiving Day, "You guys are going to get yourself killed if you keep standing there like that."

"Woody," said the half-frozen Kurcaba, "if I get down I'll never be able to get up." It was snowing hard as he was pointing out a route on his map to Lieutenant Joseph Owen when a bullet pierced his forehead just below his helmet. Kurcaba slumped to the ground. In the bitter cold there was little blood, and the dying died quickly. Woody Taylor inherited the command of Baker/7.

A hasty funeral at Koto-ri, as small-arms fire could be heard in the distance, interred the dead who could not be airlifted or trucked out. At what had been an artillery command post, a bulldozer scraped out a mass grave. The bodies of 117 Marines, soldiers and Royal Marines were to be left behind. Sergeant Robert Gault of the 7th Marines Graves Registration Section recalled, somewhat differently from General Smith,

> We had a chaplain of each faith, and the fellows had made a big hole and laid the fellows [to be buried] out in rows the best we could and put ponchos over them. As soon as each chaplain had said his little bit . . . we would cover them up and close them in. Everyone was given—I think under the circumstances—a very fine burial.

Doffing his helmet despite the weather, Smith observed the hasty obsequies with due reverence yet noting laconically in his log, "A mound was bulldozed over the bodies. It was not a very pleasant sight. It was bitter cold and during the services there was driving snow." Although recognized by those around him as a man of deep faith and his dog-tag noted his *P* as Protestant, he eschewed churches all but the first years of his adult life. His father had been raised as a Presbyterian; his mother a Lutheran who turned to Christian Science. Smith married a wife raised in Christian Science. Although there were other officiating alternatives, they were married, while he was stationed in Guam, by a Methodist missionary.

Also left behind in Koto-ri were about fifty wounded Chinese prisoners who would be a burden to the withdrawal.

A hasty funeral at Koto-ri, where 117 frozen corpses were buried in
a mass grave. *National Archives*

In a heated village hut, after being given treatment for their
wounds, they were left with food and water. A painted Red
Cross identified the location. When the Chinese came to occupy and loot, they would be able to recover their casualties.
No message was posted, but it was an implicit acknowledg-
ment of the wounded Marines who had been left behind un-
harmed in a barn after the capture of Frank Noel.

General Smith had worried as they pushed north in early
November about the narrow, one-lane concrete bridge that
crossed the steep Funchilin Pass. Under it, 2,900 feet below,
were four steel penstocks—huge intake pipes—carrying surg-
ing water from the Chosin Reservoir to a power plant. The
bridge had been damaged but not blown. An enemy failure?

It had to be deliberate, Smith thought—to lure troops beyond it, then trap them by dynamiting the span. There was
no way to protect the roadway from infiltration by night, and
while the Marines were planning to break out of Hagaru, a
twenty-four-foot section was indeed destroyed. Beyond the
gorge, the Chinese had further blocked the route by dynamiting supports for a concrete trestle, dropping it to further
impede passage.

Summoned to survey the impasse was Lieutenant Colonel
John H. Partridge, commanding the Marine Engineer Battalion. Flying low in a light plane, cockpit open in the minus-
zero winds, he hazarded Chinese fire and, Smith recalled,
"near froze to death trying to take some notes, trying to make
an estimate of what he needed. . . . He said what he had to do
was to air-drop Treadway bridge sections at Koto-ri and put
in a Treadway bridge over this gap." The Air Force, Partridge
acknowledged, had never parachuted an M-2 steel bridge section. Each weighed 2,500 pounds. At least four intact sections,
with their plywood planking, were needed. Under intermittent
fire, the 1st Battalion held the bridge site. "I got you across the
Han River [at Seoul]," Partridge assured Smith. "I got you an
airfield [at Hagaru] and I will get you a bridge."

A test drop by a Flying Boxcar from the Yonpo airbase
below Hungnam smashed the Treadway section. To allow for a
margin of error, Partridge radioed Ashiya Airfield in Japan for
eight Treadways and two large G-5 parachutes to be attached
to the ends of each span. For a drop zone near Koto-ri, a mile-
and-a-half from the Pass, each section required a C-119. Fortunately, there were Brockway trucks at Koto, with winches,
brought up from Hungnam when Almond planned to build an

Aerial view of the difficult terrain and water-carrying pipes in the Funchilin Pass area. The break is lower right. *National Archives*

advance headquarters for himself and move his elaborate compound north. Flying at a dangerous eight hundred feet above the mountain top, the C-119s were to spill the girders at 9:30 on the morning on December 7, even as some Marines were still fighting their way from Hagaru to Koto-ri.

On schedule, the oversized Treadways came down—possibly the only airdropped bridge in history. The withdrawal toward the pass, organized in sections, began early on December 7, almost as the spans arrived. Koto-ri emptied but for screaming, bedraggled Korean refugees intending to flee south, including two newborn the night before with the aid of Navy medics. By Smith's orders, Marine squads would move on foot along the ridgelines to protect the troop columns and Treadways from snipers and infiltration by refugees. Only drivers, radiomen, medics, a few reporters and the wounded were permitted to ride. Also the dead. Despite burials, there were always more dead. Four tanks were stationed to hold off the refugees, estimated at three thousand but growing daily, some of whom scavenged dangerously into dump bonfires, leaving little to the Chinese. Even a phone box was ripped of its telephone, although it was of no use to anyone.

Swirling gusts caused one Treadway to fall into Chinese hands, which raised awareness that the Funchilin Pass was in play. Another section shattered on impact. Brockway trucks hauled the others slowly to the bridge site, guarded by the Weapons Company of Chesty Puller's battalion. Windswept, most of the huge parachutes, once detached, blew away. At least one survived in part. A British commando saw wounded Marine corporal Howard Koone trussed up in red parachute cloth and asked a buddy to lend a hand. "Here, Harry, they've got this f——Yank all tied up like a Christmas present."

No other redundancy in the undertaking was possible beyond the additional Treadways. If the bridging failed, the breakout would be imperiled and the thousand-plus vehicles, from tractor-drawn artillery to trucks loaded with wounded unable to walk, would not make it across the chasm. Preparing for reconstruction, engineer troops had to erect a base of sand and timbers and rebuild the southern end of the abutment. About one hundred enemy prisoners were employed in the work crews, which began the task shortly after noon on the 8th

The blown bridge in Funchilin Pass that, unless repaired, would stop further southward movement of vehicles. *National Archives*

as the 1st Battalion, 7th Marines drove back infiltrating Chinese from approaches to the site. Realizing that a mortar shell or even a grenade could end the operation by disabling a truck or a Treadway, Litzenberg had fifty-ton tanks, in frigid gusts and risking fire, shield as much of the work as possible during the three and a half hours the complex installation required.

The last to leave Koto-ri in the early morning of crossing day were O. P. Smith and an aide, who flew over the stream of troops and vehicles heading south toward the Funchilin Pass. Although he wanted to move his CP to Chinghung-ni, down-hill from the pass, his helicopter pilot could not land in the high winds and came down farther south in Hungnam. Smith would have to jeep back up. Regimental commanders would direct the breakout, fending off Chinese sniper squads lying in wait, some crouched in place so long that they had frozen to death.

Prisoners taken and interrogated above the Treadways—if they could be trusted—revealed that seven CPV divisions were lurking in the area and more were infiltrating from above the Reservoir. The bridge area was dominated south of the pass by Hill 1081. Covered by Corsairs and mortar fire, Lieutenant Colonel Donald Schmuck's battalion of the 1st Marines, moving up from Chinghung-ni, stormed the hill, taking casualties but making the descent across the chasm possible. Another of Puller's battalions had been designated to fall behind the last tanks as the last unit, but for the demolition team, over the Treadways. Stalled tanks and intermittent Chinese attacks would disrupt the line of march.

The steel treads, which quickly iced over, were dangerous footing—and didn't quite fit. The gap over the chasm was twenty-nine feet. It had been estimated from the air as twenty-four. As the Treadways spanned only twenty-two feet, engineers built a "crib" of railway ties under plywood flooring to connect the girders and close the gap. Bolstering the subsurface when the ties ran out were "dead men." As 1st Lieutenant David Peppin, a Marine engineer, explained, "Off to the side I noticed a pile of bridging timbers [that] engineers call 'dead men.' The Japanese had prepositioned them there many years before and they were part of a system that made nearby villagers responsible for the road or bridge repairs."* When Colonel

---

*Some marchers thought that the "dead men" were the rigid, frozen corpses of Chinese soldiers and were dismayed at what they imagined to be underfoot. A tanker "recalled" that since there wasn't "enough loose rock for the bulldozers to scrape up, . . . there were enough dead enemy soldiers frozen hard as rocks stacked up alongside the road, so they bulldozed them in and covered them with dirt and we started to move."

Litzenberg came forward, barking, "What's the delay?" Peppin explained. "How long will it take?" Litzenberg asked. "About two hours," said Peppin, to fit in the dead men. The colonel looked at his watch. Dusk came early. "All right," he said, "I'll hold you to that. We cross at 1418." It would take longer.

The final obstacle was the fallen rail trestle blocking the road beyond the bridge. Peppin proposed pushing a bulldozer blade against an end of the trestle to see whether it would give way. The dozer driver gunned its engine under mortar fire. "It was like opening a farm gate," said Partridge in relief. "The whole structure just swung aside," and the ice "skated this huge object right off the road."

Final work on the bridge itself was still ongoing in the late afternoon gloom of December 9, when, as the first vehicles began crossing, a bulldozer with one of its tracks on the girder and the other on the thick plywood, broke through the panels between the Treadways. Nothing further could cross until the heavy vehicle could exit the bridge in reverse and the break was repaired. The bulldozer teetered hazardously midchasm. Firing lit up the sky as Marines fended off the encroaching Chinese while Technical Sergeant Wilfred Prosser, an expert at manipulating tractors, gingerly backed the bulldozer off the bridge. Happy cheers of relief came from onlookers awaiting their turns across.

In the dusk, John Partridge tried the passage in his jeep and confirmed to Colonel Litzenberg that the convoy could go ahead. It was nearly six when vehicles and then troops began streaming toward the bridge. Almost everyone and everything movable would have to do so in darkness, descending from an elevation of 4,500 feet while arctic gusts blew through the valley. More than 1,400 vehicles, including the huge Brockways, fifty-ton tanks and towed artillery, inched slowly forward. Partridge had calculated that the pairs of Treadways, laid parallel but apart, afforded him a maximum width of eleven feet, four inches, with a margin of two inches for tanks. The bridging work above the chasm in whipping wind, drifting snow and arctic chill—only fourteen below—had been intimidating and took until 1530 to complete. Litzenberg's hoped-for 1418 had passed.

The heavy Brockway trucks were the first to test the weight that the span could bear. Partridge realized that for weight bearing, pushing the treads closer together, using bulldozer blades, would permit the mass crossing to work. Yet he needed a total width of 136 inches. "There was a lip," Smith recalled, "on the inside of these treads to keep the wheels from going over." Partridge "measured it so a jeep would go across there with a half [-inch] in play for each wheel on either sides of these lips. Then the trucks would ride nicely on the two treads. The tanks, when they went across, had half of one of their treads over the edge of the bridge. They proceeded very slowly at two miles an hour."

Vehicles carrying materiel, the wounded and the dead crossed the chasm during the early hours of the night using headlights and guided by flank guards with flashlights. As reported by N. Harry Smith, waiting troops were

> jumping up and down, first on one leg, then the other, in a futile effort to fight the bitter wind and cold. . . . Slowly,

inch by inch, our jeep moved down the steep grade until it came to the north side of the Treadway bridge, where it was stopped. "Now take 'er easy, driver," said one of the engineers directing traffic. "Come on. . . . Easy now. . . . Got t'keep those wheels of yours 'tween the markings. . . . That's it. . . . You got it made now. . . . Over! . . . "

My jeep had been assigned to the convoy about one-quarter [mile] distance from the tail end. In front of us was a large truck carrying mortar and machine-gun ammunition, and to our rear was a jeep. The view further back was obliterated by the personal gear that was stacked to the height of the jeep driver's head. Behind the jeep came the heavy mobile equipment—dual-wheel . . . trucks, antitank guns, reconnaissance trucks with .50-caliber machine guns mounted on them, a long line of 105-mm and 155-mm cannon—followed by a few jeeps and tanks bringing up the rear.

Each section . . . was spaced a quarter-mile interval from the next. Each vehicle in the column was likewise spaced about fifty yards from the vehicle directly to its front and rear. This gave added assurance that the enemy would not be able to exact wholesale destruction of an entire section if they attacked the convoy.

As midnight approached on December 9, troops, including the walking wounded, crunched south on the slippery surfaces—slowly. According to Harry Smith, each man "looked like a walking arsenal. Aside from the rifles they carried, hand grenades were strung over their chests, around their

By evening on December 6, troops and vehicles began reaching the Treadway bridge. *National Archives*

waistlines, and even upon the sleeves of their snow-whitened parkas. Someone in the column remarked that they looked like a 'walking army of Christmas trees.'" Each Treadway was taking on a long stream of very uneasy men who could have pitched into the darkness below. "Don't look down!" one Marine shouted.

"I tried not to look down, but it was absolutely frightening," another remembered. He had looked. Apparently, he crossed toward morning on the 10th, when the blackness was fading into hazy dawn. High on the mountain ridges, then, Marines and GIs moving south could be seen on the twisting switchback road beyond the span, taking up positions to cover the descending columns from enemy fire, which had increased with growing daylight and faded again at early dusk.

Not every vehicle made it across. "Some of the tail-end Charlies," medic James Claypool recalled, "were able to grab a ride on the last trucks out, but I was afraid to ride down the mountain because I had seen a six-by[-six] slide across the ice and go over the edge. Dead and wounded Marines came flying out of it, tumbling end over end in their sleeping bags." The truck hit bottom on its rear end with its headlights streaming up the canyon wall.

"The sensation all through the night was extremely eerie," said Partridge. "There seemed to be a glow over everything." Vehicle lights and flashlights and flares from distant enemy firing glinted in the freezing murk. Passage remained slow and deliberate through the day and beyond. By 0200 on December 11, Partridge concluded that everyone who should cross had done so and that the encroaching Chinese now had to be denied access.

"I had a sense of well being," he said. "After all had gone across and I had blown the bridge." But, O. P. Smith recalled, "There is where Lewie Puller slipped up, on the loss of the [last] tanks." About forty tanks followed the 3rd Battalion, 1st Marines. "The plan was that the 1st Marines were to be left in Koto-ri to defend and come out as rear guard. . . . We had taken the precaution of putting [many of] the tanks at the rear of the column because we were afraid if something happened to a tank it would block the road and it'd be so heavy you couldn't move it. . . . Lewie just assumed the tanks would take care of the rear." But little more than a mile from the bridge,

General MacArthur with Major General Edward Almond at Yonpo airbase. *Douglas MacArthur Foundation and Museum*

the ninth tank from the rear stalled, its brakes frozen in the bitter cold. Those forward of it kept moving.

Lieutenant E. C. Hargett's Reconnaissance Platoon of twenty-eight men accompanying the last tanks held back the clamoring mass of refugees who wanted to cross. Soon after the tanks stopped, Hargett saw five supposed refugees now claiming to be Chinese soldiers bursting from the throng, shouting in English that they wanted to surrender, but intent on its opposite. Exploiting the plight of refugees, infiltrating enemy troops often created opportunities for havoc by concealing weapons under traditional peasant garb. "And the refugees kept coming forward," Smith said. "We kept them back. We didn't allow them to mix with our column . . . and there was nothing the tanks could do because of a cut-out of one side of the mountain. The tanks could shoot ahead or shoot back, but they couldn't shoot up. The enemy began throwing grenades and stuff."

Suspicious of the five Chinese, Hargett had walked toward them holding his carbine ready. As he did, one stepped aside; the four Chinese behind him drew from their voluminous peasant clothes wooden handled grenades and submachine guns. Hargett pressed his trigger but it was frozen. He lunged at the Chinese, swinging his carbine and crushing the skull of the forward infiltrator, who had thrown, erratically, a hidden potato masher, lightly wounding Hargett. Covering him with a BAR, Corporal George Amyotte shot down the other four as fire erupted from other Chinese hidden among the refugees. Crews in the last two tanks were ambushed, one tank set ablaze.

Crews abandoned five tanks, now blocked. Another grenade knocked Hargett down and blew Private Robert DeMott off the road. Most of the platoon survived—two killed, twelve wounded and one missing—because they were wearing experimental fiberglass body armor. Only the fifty protective gear issued to the Reconnaissance Company were in use.

Somehow the tank with the locked brakes began crawling again, then a second got its treads moving. When Puller's battered Reconnaissance Company seemed the final unit over the bridge, he was the last across, slowly, in a jeep. On its bumper was lashed the body of a dead tank crewman. Two other bodies were lashed to the hood. Several wounded crowded the jeep's rear. "We take our own people," Puller told his driver, Orville Jones.

Refugees crowded closer and closer to the span, almost certainly including more enemy infiltrators. Now over the Treadways, Major Bruce Williams rolled to a stop in his jeep, shouting, "Where the hell is the guy who is meant to give the word when to let her blow?"

"I don't know who he is or where he is," a tanker called back in the confusion. "Let the sonofabitch blow! We're covering you. You can't wait any longer."

Williams turned his jeep around at the lower base of the span. On the road above, the refugees and concealed Chinese among them halted as they saw warning fire streaking over their heads. Then, as they rushed forward, the fuses at the two ammo dumps prepared below were ignited. The mobs were only a few hundred yards away when explosions erupted in echoing booms, and the Treadways dropped into the gorge below.

The Marines whom Puller had inadvertently left behind attacked their way around the ridge pumping station, climbing down and then up the steep sides of the precipice to find the road beyond the pass and rejoin the withdrawal. Regaining consciousness as he heard the detonation of the Treadways, Robert DeMott realized that he had to get across some other way. He climbed back onto the road and slipped in with the refugees who, ill-clad, cold and hungry and inured to hardship, slipped out, one by one, over the ridges. The Chinese infiltrators among them vanished, to reappear again—and again.

To the north, soon after daybreak, closely packed columns of Chinese were seen approaching the pass from Koto-ri. One Marine later wrote derisively about press reports of "hordes of Chinese." His experience had been one of enemy snipers, in-filtrators, squads, and companies, and he mocked, "How many hordes are in a Chinese platoon?" Yet the Chinese at Chosin had suffered tens of thousands of dead, tens of thousands of wounded and tens of thousands of weather-related casualties, impossible numbers if only platoons were involved. When Lieutenant Colonel Donald Schmuck of the 1st Battalion, 7th Marines, his unit positioned below Funchilin to protect the breakout, radioed for air strikes and his artillery fired salvos at the columns—not platoons—of Chinese, they stoically kept coming, even over the bodies of their dead.

Assured by radio that no more American troops were at hazard above the pass, carrier planes descended and destroyed what remained of the Funchilin span and the turbines below.

In a message to Marine commandant Clifton Cates, O. P. Smith reported that his men "came down off the moun-tain bearded, footsore and physically exhausted, but their spirits were high. They were still a fighting division." Musing about the breakout long after, he acknowledged the determi-nation and resilience of the troops and, perhaps, he thought, also, of the adage that there were no atheists in foxholes. "One of my regimental commanders summed it up in this fashion. He stated that he was not a religious man, but he felt that we had walked in the hand of God."

9

Downhill All the Way

*"We've walked this far; we're going
to walk the whole way."*

"WASHINGTON GUM" read a headline on the front page of *The New York Times*, a typographical error for "GLUM." Yet a word suggesting *adhesive* seemed somehow as correct in the circumstances as the term for *morose*. Otherwise antagonistic, Democrats and Republicans were sticking together in what the President described as a state of emergency. The House of Representatives even voted, 378–20, for a 75 percent excess war profits tax. To little opposition, the Department of Commerce exerted its right to block shipments of goods to Russia and China and their Communist satellites, including cargoes that American ships might acquire in foreign ports. In the Korean northeast, the Marines almost out of danger were sticking close to the troops coming up to accompany them toward safety. The collective convoy seemed thirty miles long.

South of the blown Funchilin span, the rubble road along the icy ridgeline had to be traversed cautiously by troops and tanks, taking and returning fire from Chinese on their flanks. Marines and the improvised army battalion took more casualties and inflicted even more as they descended. "Walked down the mountain," Corporal Frank Bifulk recalled. "It's hard to believe but honest to God, when we hit the valley [toward Chinghung-ni] it was like going from Minnesota to California. Boom! It wasn't cold anymore."

The 5th Marines followed the 7th Marines, wary of reports of concealed North Korean guerrillas—the residue of shattered army units. Chinese troops seemed everywhere on the flanks, some coming forward and offering to surrender. The Marines were inured to enemy fakery, but the Chinese were frostbitten and out of food. The 7th Battalion headquarters radioed, "Send the prisoners down for interrogation." According to Sergeant Sherman Richter, "We said, 'Fine.' The Chinese did not make it. A message was sent back down to battalion, 'The Chinese tried to escape and we shot them.'" However inhumane, extinguishing the burden of unwanted prisoners was hardly new to war. The exhausted troops coming down from the pass needed a covering force southward that did not draw POW guards from their own depleted strength.

On December 5, Almond had met with Major General Soule of the 3rd Division to form the provisional Task Force Dog, including infantry, engineers and artillery, under Brigadier General "Red" Meade. Activated the next day, "Dog" made contact with the men descending from Funchilin, relieving the 1st Battalion, 1st Marines, keeping the road open—almost open—despite continuing enemy mortar and sniper fire. Disabling vehicles athwart the MSR could create roadblocks around which the Chinese could target halted troops. During the withdrawal from Koto-ri across the chasm and down to Chinghung-ni, the harassed Marines had taken 347 additional casualties—75 killed, 16 missing and 256 wounded. Traversing Funchilin and beyond had not been a cakewalk.

Nor was the aftermath easy. As troops began entering Sudong, just below Chinghung-ni, during the night of December 10, Chinese concealed in houses in the village emerged with grenades and burp guns. Although ambushed, surprised riders and truck drivers fired back. In the melee, eight Americans were killed and twenty-one wounded. Nine trucks and personnel carriers that had crossed perilously over the Treadway bridge were wrecked. Flickering fire from the burning trucks lit up the village. Visible in a heap of sixteen Chinese bodies was Lieutenant Colonel John U. D. Page, forty-six.

An army engineer, Page had been in Korea only twelve days, attached to the 52nd Truck Transportation Battalion. Flown to Koto-ri as a replacement, he was assigned by Chesty Puller of the 1st Marines, anticipating C-47 landings, to oversee extending the airstrip a thousand yards beyond the perimeter into an area in range of Chinese snipers. To get the job done meant more than watching the work. He mounted a tank, operated the topside machine gun against the Chinese firing upon the airstrip and directed the tank's crew. Transports were soon able to land and take off.

Page descended the Funchilin Pass a few days later. When his column was stopped by enemy fire as they came down, he clutched a Thompson gun and silenced the attack. Confronted again at Sudong, he hurried to the head of his column and broke up the ambush before he was cut down. Although not a Marine, the Corps would award him posthumously its highest honor, the Navy Cross. When his audacity in a combat career as remarkable as it was brief was finally recognized at home in 1957, Page would receive a posthumous Medal of Honor.

The withdrawal route remained insecure, as any outcrop could conceal a sniper and any seemingly vacant dwelling could house guerrillas. The welcoming vehicles from "Dog" provided those still on foot with some cover. Lieutenant E. C. Hargett's platoon, the last unit of the Marine Reconnaissance Company, had been in a firefight at the Treadway bridge but reached Chinghung-ni without incident late in the morning of December 11. Armored personnel carriers and a string of trucks from "Dog" had been picking up willing and weary marchers, offering them rations and hot coffee. Some Marines remained proudly stubborn. "Do you wanna ride into Hamhung?" shouted Lieutenant John Cahill.

"No, no," said a scruffy bearded Marine. "We've walked this far; we're going to walk the whole way." Some could not. Of the original 192 men in Fox Company, 2nd Battalion, 7th Regiment, only 30 had survived. No officers were left standing. A platoon sergeant, Richard Danford, led the abbreviated company. The Marine combat role had ended at Chinghung-ni, still forty-three miles from the sea, on entering the 3rd Division's defensive perimeter. Weaponry and weather had put twelve Chinese divisions out of action, while the Marine division had lost a third of its strength from deaths, wounds and the numbing cold.

Still a mile and a half from the village, down a knob identified as How Hill, probably after Read's "HOW" battery, was a hairpin loop of a thousand yards, the bottom of a ridge that extended north, above the chasm, to Koto-ri. To keep concealed Chinese at a distance, the division's 155s fired hundreds of rounds over the incoming Marines. It was a dangerous strategy. Although the theoretical range of the guns was ten miles, in the frigid air the volleys could fall short. As Lieutenant Colonel Kenneth Dawalt of the 999th Field Artillery worried, "A error in deflection would have killed our own troops. I got a few gray hairs."

For the AP, Hal Boyle wrote, "Seen from the air, [the] march held both magnificence and pathos. There was a Biblical pageantry about it. In a plane at 4,000 feet the great retreat looked like a scene from a silent movie epic. . . . Everything seemed frozen—grey clouds. . . . The evergreen mountains . . . the yellow roads . . . the dusty battle cars . . . the whiteclad groups of refugees wading the rivers or huddling together in the hills . . . the endless columns of troops in olive drab. But as the plane came lower, the tableau surged with swarming life."

At a rail siding below the village of Majon-dong, thirteen miles south of Chinghung-ni, the remnants of Fox Company boarded a gondola car which had neither seats nor roof and sucked in the acrid coal smoke of an ancient steam locomotive. Truck drivers disgorging the Marines honked their horns in response to the shrill "peanut whistle." Doc Litvin recalled the "wonderful, jubilant sound" of the locomotive's shriek as it tooted along, its passengers unconcerned that the fumes blowing back carried sparks that burned holes in parkas which, in a milder climate, would soon be obsolete.

Because of Chinese hidden on cliffs and in crevasses down from Funchilin, Chinghung-ni was the northernmost safe place to assemble rail equipment. Ten old locomotives and fifty-eight cars in various states of dilapidation had been parked at sidings on the narrow-gauge tracks. Also, an eight-car hospital train awaited to carry wounded directly to the coast, and more antique but serviceable rail cars were stacked up at Oto-ri, twelve miles farther south. Much of the Korean rolling stock, even after Japanese colonization, had seen better days. The trolleys in Pusan had labored on tracks in Philadelphia for decades.

A soldier had discovered a stockpile of familiar cocoa-flavored candy in wrappers piled under a canvas covering at the Sudong railhead and shouted for takers. Lieutenant Colonel Raymond Davis of the 7th Marines sent men to distribute boxes down the crowded carriages. Cases of Tootsie Rolls were emptied, as half-starved men grabbed them and filled their pockets. An officer walked down an aisle and admonished, "You don't have to steal that. It's all yours. Just help yourselves." Tootsie Rolls had been doubly valuable since departing Yudam-ni. When softened by body heat, the chewy candy had plugged bullet holes in engine blocks and vehicle radiators.

From the breakout onward, there had never been a shortage of Tootsie Rolls. When Marine weapons companies were running out of 60mm mortar rounds, radiomen began requesting urgent air drops of ammo under the code name *Tootsie Rolls*. (The confection was, indeed, round.) They did not want to alert the Chinese nearby that Marine mortar sections were at risk. Crates by the dozens were duly airlifted, but their loaders in Japan may have been Japanese warehousemen unaware of supply specialist codes. Rather than 60mm shells, to the bafflement of mortar crews the emergency containers were filled with Tootsie Rolls. Those air-dropped out of Marine reach must have also puzzled the enemy. Their Russian-made mortars could have fired American shells, but not the thousands of frozen Tootsie Rolls.

After dark on the 11th, troops reaching Hungham were disembarked to a bivouac area near the harbor, with tents, stoves and galleys dispensing hot food. (The tanks had yet to clank in.) Davis himself recalled eating "something like 17 or 18 pancakes in two hours."

Above Chinghung-ni, Task Force Dog as rear guard continued to keep at bay thousands of clamoring refugees who were slipping around the pass and the ridges, at hazard to their lives. The valley had been mined and strung with barbed wire as a perimeter defense line. As the Marines cleared Chinghung-ni and the Sudong, weapons in hand, any vehicle that became inoperative was pushed to the side of the road and destroyed. Air reconnaissance scoured the ridgelines for enemy sightings, rocketing and strafing concentrations of Chinese observed lying in wait. Supply dumps en route which had to be abandoned because of a shortage of trucks were destroyed by explosives or burned. Still, the refugees, although kept at a distance by overhead fire, kept coming. With them, in Korean garb, the 3rd Division's 65th Infantry worried, with reason, were more concealed and armed Chinese.

According to Corporal Ray Mighells (he pronounced it *Miles*), troops on reconnaissance looking for signs of the enemy were under orders not to reveal their own presence unless absolutely necessary. When his cold and hungry platoon, on

C-rations and dried seed corn liberated from root cellars, came across a small pig they estimated at twenty to thirty pounds, they chased it down. "Being beaten with M-1 and Carbine butts while very actively struggling made it pretty hard to get a knockout blow. I never knew a pig could squeal that loud or long." Roasting it hurriedly over a forbidden fire, which could have been a giveaway of their location, they enjoyed the carved-up porker "half-raw."

With a newly protected perimeter beginning at Hamhung established by the close of December 11, Task Force Dog was disbanded and its elements folded back into the 65th Infantry. The perimeter, several arcs at first including Yonpo airfield in its southeast, would gradually shrink as troops moved toward the embarkation area at Hungnam. Almond had maintained to the *Dai Ichi*, even as the fighting withdrawal from Chosin proceeded, that X Corps could hold a substantial bridgehead, including Hamhung, Hungnam and Yonpo, indefinitely with sufficient land and sea firepower and air cover. That strategy, he offered again and again to no one's interest, might, he contended, impede a Communist takeover of all of Korea. Yet the constant resupply of the proposed enclave, requiring a substantial naval and air presence, would have been a logistic drain of little strategic or political value—unlike the dramatic and highly successful Berlin airlift, which thwarted Soviet ambitions in Germany and western Europe. The presence of Major General William H. Tunner of the FEAF Combat Cargo Command, who had overseen the remarkable Berlin airlift, was a reminder of what extreme measures might accomplish—if the consequences warranted the effort.

Before Yonpo was abandoned, General MacArthur flew in just before noon on the 11th for a photo-op of three-quarters of an hour to suggest his active involvement in the retrograde operation. He brought with him, for little strategic reason, some of his GHQ staff. (Regulations provided a month's income tax relief for as little as a day's presence in a combat zone, a tourist opportunity often taken by opportunistic brass.) None of the Marine command was present at Yonpo, and none of the *Dai Ichi* "Bataan Gang" had any role in the discussions with Almond. The Tokyo press and an AP wirephoto of MacArthur with Almond described the site as Hungnam, which suggested that MacArthur had observed the evacuation process, but Yonpo was a jeep ride to the south, and in his forty-five minutes on the ground, the general never left the airfield. Flying back to Japan, he penned an assessment of his "inspection of the front"—the outloading situation as described by Almond—and read it to reporters waiting at the Haneda runway. Because of circumstances beyond his control, MacArthur asserted, "our forces were unable to fulfill the prescribed mission" authorized by the United Nations but were efficiently following orders.

O. P. Smith had learned from Almond that the Marine division would embark almost immediately on arrival at Hungnam. Almond viewed the battered Marines as no longer combat effective, assigning them priority for redeployment. However, that was not what Smith had anticipated. Because of their amphibious expertise, he expected to defend the beachhead and be the last troops out. It was, after all, a Navy operation, and the Marines were Navy.

As the withdrawal from Chosin was in preparation, Admiral Arleigh Burke, the deputy Navy chief, Far East, informed Washington that he was going to hold "every fifth merchant ship" arriving in Japan for the inevitable evacuation as well as five ships "that had heavy-lift cranes that could raise a tank [on board]." By early December, he had collected "sixty or seventy large empty ships." And there would be more, despite a nationwide rail strike for higher wages in which the President had to intervene. The ships were proceeding to Hungnam even before the Treadways were in place.

Task Force 90, the evacuation fleet, was commanded by Rear Admiral James H. Doyle. Colonel Edward Forney, who advised Almond on Navy and Marine operations, was designated as X Corps evacuation control officer. The Army's 2nd Engineer Special Brigade was to operate port facilities and handle traffic control. With the arriving ships were 1,200 Japanese dock workers long experienced with American merchantmen. Working round the clock, they would sleep in shifts on their mother ship, the *Shinano Maru*. By December 14, wirephotos depicting cranes lifting tanks onto ships in Hungnam harbor had reached American newspapers. Praising Forney's organizing skills, Almond said later, "*Colonel* Forney, he should have been a *General*!" Shortly, he did earn a promotion to Brigadier General.

Smith's anticipated functions were formally "changed" to outloading by Almond's order 10–50 on December 11. But for the 7th Division's battalions "that were messed up at the Reservoir," Smith understood, the Marines had taken most of the casualties and had earned evacuation priority. Nothing operational had changed but for MacArthur's token flight to Yonpo, which suggested, for the sake of appearances, that he had formally ordered what was already ongoing. Following the Marines out, what remained of the 7th Division would board with the 3rd Division, which had seen the least combat, securing the perimeter to the last outgoing ship. South Korean troops below guarding Yonpo airfield until its imminent closure would go out from nearby Wonsan. The 1st Marine Air Wing, afloat on the *Bataan*, the *Badoeng Strait* and the late-arriving *Sicily* and also ashore at Yonpo, would go to bases in South Korea west of Pusan, at Masan, where the Marines were scheduled to bivouac. Smith would write later to Field Harris, "During the long reaches of the night and in the snowstorms many a Marine prayed for the coming of day or clearing weather when he knew he would hear again the welcome roar of your planes."

At Yonpo, MacArthur had asked Almond whether he wanted to return to the Far East Command in Tokyo as chief of staff or remain with X Corps once it merged with Walton Walker's withdrawing forces in the west. Almond chose Johnnie Walker. He and Almond had no love for each other, but Almond may have assumed that MacArthur would shortly relieve a general he disliked and whose forces had faltered and put his own protégé in Walker's place. Even so, the acting FEC chief of staff, Major General Doyle Hickey, was not elevated to the position Almond still nominally held. MacArthur may have been keeping the title for Almond as a postwar plum.

Walker's disintegrating army, its morale at bottom after its "Big Bugout," had retreated over 120 miles in ten days. While the Chinese remained out of contact, Eighth Army had some of its lost equipment and ammo replenished by airlift. Forward troops had withdrawn largely below the 38th parallel. Walker's rear guard had halted at the Imjin River about 30 miles north of Seoul, with the Chinese still distant, their momentum slowed by primitive logistics. Rail trackage in the north was rare, and trucks were in short supply. Enemy armies were running low on rations and ammunition, transported on the backs of thousands of bearers using foot power or pilfered from undestroyed stores chaotically abandoned.

On Walker's front, General Peng had paused at Pyongyang, the recovered North Korean capital, so that Kim Il Sung could symbolically review his reconstituted troops from a soccer stadium—a gesture performed hastily because of concerns about American warplanes. Soon after, on December 13, Mao radioed Peng, "If the enemy plans to give up Seoul without a fight, our armies on the western front should stop between Seoul and Pyongyang for a few days to give our exhausted troops the rest they need." Stalin's resident proxy, Colonel General Terenty Shtyov, the Soviet ambassador, objected when he learned of the order. The Chinese, he advised Peng, should push into South Korea. "Such hesitation in fighting a war has never been seen in the world." Shtyov was unaware that the Chinese had already lost a third of their combat troops to enemy action and extreme weather. But Peng knew.

"Chasing a modern army on foot makes no sense," Peng retorted without reference to his excess of casualties. Radioing Mao in Beijing, he explained, "After two victories the mood of quick victory and blind optimism has been growing out of proportion in all aspects. The Soviet ambassador insists the U.S. troops will flee quickly and demands that we move forward quickly. I am convinced that the war will be a protracted one and we should not go forward without calculation."

Going forward in the east was a different matter from the headlong rout in the west. Peng would cautiously fill the imminent vacuum. Third Division commander Robert Soule, in charge of perimeter security in the Hamhung-Hungnam area, knew that the Chinese would test his defenses, but there was only light contact until dawn on the 13th, when about two hundred enemy troops attacked E Company, 7th Infantry. Surprising the Americans, the Chinese wore GI parkas and uniforms taken from prisoners or the dead. About fifty Chinese were killed. The next night, a larger force attacked B Company, 65th Infantry, which fell back until artillery fire drove off the enemy. Anti-aircraft guns were sited low to sweep the hills and ravines beyond the perimeter, as sizable Chinese forces seemed to be closing in, attacking largely after dark, and the perimeter which X Corps occupied would continue to contract with evacuations limiting the need for space.

A dispatch from Tokyo by Lindesay Parrott of *The New York Times* on the 15th reported that "seven to twelve Communist divisions rolled yesterday toward the beachhead around Hamhung and the seaport of Hungnam," but that was inflated *Dai Ichi* verbiage from a handout. (The next day, it was "at least ten divisions.") To slow whatever Chinese were moving in, bridges were destroyed, including rail crossings. No longer needed, rolling stock, including 15 locomotives and 275 cars, were wrecked. Nothing useful was to be left behind.

On the 15th, General Peng convened commanders of his divisions to report that Chairman Mao was insisting that, "because of political considerations," they drive on both fronts across the symbolic 38th parallel. "If we succeed in doing that," said Peng, "we will claim a victory, and what to do next will depend on circumstances." That would be no problem for the "Northeast Command"—the Chosin front—as "according to the news reports from the foreign presses," the enemy was in the process of evacuation, and Eighth Army in the west would be pulling back below Seoul.

Deputy commander Hong Xue Zhi was skeptical that his depleted forces could go further. General Nie Rongzhen, chief of the PLA general staff, proposed another reason for caution, believing that "if we pushed back too far, there could be another Inchon[-type] landing." After further discussions, Peng responded to Mao on the 19th that shortages of supplies and transport, the lengthening distances, the exhaustion of troops and the frigid winter were all daunting. Collectively, all their armies had "no more than 300 trucks at their disposal." Their soldiers lacked winter coats, and the 42nd Army did not have reinforced cotton boots. "Those who had cotton boots have worn them out. Many cotton jackets and blankets were burned by the enemy incendiary bombs, and with no cotton boots, many [soldiers] have been barefooted." Further, "The supply of food, vegetables, salt, and [cooking] oil is so low that the troops' health condition is deteriorating and more and more troops are getting sick."

Beyond village informants, infiltrators and the American media, on occasion, the Chinese, as they would do throughout the war, employed, as darkness turned to dawn, small, nearly antique PO-2 biplanes to reconnoiter below the radar the disposition of enemy troops and equipment and the progress of withdrawal. Sometimes, before exiting, the slow, low-flying "night hecklers" would drop small fragmentation bombs.

Mao conceded that Peng's realistic assessment meant "protracted war," although "the United States and Britain are exploring the old status quo of the 38th parallel . . . for political propaganda purposes and trying to force us to accept a cease-fire." The outlook for a Christmas victory had receded to a forlorn hope for a Christmas truce. The military conditions for a political solution remained remote.

The UN command—in effect, MacArthur—knew little beyond guesswork of Chinese logistics problems, although it was obvious that lengthy distances and miserable weather increasingly hampered their supply chain. MacArthur reiterated his claim that the deep withdrawal of his armies was deft strategy to stretch enemy resources and supply lines.

An unanticipated problem for backtracking troops remained the ever-increasing numbers of civilian refugees desperate not to be left behind. On the EUSAK front, they could trek by land. In the northeast, they were blocked by Chinese forces and North Korean irregulars who had infiltrated below the fluid front. X Corps kept them at a distance on all sides by the threat of mines, barbed wire, air strikes, artillery and automatic weapons. Almost certainly the masses of fleeing Koreans continued to conceal enemy soldiers in peasant garb, even to long white papa-san coats traditionally worn by many of the elderly. The desperate thousands who had survived numbing cold and lack of food and water had no means of thwarting the infiltrating Chinese and feared being killed by the Communists or left to die by the Americans.

Almost daily, a Korean civil affairs official, Dr. Hyun Bong Hak, had been pleading with Almond to help them leave. Hyun, an MD, later a medical school professor in the United States, had credentials to take very seriously. Many refugees, he claimed to Marine colonel Edward Forney, long had been devout Christians, converted by zealous missionaries. Tens of thousands were crowding in the wintry chill around the Hamhung railway station, intending to walk if necessary, even shoeless, the ten or so miles further to the sea. Forney agreed to intercede with Almond. "Doc," he told Hyun, "it's going to be difficult, but let's give it a try. Napoleon didn't find the word 'impossible' in his dictionary."

The refugee problem was not only a moral and a strategic matter but also potentially a politically sensitive issue at home. The American-led command could not be perceived in the States, especially as Christmas approached, as abandoning Christians to the less than tender mercies of nonbelieving Communists. Powerful Americans of conservative bent, like Henry Luce, publisher of *LIFE* and *TIME*, were offspring of Christian missionaries in China. DeWitt Wallace, publisher of the mass-circulation *Reader's Digest*, was the son of a Presbyterian minister, and John Foster Dulles, foreign policy guru to the Republican elite, was the most influential Presbyterian layman in America. The *Dai Ichi* could not be unaware. MacArthur, as viceroy in Japan, had actively encouraged Christian missionaries to come to Japan and even forced the docile

Japanese government to accept them. He had convinced himself that the Japanese could be converted in large numbers and encouraged the American Bible Society to furnish Bibles. To disappointing results, 10 million translations would be distributed during the occupation.

Almond agreed to meet with Forney and Hyun. All available ships, the general explained, were needed to bring out his troops on ships collecting at Hungnam. MPs were already holding the swelling numbers of Koreans back. Yet the refugees, Hyun pleaded, had no shelter, water or cooking facilities. Almond promised to issue orders to feed them with whatever stocks remained. The case for evacuation seemed lost when, on December 9, X Corps headquarters—in effect, Almond—informed Hyun to ward off his further importunities, that it might not even be able to evacuate its own Korean civilian employees. Hyun then tried another strategy. He met with a sympathetic priest, Father Patrick Cleary, a chaplain with X Corps and a former Maryknoll missionary. The persuasive Father Cleary understood that the pressure of the civilian throngs on the perimeter troops as the defensive line shrank had to be relieved, and that Hamhung, where most of the refugees had clustered, was soon to be abandoned. Approaching Chinese could already be seen on the ridges.

The appeals led Almond, reluctantly, to seek approval from Tokyo to outload refugees. Noting that many were Christian converts helped secure MacArthur's go-ahead. Giving in to necessity, Almond ordered trains still under steam at Hamhung to bring the Koreans to the dock area. (Many thousands more had already made it on their own.) A few ships in harbor were diverted to refugee outloading. Dr. Hyun, their self-appointed spokesman, found fifty refugees praying in the basement of a soon-to-be-vacated Presbyterian church in Hamhung. When he alerted them to spread the word about rescue, one of the desperate worshipers cried out, "Moses has come to evacuate us!"

Thousands of Koreans entrained from Hamhung began crowding close to the docks. Rescue ships for refugees arrived on December 17 and December 18—three LSTs from the South Korean Navy and more transports from Japan. Beginning on the 19th, as each arrived, they would be loaded far beyond official capacity. Dr. Hyun would board the Victory ship *Sergeant Andrew Miller* on December 21, recalling that, at night, watching from the deck, naval gunfire volleying inland was "like shooting stars falling on the horizon."

10

Christmas Eve

On the banks of the Yalu,
General Sung Zhi Lun . . . took off his helmet
"and bowed deeply toward the Chosin Reservoir,
to his fighting comrades."

The withdrawal from northeast Korea was no Dunkirk. A carefully planned operation, it began with the Marines twelve days before the last ship outloaded. No motley armada of small craft piloted by civilian volunteers converged in the bay at Hungnam as occurred on the English Channel from May 27 to June 4, 1940. No desperate brigades waded out into the surf to board whatever floated. No mountain of weapons and gear were abandoned to the enemy. No pressure from the enemy forced any desperate urgency, as ground artillery and offshore warships protected the beachhead.

The closest parallel to the escape of an army with most of its weaponry was an embarrassing episode that Generals Eisenhower, Montgomery and Alexander, three years after Dunkirk, would have preferred history to forget. Evacuating

Sicily in August 1943 across the Strait of Messina to the peninsular boot of Italy, the *Wehrmacht* exploited the bizarre incompetence of Allied air, sea and land leadership. "The last German soldier [has been] flung out of Sicily," General Harold Alexander radioed Winston Churchill. Yet no one was flung. The Hermann Göring Panzer Division and other units, complete to their tanks and artillery, crossed the strait unopposed. From August 10 through August 16, 1943, one-armed Lieutenant General Hans Hube (a casualty, earlier, in Russia) evacuated 39,569 Germans and 62,182 Italians as well as tens of thousands of vehicles, guns, ammunition and supplies to keep the war going in Italy for nearly two more years.

The ongoing withdrawal from North Korea, unconcealed from the media, was compared (first by *TIME* in its issue of December 18, 1950) to the classic march of the ten thousand in Xenophon's *Anabasis*, or *The March Up Country*, the account of the epic retreat of a Greek mercenary army in 401 BC. General Smith's frigid fighting retreat, Roy Appleman wrote in *Escaping the Trap*, was "a textbook application of Xenophon. . . . The prime lesson, if there was a single most important one, was that enemy-held high ground along the route of march must be seized before a column attempts to pass below it."*

At the Hamhung beachhead, Air Force, Navy and Marine aircraft provided a curtain of safety, and warships offshore in

---

*Napoleon's desperate retreat from Moscow in October-December 1812 as the Russian winter came early belies comparison. Huge in numbers, dwindling as men marched over devastated ground while harassed by the enemy, and abandoned by its commanding general, the Grand Army was only a remnant when it crossed back over the French frontier.

the Sea of Japan, including massive sixteen-inch cannon from one of the last missions of a battleship in warfare, pounded sites from which the Chinese might disrupt the outloading. There were 109 ships, ranging from LSTs to haul men to anchored ships and to ferry equipment to the battleship *Missouri*, a late arrival, and the cruiser *St. Paul*, crowding the sea approaches.

Wonsan, below, had closed as a port of embarkation on December 10, and flights from there and from nearby Yonpo ended on the 17th. Until the last, the 17th Combat Cargo Command at Yonpo flew around the clock, with aircraft, mostly C-119s, taking off and returning—often at five-minute intervals. At the last, 393 sorties were flown from Yonpo, evacuating 228 casualties, 3,891 troops and 2,086 tons of cargo. Soon shorthanded, flight crews had to pitch in to load the departing planes. Four with mechanical problems remained. Two were repaired on site. For the third, two engine assemblies were removed from a plane at Ashiya and flown from Japan to install on a Flying Boxcar. The fourth aircraft, approaching takeoff, suffered a sudden pump failure and had to be destroyed.

Until it was abandoned, the vast Kimpo airbase near Seoul was the home strip for the new, high-speed F-86 Sabrejets, based like the MIG-15 on a *Luftwaffe* ME-262 swept-wing design. The Sabrejets flew their first missions on the 17th. They were of no use, however, in the shrinking northeast, where a small field for emergency use was opened in the Hungnam harbor area.

From the Wonsan beachhead before shutdown, the 1st Shore Party Battalion and associated units offloaded 3,834 troops, mostly Army; 1,146 vehicles, 10,013 tons of bulk cargo, and 7,009 Korean civilian workers. A field hospital at Hungnam took casualties who were unable to board ships, preparing them for air evacuation. Some struggling aboard were also in poor shape. Staff Sergeant Lee Bergee heard a corpsman being directed, "Put that man over there. He won't make it." Bergee hoped "it wasn't me he was talking about." Sergeant Sherman Richter, in the first group of Marines to debark, recalled, as he gratefully came up the gangway, his fright at first encountering the Chinese—that "you stop thinking, your mind goes berserk. . . . I knew they were trying to kill me. I pumped bullets into them. I mean, how many times can you kill a guy? Until the battle is over, until you stop pulling the trigger, you're crazy. When you stop, you return to reality."

On the 11th the evacuation from Hungnam had begun with the outloading of the 7th Marines on the *Daniel I. Sultan*. They had hardly set down in Hamhung after their embattled trek from the Treadway when trucks arrived to take them ten miles further to the docks at Hungnam, which could berth only seven ships at a time. As the Marine magazine *Leatherneck* would describe them on boarding, "They were filthy— scroungy beyond belief. Most had not had their clothes off for the better part of two months. They smelled like a herd of wet water buffalo." Sergeant Richter boarded realizing that he and his buddies, hurried up to the decks, were "filthy, crummy, had scales on our flesh. They cut our boots off. A doctor walked down the line looking at frostbitten toes. 'Treatment. Treatment. Amputate. Treatment. Amputate. Treatment. Treatment. . . . ' Everyone held his breath. If your toes were black, it was bad for you." Beyond combat losses, the Marines would report 7,338 nonbattle casualties, almost all from severe frostbite. Many of the immobile had been flown out earlier.

The 5th Marines followed on the 12th, and the 1st Marines on the 13th. When Doc Litvin, boarding, "reached the top of that [gangway] ladder, those Navy boys just grabbed hold and shoveled me over the railing like a sack of potatoes. I've never been happier before or since." Haste and efficiency counted. Some ships would dock at Pusan, offload, then make a quick turnaround to return, lifting out more troops or equipment. About 1,400 vehicles had been brought down from Chosin, "the same number," said Smith, "as had gone up, but now some of the complement bore U.S. Army markings." Also loaded, according to a photo shot against a background of freighters in the harbor, were captured self-propelled 76mm Russian-made guns, evidence of a little-seen enemy mechanized dimension and now identified as ROK equipment. Vehicles would go out from Green Beaches One and Two, which could handle eleven LSTs. (Charts also identified a Yellow Beach and a Pink Beach.)

Almond had ordered his posh trailer compound dismantled and moved from Hamhung to the reduced perimeter, and on December 12, as evacuation was underway, he called his generals together there for a conference and dinner. Was he using up some of the steaks and wines and other delicacies he would otherwise have to return aboard the waiting *Mt McKinley* along with his trailer and bath? (He had ordered the flagship used for the Inchon invasion—employed then by MacArthur—for his own embarkation.) Was he convening his upper echelon to thank them in a splendid farewell for their effective service? It seemed awkward in the circumstances, as the beaches of Hungnam bustled with the grimy survivors of Chosin. Nevertheless, the division commanders—Smith, Barr and Soule—came and listened dutifully without comment to Almond's briefing, explaining what they already knew. Then they learned that the purpose of the dinner was to mark Ned Almond's fifty-eighth birthday.

Although unseemly in the circumstances, white-jacketed stewards served, and Almond's chief of staff, Major General Clark Ruffner, presided. In a letter to historian Eric Hammel much later, in 1979, Ruffner would characterize MacArthur's aborted rush to the Yalu, abetted by Almond, as "an insane plan," but at the birthday festivities, Ruffner eulogized the general, claiming that never in the history of the American Army had a corps in such a short time done so much. He was obviously referring to the success at Inchon in September more than the failure at Chosin. Almond replied warmly, and Marine Far East commander Lem Shepherd, who had flown in for the occasion, added complimentary remarks.

In the background could be heard the tumult of the simultaneous, floodlit outloading of men and gear, watchful flyovers of F4U Marine Corsairs, and the thunderous interdiction of naval gunfire and perimeter artillery to prevent the Chinese from thwarting the evacuation. Third Army units continued their patrols.

By December 13, the 5th and 7th Marines were aboard and ready to depart. The division had loaded 22,215 Leathernecks and equipment in four transports, sixteen landing craft, an assault cargo ship, and seven merchant ships. Happily, all hands were all now on relatively sumptuous Navy rations. In winter parka and boots, which concealed how gaunt he had become, General Smith paused before closing his command post to attend a memorial service at the beachhead cemetery where the dead not to be disinterred were buried. In the bright late-afternoon sun, his submachine gun lay on the bare ground in his long shadow. Protestant, Catholic and Jewish chaplains officiated against the backdrop of a low hill that held the earth scooped out to make the graves. From a white pole hung a flag at half-mast, limp in the still air. Led by a bearded sergeant, a Marine firing squad in parkas and helmets marched forward and stood at attention.

Tom Lambert filed an AP dispatch from the scene:

The general arrived early for these had been his Marines and he owed them more than the few brief words he would speak during the ceremony. He walked slowly up the hill, the red clay mud gathering in great lumps on his shoepacs, and stood very still for a moment at the foot of the plot of graves.

The white crosses and the Stars of David gleamed on the hillside against the rust-colored moldy ground. . . . The mud was fresher on the new mounds and the crosses were lustrous. To the north lay the mountains. Here [lay] these Marines [who] had died fighting for towns with strange names like Koto and Hagaru and Yudam. To the south lay the sea. . . .

The Marines' chaplains came forward then, looking north. . . . One of them said, "May hate cease and wars be forever ended."

Now a sudden breath of wind arose and unfurled the flag from the pole. . . . A flight of Marine Corsairs drummed north, flying very high. Then General Smith stepped toward the graves. He is a tall thin man and he looked lonely against the background of white crosses. He took off his fatigue cap and the sun glinted on his white hair. . . . "It is regrettable that their last resting place must for the time being be in foreign soil," he said. "But the memory of what they did here will remain with us always."

Once the Marine sergeant barked his commands, three volleys were fired over the cemetery, and a lone bugler, also behind the last row of graves, stood at attention and blew the mournful "Taps." The wind died down as the last notes faded, and the flag fell back. With the ceremony over, the outloading, briefly suspended, continued.*

By December 15, in the United States—the 16th in Korea—newspapers across the nation would publish a photo, "WHERE MARINES LIE IN NORTH KOREA. Crosses mark the graves of Marines who won't be home for Christmas, during a solemn burial ceremony at Hungnam." On the same day, a syndicated editorial cartoon appeared, showing the eruption of a volcano christened "Korea." Flying skyward from its cone were balloon-labeled question marks:

---

*Historians continue to write—this is from a book published in 2013—that O. P. Smith "conducted the retreat . . . leaving no man—the dead included— behind." But from Yudam-ni to Hungnam, mass field burials became logistically necessary in the circumstances and are on record by word and by camera. Smith witnessed, regretfully, at least two.

Syndicated editorial cartoon showing the "eruption" of the conflict and the questions it raised.

Should we have intervened in Korea?

Should we have crossed the 38th parallel?

Who was to blame?

Can we make another stand in Korea?

Should we withdraw from Asia?

What is Mao up to?

Is this the start of a third world war?

Are we prepared for a full-scale war?

Should we now concentrate all our resources on
   rearmament?

Will we? . . .

Will it be another Dunkirk?

Another cartoon, emphasizing the positive, portrayed a contented Uncle Sam reading a newspaper headline, "YANKS BREAK OUT OF RED TRAP!"

Smith boarded the *Bayfield*, an attack transport, on the 14th and sailed at 1030 on the morning of the 15th. Marines had boarded not only with their backpacks but also with souvenirs of Chosin. One leatherneck carried up the gangway, in addition to his M-1, a Russian-made carbine. General Shepherd left Hungnam the same day for Hawaii by way of Tokyo. Marines still ashore were an air-naval gunfire liaison company, a shore party company, the reinforced 1st Amphibian Tractor Battalion manning eighty-eight amphibian tractors ferrying vehicles and the remaining men staffing X Corps. Smith had not wanted his engineer battalion left behind, but General Shepherd had insisted it was still needed, and Admiral Doyle earmarked several LSDs (landing ship docks) to lift off the

Portsmouth Herald (New Hampshire) cartoon heralding the "breakout."

Marines board USS *Bayfield* at Hungnam. *Naval Historical Center*

tractor battalion and its vehicles. The final Marine presence would be a standby air control center, maintained on a LST until the day before Christmas.

A last serious attempt to break through the covering force occurred when the 1st Battalion of the 3rd Division's 15th Regiment was struck shortly after midnight on December 18 by about five hundred Chinese firing mortars and automatic weapons. After about three hours, the attackers broke off contact in the darkness, leaving seventy of their dead and twenty-three prisoners.

While guns still fired to keep the Chinese away from the perimeter, the last of the ROK army units not part of the 7th

Division outloaded after sunrise on the 18th and sailed the same day. Before boarding the *Mt McKinley* on December 19, from which he would observe the remaining evacuations, continuing with the 7th Division, General Almond presented a Distinguished Service Cross to General Barr, who had apparently earned it for something. Once offshore on the *McKinley*, Almond was reminded by Admiral Doyle that, according to military doctrine, all troops still on the ground as well as those on ships in the harbor were now under his command as task force commander. Almond had become a passenger.

On the 20th, David Barr's 7th Division was embarked, leaving most of the final preparations for withdrawal to Soule's 3rd Division. Writing from Korea, Associated Press reporter Stanley Swinton, later an AP executive, dispatched home in baffling hype, "A stubby, two-star general named Robert H. Soule is the man of the hour here. Soule is the human dynamo who commands . . . the Johnny-come-lately Third [which] has emerged as the fighting heart of this besieged beachhead." Swinton noted admiringly that Soule's "personal slogan" was "get tough."

—⚊—

Christmas began prematurely at POW Camp No. 10, eight miles from Kanggye, just below the Yalu, in what was once a warehouse. There, the first collective meeting of brainwashed POWs, ordered by the camp commander for December 21, was called "a Christmas party." A Chinese indoctrination officer who spoke some English offered the men an already familiar lecture on Chairman Mao's "Lenient Policy for Prisoners of War." To their surprise, the room in which they were harangued was decorated with wreaths, red paper bells, and a sign, "MERRY CHRISTMAS." A large placard under it read,

If it were not for the Wall Street Imperialists
you would be home with your families
on this Christmas night.

Marine private Theodore Hilburn recalled as a holiday treat the best meal most POWs would have during three dreary, hungry years behind barbed wire—servings of hot rice and boiled fatty pork. Candy, peanuts and packs of cigarettes were distributed—very likely from captured stocks. Recorded Christmas music was played. "They had a banner tacked up on all four walls," Marine sergeant Leonard Maffioli remembered, "with 'Fight for Peace' and such slogans as that. They had two Christmas trees with little candles burning on them."

After the fake festivities came the servile payback. Volunteers were encouraged to come forward and speak. Master Sergeant William Olson, who had seventeen years of Army service, including D-Day in Normandy, and experience as a German POW, was first to rise. "The Germans were Christians," he began. "But they did not allow us to spend our Christmas happily. The Chinese do not observe Christmas, but they have arranged this fine party for us. The Nazis beat their prisoners. They spat on us and forced us to stand for intolerably long hours at a time. . . . The Chinese have given us warm clothes, bedding and even hand towels. They have shared their food with us and given us the best they had. This has taught me a lot of things, I can tell you. When I get home this time, they would not get me in the army again. If the millionaires want war, let them take up guns and do the fighting themselves." Other men rose to echo the propaganda line.

On March 1, the indoctrination camp would be closed and the "reeducated" prisoners transferred to other locations to spread their anticipated contagion. Major John McLaughlin, the senior officer at Camp 10, who had been ambushed and surrendered near Hagaru with correspondent Frank Noel and British commandos, advised Lieutenant Charles Harrison, vocally angry about the turncoat behavior, that, to save lives, he saw nothing wrong with "going along with the program to a certain extent." The testimonies procured, he rationalized, were only "a parody of Communist ideology."

—⁓—

Almond would leave the *Mt McKinley* at 9:15 a.m. on the 24th, going ashore to observe the final withdrawals and to award Soule the Distinguished Service Cross for "extraordinary heroism" in

> covering the withdrawal of those elements of the X Corps in the Chosin Reservoir and Hagaru-ri areas. . . . Although faced with a numerically superior force, freezing temperatures, and an aggressive foe, General Soule's actions enabled the successful withdrawal of the entire First Marine Division and elements of the Seventh Infantry

Division. Subsequently, General Soule continued his covering mission so successfully that the enemy was . . . beaten back from the beachhead allowing a complete and orderly withdrawal. . . . His continuous presence at the front under bitter conditions with total disregard for his personal safety . . . was an inspiration to his men.

In reality, Soule was never at Chosin, nor was he even at Hagaru. His division had furnished the post-Funchilin covering fire below the pass and the perimeter patrols to enable the evacuation. On the morning and early afternoon of the 24th—Christmas Eve—Soule's 3rd Division embarked from seven beaches at Hungnam into landing ships, its departure marred only by the premature explosion of an ammunition dump set of by the careless discard, probably by a Leatherneck tractor driver, of a lighted cigarette onto a stack of four thousand rounds of mortar ammunition. A Marine lieutenant and a Navy seaman were killed, and thirty-four others wounded. Three Marine "Amtrack" amphibian tractors were lost in the massive explosion.

As the outloading continued, a day's steaming brought the Marines to Pusan, from which they were trucked toward Masan, to the west, where a sea of tents was being erected. Smith was lodged in a Japanese-style house at Masan, reporting, "The toilet works, but the radiators are not in operation." The milder chill of a South Korean December did not bother him, but he had a thing about toilets. At Hagaru, John Y. Lee, an ROK lieutenant recruiting village labor for Smith's command post, had ordered workmen to construct a wooden toilet

5th Marines move from landing craft to transport ship on their way out of Hungnam harbor. *National Archives*

for the general. (Unlike Almond, Smith shared the rations doled out to his men, but rank had some privileges.) After a Korean carpenter hammered the last nail, he sat on the seat himself—just as Smith entered to use it. Lee was appalled, but the general "told me to let the man finish his need. Smith was a modest gentleman."

At Hungnam, with boarding continuing under an umbrella of naval gunfire, thousands of wretched Korean refugees crowded the harbor, pressing to board the remaining ships. In the two weeks of outloading, the *Missouri* had hurled 162 sixteen-inch shells, and total naval fire intimidating the Chinese included 2,932 eight-inch, 18,637 five-inch and 71 three-inch rounds as well as 1,462 five-inch rockets. The 109 vessels of all kinds would take 193 boatloads, some ships returning for additional sailings. There were 105,000 U.S. and ROK troops boarded as well as 17,500 vehicles and nearly 350,000 tons of supplies and equipment, including 29,400 fifty-five-gallon drums of fuel, were stowed away. Everything left on the beaches was to be rendered unusable.

The ships still in harbor seemed unable to hold all the despairing refugees, their possessions and their small children strapped to their backs. Families resisted being separated on boarding. The last vessel left was the World War II–vintage *Meredith Victory*, its gangway jammed with embarking Koreans. As a cargo ship, it was designed to carry a crew of fewer than sixty, but circumstances rendered the rule book inapplicable. An officer from the outloading team came aboard to help coordinate arrangements from the dock, and Merle Smith, a junior engineer fresh out of the Coast Guard Academy, greeted him and asked—assuming that he hadn't sampled tasty fare since Thanksgiving Day—if he'd like "something good to eat."

"I want an onion," he said. "I've been thinking about an onion for weeks." Handed an onion, he bit into it like an apple.

From midnight to 7:30 a.m. on the 24ᵗʰ, Captain Leonard LaRue's crew loaded rice aboard to feed the desperate refugees.

Korean refugees crowd the SS *Meredith Victory* at Hungnam.

They were instructed at Hamhung to bring their own food and water, as J. R. Lunney, a staff officer and ship's engineer, wrote home, yet "whatever the poor people could scrape together is beyond me, for the whole dock area was completely leveled." Realizing that all the pushing and pleading refugees could not be squeezed below and that there were no further ships going out, Captain LaRue, overseeing the embarking, permitted thousands to fill every space on the decks not required for the ship's navigation. There were five holds with three decks, but as a cargo ship, it had no hold lights nor heat below.

Of the 91,000 civilian refugees at Hungnam, 14,000 vastly overcrowded the *Meredith Victory*. Food and water were short to start and soon unavailable, and the voyage south, slowed by its onboard weight, would take three days. One refugee stand-ing near the ship's galley got his hands on a hard-boiled egg. He swallowed it, shell and all. Other grabbed at oranges and chewed at them unpeeled. Hundreds of drums of jet fuel were on deck, and some chilled refugees began lighting fires on the steel drums. Since an explosion would have destroyed the ship, crewmen, knowing no Korean, frantically used hand signals to warn the incendiaries, and when that failed, pushed through to douse the flames. Another scare emerged at sea when an ROK military policeman in uniform turned out to be a Com-munist infiltrator. He was shackled to a post. A baby boy was born on deck and midwived by the women crowding nearby. During the sailing, four more infants were delivered, the five babies aboard being the best fed—at the breast. There were no sanitary facilities available, Merle Smith wrote home in a Christmas Day letter from the ship, "but the few containers we could find for them. The stench became overpowering—al-most makes you sick." Rumors spread that some refugees had died and that their corpses—actually there were none—were the cause. The ship would be watered down after offloading.

—◊◊◊—

The curtain on the Chosin operation was scheduled to come down as the last ships cleared the harbor. A demolition team had prepared explosive charges to destroy docks and cranes and the ammunition and stores abandoned on the beaches— potential Christmas Eve fireworks like no other. The residue included five hundred 1,000-pound bombs, likely to create a tremendous roar and cloud, and crater the beach. The demolition zone was a mile wide, to be fired upon on departure by offshore warships as explosive insurance. At 2:36 p.m. on Christmas Eve, the outloading beaches were declared cleared of personnel. Observers aboard the ships that were the rear guard could see, with binoculars, Chinese troops on inland ridges preparing to move in. Volleys of shelling continued to give them pause.

Far to their north, CPV headquarters was issuing an operational order for the next offensive, to target weak South Korean divisions. The Chinese command had checked the calendar and found that the moon would be full between late December and early January, which would favor night attacks. Also it was a holiday time in the West, which would reduce alertness.

—⧓—

At 2:40 p.m., a radio message from Almond aboard the *Mt McKinley* to the *Dai Ichi* reported that all elements of X Corps had been successfully evacuated from Hungnam. The beachhead pyrotechnic display that followed would be spectacular. However, Almond's radio to MacArthur was slightly inaccurate. Safely out of range at the emergency airstrip, an engineer officer, Lieutenant Colonel Ed Rowny, and two enlisted men had been waiting for the last LST to fetch them, and, Rowny recalled when a retired lieutenant general in his nineties, "It's coming for us and 200 yards before it comes to us, it blows up. . . . We were sitting on the beach watching and Doyle and

A Navy transport ship, the USS *Begor*, stands by during the demolition of the port of Hungnam. *Naval Historical Center*

Almond out on the flagship believed that I am in that, so they sail south.''[*]

The radio with Ed Rowny seemed "inoperative; well it wasn't meshing with [Admiral] Doyle." Since they could not put an SOS on the air and the Chinese were certain to come after them, Rowny's sergeant came up with a desperate suggestion. "Look, you have all this powdered milk here. We'll make a big SOS on the runway here about ten feet tall." The strategy was chancy. They knew that demolition crews had booby-trapped what could neither be removed or destroyed, from portable toilets to food stocks, including frozen juice cartons. Fortunately, the explosives experts had missed the milk.

---

[*] The LST loss, apparently from a mine, was unreported, and the reason for the abandonment of Rowny's crew is from his recollections.

Dragging sacks of powdered milk that had not made it aboard but were piled up nearby, they "spelled out SOS and a reconnaissance plane comes in and sees that and lands and picks us up . . . and the three of us go back, and Christmas Eve, I'm back in Tokyo with my family. . . . Christmas Day, I get a message from Almond saying, thought you were dead; so glad you're alive. I want you to catch an airplane and get back over here."

Almond was in a base camp outside Pusan, having disembarked on Christmas Day. His message to MacArthur from aboard ship had been forwarded to the White House, where a relieved President Truman was quoted as calling it "the best Christmas present I ever had."

—⁀ɷ⁀—

On the banks of the Yalu, General Sung Zhi Lun, who had commanded the IX Army Group, paused on his return to China, took of his helmet "and bowed deeply toward the Chosin Reservoir, to his fighting comrades he knew or did not know." His huge losses* had required forced marches of reinforcements, who had arrived only after the Marines had withdrawn to the coast. His four fresh divisions had replaced the wounded, the frozen and the dead. "When he raised his head and put his helmet back on, saluting them solemnly, tears were running down his face."

---

*General Peng estimated (probably underestimated) Chinese losses as thirty thousand killed, tens of thousands wounded and fifty thousand lost to the weather.

Epilogue

"It was around Christmas and we got all this turkey. . . . [Admiral Joy] also sent us a bunch of Christmas trees."

As the 3rd Division prepared to outload from Hungnam, General Johnnie Walker in the west was boarding his shiny black command jeep at Seoul, the battered capital soon to be evacuated once more, to visit I Corps at Uijongbu, just to the north. It was midmorning on December 23. Army logistics was already shipping from Japan Christmas dinners identical to those which had filled mess kits on Thanksgiving Day. EUSAK troops in the Han River valley, with the Chinese encroaching, would have to dine rapidly and run.

Walker's veteran driver had been with him since France in 1944. The open jeep sported flashing red lights and sirens mounted on each front fender to speed the general past ordinary traffic and a steel handrail mounted at the passenger seat so the general on occasion could stand gripping the bar. Wearing a pile-lined cap with earflaps he sat, on this journey, with a rug around his knees to keep out the cold.

In the opposite direction—the South Koreans seemed always to be going in the other direction from the action—came a solid line of ROK trucks and jeeps fleeing south. Rumors about Syngman Rhee's presidential proclamation scheduled the next day to abandon the capital had already set off a frantic exodus. An ROK weapons carrier ferrying troops away clipped the left rear of the general's speeding jeep, which hurtled off the icy road and flipped over. Walker and his driver were killed instantly.

Doyle Hickey at the *Dai Ichi* telephoned Washington as soon as he knew, and MacArthur then lavished more praise on Walker than he ever had done in life. Ned Almond would not inherit the command. Lieutenant General Matthew Ridgway, a tough former paratroop commander fifty-five that December, would miss his Christmas dinner at home. Telephoned by General Collins at Fort Myer in the Virginia suburbs of Washington, Ridgway was ordered to depart for Korea without delay. Truman and Marshall had signed on to the appointment.

At the time of Walker's death, Almond was berthed on the *Mt McKinley*, nearing Ulsan, a port about thirty miles north of Pusan. Exhausted, he "went into a dead sleep" after Christmas Eve dinner aboard. Three days later, still commanding X Corps, he would report to Ridgway, who kept him on. Reassigned home in July 1951, Almond would retire in 1953. Preceding him to the States would be General MacArthur, relieved of command in early April by President Truman after many provocations and on recommendation of the Joint Chiefs of Staff on grounds of continuing insubordination. Ridgway would replace him in Tokyo.

Far from home, evacuated troops ate Christmas dinner in South
Korea. *National Archives*

Bivouacked in Masan, where the Marines were trucked from
the harbor at Pusan, O. P. Smith hoped "to get some fresh
meat and stuff to rehabilitate these men who had been living
on C rations and what not up north there. . . . Admiral Joy [in
Japan] loaded up a ship with turkeys and sent it around to Masan, and at the same time the Army made good on its promise and we had turkey coming out of our ears. . . . We didn't
get much fresh beef, but it was around Christmas and we got
all this turkey. . . . He also sent a bunch of Christmas trees."

Outside one tent, Marines arranged small, bleached rocks into "Merry Christmas." Otherwise, it was not a white Christmas. There was no snow then in the south of South Korea.

Smith held an open house for his senior unit commanders. Marine lieutenant James P. Soper, at the harbor in Sasebo which shipped men and materiel from Japan to Korea, had sent the general a case of Old Grandad bourbon. Mixed by his staff with powdered milk, sugar and Korean eggs, it made a passable holiday eggnog.

Sergeant Emilio Aguirre would miss Christmas with his battalion. He was in Corpus Christi Naval Hospital in Texas on Christmas Eve, with his wife at his bedside. It wasn't home, but it was nearly so. Walking into his room, recovering from shoulder surgery, was Willie, his fire-team buddy Kenneth Wilson. For some troops, General MacArthur had kept his promises.

—◊◊—

The *Meredith Victory*, with 14,005 passengers aboard—including the five infants born at sea—was turned away at Pusan, already overcrowded with refugees. It steamed fifty miles southwest to Koje-do, the island off the coast which would soon house tens of thousands of prisoners of war. There, on Christmas Day, two Navy landing craft assisted in offloading the crush of passengers. The operation, concluded, would change Captain LaRue's life. In 1954, after the *Meredith Victory* was decommissioned, he became, as Brother Marinus, a Benedictine monk. He died, at eighty-seven, in 2001.

—⫘—

Peng Dehuai remained Chinese commander in Korea until 1953 and became a Marshal of the People's Liberation Army and Minister of Defense. In 1959, as Chairman Mao became more and more paranoid, he accused Peng of forming a "Right opportunist clique" and put him under virtual house arrest. Publicly humiliated and then tortured, he was sentenced to life imprisonment in 1970, dying in prison in 1974. Before his jailing he managed to write a memoir, including his services in Korea, completed in 1970, but only published post-Mao in 1981.

—⫘—

When O. P. Smith was reassigned to the States, he was named head of Marine forces in the Atlantic, where they had little active presence. Lem Shepherd had become commandant of Marines in 1952, closing off any future for Smith, for whom Shepherd's faint praise was, "[He] went up to the reservoir in an orderly manner and he came back in an orderly manner." Having never owned a house and without a credit history, Smith and his wife, on his retirement from the Marine Corps as a lieutenant general at sixty-two in 1955, found it difficult to obtain a mortgage. After his wife rediscovered an expired department store credit card, they finally succeeded. Settling in Los Altos, California, Smith read and wrote in a study, where, behind his green leather chair, was a large map of the Chosin Reservoir; and he gardened in the combat boots he had worn at the close of the campaign. He died in 1977, on Christmas Day.

Sources

Four major archives stand out as prime documentary sources for Korea November–December 1950. The MacArthur Memorial and Archive in Norfolk, Virginia, directed by James Zobel, has assembled an immense quantity of related material and done so without bias, although it is natural that the papers of the general's longtime aides reflect loyalty to him. The National Archives Record Group 407, Federal Records Center, Suitland, Maryland, is especially complete on war operations and is a massive file representing all levels of command and service. The U.S. Army Military Research Collection at Carlisle, Pennsylvania, includes crucial papers by Edward Almond and Matthew Ridgway and exit interviews with many general-level officers who served then in Korea. Especially valuable because the Marines were the vital center of X Corps is the Marine Corps Archives and Special Collections, History Division, Marine Corps University, Quantico, Virginia. Happily, much documentation at these locations and elsewhere now is accessible online.

The vast published literature, including volumes of facsimiles from the Truman Presidential Library and a plethora of online resources, belies the "forgotten war" tag. Memoirs, interviews and special unit histories continue to appear, in print and online. Extensive official and quasi-official studies include Roy Appleman, *Disaster in Korea: The Chinese Confront MacArthur*, *East of Chosin: Entrapment and Breakout in Korea, 1950*, and *Escaping the Trap: The US Army X Corps in Northeast Korea, 1950* (all College Station: Texas A&M University Press, 1961, 1989, 1990). For the Air Force, the basic history is Robert Frank Futrell, *The United States Air Force in Korea, 1950–1953* (Washington, DC: Office of Air Force History, 1983). For the Navy, there is Malcolm W. Cagle and Frank A. Manson, *The Sea War in Korea* (Annapolis, MD: Naval Institute Press, 1957). For the Marines, there is the multivolume series by Lynn Montross and Frank Canzona, *The U.S. Marine Operations in Korea, 1950–1953* (Annapolis, MD: Naval Institute Press, 1954–1956); and Charles R. Smith, ed., *U.S. Marines in the Korean War* (Washington, DC: History Division, U.S. Marine Corps, 2007).

Since many sources cite the same or similar documentation, citations which follow, chapter by chapter, refer largely to unique locations. Many other sources are cited in the text, especially those from newspapers, news magazines and press agencies.

Place names in Korea may differ from present usage. *Pusan*, for example, is now *Busan*. For verisimilitude I have used 1950s geography.

Preface

The Marine quoted about "tomorrow" is from David Douglas Duncan, *This Is War!* (New York: Harper, 1951). SW's Korea memoir is *War in the Wards* (New York: Doubleday, 1964; augmented ed. San Rafael, CA: Presidio Press, 1976).

1: A Turkey for Thanksgiving

The Wake Island transcript by Laurence Bunker is in the MacArthur Archive, Norfolk, Virginia. The ham radio crank episode was reported in *The New York Times*, November 5, 1950. Peng Dehuai's memoirs, translated by Zheng Longpu and edited by Sarah Grimes, are *Memoirs of a Chinese Marshal* (Beijing: 1984). Further details about his entry into Korea and subsequent events are quoted by Tang Bao Yi and Qin Shu Lan in *Bombs and Fresh Flowers*, ed. Li Zhi Min, Chan Yan and Zhang Yi Sang (Beijing: 1983), translated for SW by Wan-Kay Li; and in Shu Guang Zhang, *Mao's Military Romanticism: China and the Korean War, 1950–1953* (Lawrence: University Press of Kansas, 1995). Further Chinese accounts of the early days of intervention are from Kim Chullbaum, ed., *The Truth About the Korean War: Testimony 40 Years Later* (Seoul: Eulyoo Publishing Company, 1991), which includes firsthand reminiscences by a participant, Ye Yumeng. These Chinese sources are utilized throughout except where other sources are cited.

Bob Hope's arrival in Wonsan ahead of the landing forces is from his *Have Tux, Will Travel*, as told to Pete Martin (New York: Simon and Schuster, 1954). Rumors about Syngman Rhee's extracting rail transport fees were heard often by SW while serving in wartime Korea. MacArthur's pre-Christmas 1941 departure from Manila to Corregidor is described by SW in *15 Stars: Eisenhower, MacArthur, Marshall* (New York: Free

Press, 2007). Russian bridges constructed below the water line in the Manchurian war with the Japanese are described by Phil Zimmer, "Armored Strike at Nomonhan," *Military Heritage*, September 2013. The description of Chinese underwater bridge building at the Yalu and soldiers like river gods is from Hu Hai Bo, translated by Wan-Kay Li, *Korean War Memorandum: True Records of the War to Resist the U.S. and Help Korea* (Beijing: Huang He, 1953). MacArthur's cables to Washington and those of his staff, quoted in many accounts, are in the Norfolk archive. Marshall's responses are quoted by SW in *MacArthur's War* (New York: Free Press, 2000). For Chinese troop strength, see Xie Fang in Chapter 2, below. Almond's posh compound is referred to in many Korea accounts, including David Halberstam, *The Coldest Winter* (New York: Hyperion, 2007). Maurice Kaye, then a major on Almond's staff, described the compound to SW in an interview in 2010.

MacArthur's alleged broadcast from his *Constellation* is reported from Chinese sources by Edwin P. Hoyt in *The Day the Chinese Attacked: Korea 1950* (New York: Paragon House, 1993), attributed to Peng's memoirs and "materials translated by Ellis Melvin from various Chinese publications. This material did not begin appearing until the middle 1980s. . . . They have been suppressed in the [Chinese] used book market, although hundreds of volumes exist in the Lenin Library in Moscow and in the Beijing and Beijing University libraries." Hoyt accepts the impossible broadcast from the sky without skepticism.

Bob Hammond is quoted from *MacArthur's War*. Dwight Eisenhower's Thanksgiving dinner with Alfred Gruenther is described by John S. D. Eisenhower in a letter to SW and in his *General Ike: A Personal Reminiscence* (New York: Free Press, 2003). A Chinese spin on the American military Thanksgiving dinners is by Hu Hai Bo (see Chapter 2). Lee Bergee, Raymond Davis and Cornelius Griffin are quoted in Donald Knox, ed., *The Korean War: Pusan to Chosin: An Oral History* (New York: Harcourt, Brace, 1985). Emilio Aguirre's memoir is *We'll Be Home for Christmas* (New York: Greenwich Book Publishers, 1959). Fox Company and Baker Company personnel, 7th Marines are quoted from Martin Russ (see Chapter 2). Lawrence Schmitt is quoted from Knox, above. Almond's festive banquet is quoted from O. P. Smith's oral history. Almond is quoted from his papers and interviews (above). "How soon? . . ." is quoted in William Stueck, *The Korean War: An International History* (Princeton, NJ: Princeton University Press, 1995). See further at the close of Chapter 3, below.

2: Upbeat Thanksgiving

Private Lockowitz's mock broadcast is from Martin Russ, *Breakout: The Chosin Reservoir Campaign, Korea, 1950* (New York: Fromm International, 1999). The Chinese spin on the military Thanksgiving dinners, the description of the death of Mao An Ying, and the alleged capture of 218 abandoned trucks and many prisoners are from Hu Hai Bo.

Xie Fang's estimate of comparative troop strength is quoted by Charles R. Smith, above.

James H. Dill is quoted in *MacArthur's War*. Muccio's notes are in the MacArthur Archive. O. P. Smith's command diary is quoted from liberally by Gail B. Shisler in *for Country and Corps: The Life of Oliver P. Smith* (Annapolis, MD: Naval Institute Press, 2009). (Her title begins with a lower-case *f*.)

Most MacArthur biographies detail the flight of the *Constellation* over the Yalu. Relman Morin wrote the AP dispatch, November 24, "MacArthur Shows No Fear." The ludicrous Chinese version including the broadcast from the air is from Hu Hai Bo (above). Peng's "Liar!" ejaculation is from Ye Yu Meng in *Black Snow* (1989), in a Korean translation in *Chosun Ibo* (1989), quoted in *MacArthur's War*, above.

The cautious *LIFE* third-person interview appeared under a December 4 date. The British report, by someone identified only as "Spey," was sent to John Raynor of the Office of the Commissioner General for the United Kingdom in Southeast Asia for forwarding to F. R. H. Murray of the Foreign Office in London, and quoted in Stueck, above, Chapter 1.

3: The Pincers Parlay

Stanley Lockowitz's "Mystery Voice" mock-radio program is from Martin Russ, above. The Chinese difficulties in the cold are from Hu. Ed Mifsud was interviewed by Phil Zimmer on August 29, 2012. O. P. Smith's message to Clifton Cates is in Shisler, above. Ridgway is quoted from his *The Korean War* (Garden City, NY: Doubleday, 1967). The interrogated Chinese soldiers agreeing, "Many, many" is from Bob Drury and Tom Clavin, *The Last Stand of Fox Company* (New York: Atlantic Monthly Press, 2009). The Chinese *Military Lessons* bulletin, November 20, 1950, is quoted by Russ, above. Harold Dill is quoted from Donald Knox, above. Keyes Beech is quoted from *Tokyo and Points East* (Garden City, NY: Doubleday, 1954). Joseph Owen's memoir is *Colder Than Hell* (Annapolis, MD: Naval Institute Press, 1996). Eugene Timseth was quoted at a "Chosin Few" reunion in the *Yuma (Arizona) Sun*, October 23, 2012. The message traffic to X Corps is from Shisler, above. The cautious third-person "interview" with MacArthur appeared in *LIFE* on December 4, 1950.

4: Mission Impossible: The Offensive Short-Circuits

"The whiplash of MacArthur's known wishes" is from Ridgway, above. William F. Pounder is quoted on winter clothing shortages in Rod Paschall, *Witness to War: Korea* (New York: Berkley Publishing Group, 1995). Leith Crue's account of MacArthur's broadcast is from Knox, above. Almond bringing Smith a revised offensive plan is from Shisler, above, as is his letter to his wife, "All hands have done a splendid job." James Hunt was interviewed by Phil Zimmer on August 17, 2012. The POW Camp 10 newsletter was *New Life*, January 1951, described in Sheila Miyoshi Jager, *Brothers at War: The Unending Conflict in Korea* (New York: Norton, 2013). Peng's complaint to Mao that "fighting cannot end in a night" is also from Jager. Owen Rutter's footnoted *The Song of Tiadatha* was first printed in Salonika in 1919 (London: Fisher Unwin, 1920). Robert Foelske's fall from a C-119 was reported in an unsigned AP dispatch from Tokyo, December 7, 1950. The attrition of Task Force Faith and the defense of Hagaru are from Charles Smith, above. The Allen-Keiser interchange is from *MacArthur's War*, above. Kennemore and Yancey are from Russ, above.

5: An "Entirely New War"

Jack Wright's exclamation is from Knox, above. Peng's telegram requesting authority to release prisoners for propaganda reasons is quoted in *Mao's Generals Remember Korea*, translated and edited by Xiaobing Li, Allan R. Millett and Bin Yu (Lawrence: University Press of Kansas, 2001). Kim Il Sung's plea to Mao is in Jager, above. The "dreary" Pentagon conference on Korea, December 3, 1950, is described by Ridgway, above. Don Huth's report about the difficulties of correspondents to keep up with the EUSAK retreats and the "shifting front" is from an AP dispatch dated December 2, 1950. The suicide attack by Yang Gan Si is described in Hu, above. Kennan's memo to Acheson and the Acheson, Kennan and Truman meeting are from Jager, above. The diatribes from McCarthy and Jenner are also from Jager. Gavin's Korean study group on atomic weapons is from Ray Monk, *Robert Oppenheimer: A Life Inside the Center* (New York: Doubleday, 2012). Truman's misspoken press conference on atomic weapons was widely reported in the press and summarized in detail in *MacArthur's War*, above. For the FEAF Cargo Command, see Futtrell, above, and Smith, above. For Ed Rowny's interview by James Zobel, see notes to Chapter 10. Marine backtracking in early December is from Charles Smith, above.

6: Beginning the Breakout

Correspondent Frank Noel's capture is described in Russ, above; Stan Swinton's AP dispatch of December 4, 1950; and many other sources, including his obituaries in 1966; the recovery of his lost lens is from an unsigned AP dispatch, December 6, 1950. O. P. Smith's movements are from his long interview, above; from Shisler, above; and from Smith, above. Doug Michaud is quoted from Knox, and the self-destructive actions of the RCT leadership and the Army leadership above are excoriated in detail in Thomas Ricks, *The Generals* (New York: Penguin, 2012). Emilio (Ray) Aguirre's account is from his *We'll Be Home for Christmas: A True Story of the United States Marine Corps in the Korean War* (New York: Greenwich Book Publishers, 1959). The reburial of Don C. Faith's remains was reported in the national press on April 17, 2013. His posthumous Medal of Honor citation was reported in Army General Orders No. 59, August 2, 1951. Jerome McCabe is reported in Knox, above, and in a *Washington Post* obituary, September 3, 2010. Joe Quick's wounding and evacuation and his reporting of the air drop of condoms is from Don Moore, *War Tales*, http://donmooreswartales.com/2010/06/21/joe-quick. James Mortrude's survival is recounted by Rod Paschall, above. The Drysdale convoy's watching their trucks looted by the Chinese is from John Toland, *In Mortal Combat. Korea, 1950–1953* (New York: William Morrow, 1991). Drysdale's actions in detail and his receipt of the Presidential Unit Citation awarded to the Marine Division are in Shisler, above, as is the saga of C. V. Irwin, also recalled in O. P. Smith's interview, above.

"Look at those bastards, those magnificent bastards" is
from Andrew Geer, *The New Breed: The Story of the U.S. Marines in Korea* (New York: Harper, 1952). Also in Geer is the
account of a four-engine R5D making it astonishingly into the
Hagaru airstrip.

7: Hagaru to Koto-Ri

Tom Stone's AP dispatch is dated December 2, 1950. Bob Drury
and Tom Clavin describe John Audas and others in his unit in
The Last Stand of Fox Company (New York: Atlantic Monthly
Press, 2009). O. P. Smith is quoted from his long interview,
above. FEAF flights are from Futtrell. Olin Beall and Vincent Fosco, Chester Lessenden and Henry Litvin are quoted
by Russ, above, and by Keyes Beech, above. The assassination
attempt on Truman, November 1, 1950, was widely reported.
Truman's diatribe to critic Paul Hume, December 6, 1950, was
widely covered in the press. The unmailed diatribe to Truman
by William Banding is reproduced in www.freerepublic.com
/focus/f-news/579194/posts. An interview with Martin Russ
about his Chosin experience by Scott Holleran can be accessed
at www.scottholleran.com/old/interviews/martin-russ.htm.
O. P. Smith's Genghis Khan remark and the letter from Grace,
his wife, quoting Exodus 23:20, are in Shisler, above. Hoyt
Vandenberg at a Pentagon conference is quoted by Ridgway,
above. Edward Almond's diary is at the MacArthur Archive.
George Crotts is quoted by Russ, above. Ray Davis is quoted
in Knox, above. Maggie Higgins is quoted by Smith in his
interview, Martin Russ, Keyes Beech, and by Antoinette May,

Witness to War: A Biography of Marguerite Higgins (New York: Beaufort Books, 1983). Higgins's own book is *War in Korea* (Garden City, NY: Doubleday, 1951). Ray Aguirre's evacuation, wounded, is in his *We'll Be Home for Christmas*, above.

8: A Bridge Apart

James L. Polk's letters from the *Dai Ichi* to his wife are quoted in *MacArthur's War*, above, as is the 25th Division G4 report. O. P. Smith is quoted throughout from his interview and from his diary in Shisler, who also describes his religious background. Marshal Nie Rongzhen is quoted from Jager, above. Paul Martin and Ernest Gonzalez are quoted in Knox, above. Emilio Aguirre is quoted from his *We'll Be Home for Christmas*, above. David Halberstam is quoted from his *Coldest Winter*, above, and David Douglas Duncan from his *This Is War!*, above (preface). Woodrow Wilson Taylor and Joseph Kucaba appear in Russ, above. Robert Gault and O. P. Smith are quoted about the Koto-ri burial in Shisler, above. Howard Koone is quoted in Charles Smith, above.

The Treadway bridge engineering saga is described fully in Charles Smith and by O. P. Smith. The misunderstanding of "dead men" is that of Private Jack Erickson, quoted in the unsigned "Saga of Epic Heroism: Chosin Reservoir," *1950–1953, 60th Anniversary, Korean War, A Special VFW Publication* (Kansas City, MO: VFW, 2013). David Peppin describes the Treadway engineering and correspondent Harry Smith describes his crossing in Knox, above.

The last flight of Lieutenant Jesse Brown is in *MacArthur's*

War. The failed attempt by Thomas Hudner, at eighty-eight, in 2013, to retrieve his remains is reported by Jane Perlez in *The New York Times*, July 22, 2013. Other press accounts follow up the mission.

The postretirement letter in which O. P. Smith notes one of his nonreligious commanders referring to "the hand of God" is in Shisler.

9: Downhill All the Way

Frank Bifulk and Sherman Richter are quoted in Knox, above. Kenneth Dawalt is quoted in Glenn C. Cowart, *Miracle in Korea: The Evacuation of X Corps from the Hungnam Beachhead* (Columbia: University of South Carolina Press, 1992). Ernest Hargett is quoted in Russ, above. Ray Mighells was interviewed by Phil Zimmer on September 18, 2012, and a year later by SW, by e-mail. Hal Boyle's AP dispatch was dated December 13, 1950. Robert McMahan and William F. Duncan alerted me to the Tootsie Roll and mortar fiasco, which is further described in http://en.wikipedia.org/wiki/Tootsie_Roll.

Close descriptions of the march south from the pass are from Allan R. Millett, *The War for Korea, 1950–1951: They Came from the North* (Lawrence: University of Kansas Press, 2010); and Roy E. Appleman, *Escaping the Trap: The US Army X Corps in Northeast Korea, 1950* (College Station: Texas A&M University Press, 1990). The life and death of John U. D. Page is described by Appleman. O. P. Smith's oversight of the march is in Shisler, above, and in his interviews. Peng's and Nie's exchanges with Mao are in Shu Guang Zhang, *Mao's Military Romanticism:*

China and the Korean War, 1950–1953 (Lawrence: University Press of Kansas, 1995). Hyun Bong Hak's interventions with Almond are from Hyun's recollection, with Marian Hyun, "Christmas Cargo: A Civilian Account of the Hungnam Evacuation" (Norfolk, VA: The General Douglas MacArthur Foundation, 1997), as drawn from in Bill Gilbert, *Ship of Miracles: 14,000 Lives and One Miraculous Voyage* (Chicago: Triumph Books, 2000).

10: Christmas Eve

The German Army's escape from Sicily amid Allied incompetence in 1944 is described in Douglas Porch, *Hitler's Mediterranean Gamble* (London: Weidenfeld and Nicolson, 2004). The scroungy appearance of the Marines is described by Allen C. Bevilacqua "Chosin 1950: When Hell Froze Over," in *Leatherneck: Magazine of the Marines* 2013. The outloading from Hungnam is described in Appleman, above; Shisler, above; Cowart, above; and Millett, above. The refugee outloading is described in Gilbert, above. The role of air cover and aircraft evacuation is in Futtrell, above. Prison Camp indoctrination is from Jager, above. Jager also wildly overstates the success of the withdrawal, alleging that no man was left behind, the dead included. Robert H. Soule's DSC award is described in General Orders No. 72, HQ X Corps, December 24, 1950. The memorial service at the cemetery on the Hungnam beachhead is described by Tom Lambert for AP, December 24, 1950.

Ed Rowny's abandonment and rescue is drawn from his interview with James Zobel of the MacArthur Archive and Museum on February 28, 2012, supplied by Zobel.

Epilogue

O. P. Smith recalls Christmas in Masan in his long inter-
view. Almond is quoted from his interview, above. Jack Mac-
Beth also described the Marines at Masan in an AP dispatch,
"The Bruised Marines Relax," on December 26, 1950. General
Peng and General Shu are quoted from Zhang, above. Lem
Shepherd is quoted from Shisler, above, who also recounts
O. P. Smith's last days. Ed Rowny is quoted from his Zobel
interview.

Acknowledgments

I am indebted for access and for assistance in data collecting to Robert C. Doyle, William H. Duncan, Robert S. Elegant, Dennis M. Giangreco, Robert Guinsler, James Hunt, Maurice Kaye, Wan-Kay Li, Michael Lipschutz, Gary Lustig, Robert McMahan, Ed Mifsud, Ray Mighells, Robert Pigeon, Martin Quinn, Holly Reed, Cisca Schreefel, Ira Simon, Richard Swain, Mark T. Weber, Rodelle Weintraub, Richard E. Winslow III, Phil Zimmer, and James Zobel. Also all those cited earlier as interviewees. Also all those cited earlier as interviewees.

Index

Eighth Army (EUSAK), X Corps and First Marine Division, and "Chinese People's Volunteers" (CPV), are too ubiquitous in these pages to be indexed. Subordinate units will be identified.

Korean and Chinese names, American troops excepted, are set surname first.